# The Dismemberment of *Orpheus*

Books by Ihab Hassan

*Radical Innocence: The Contemporary American Novel*, 1961
*Crise du héros américain contemporain*, 1963
*The Literature* of *Silence: Henry Miller and Samuel Beckett*, 1967
*Liberations: New Essays on the Humanities in Revolution*, 1971 (Editor)

IHAB HASSAN

TOWARD A

NEW YORK

# The Dismemberment of Orpheus

POSTMODERN LITERATURE

OXFORD UNIVERSITY PRESS · 1971

Library of Congress Catalogue Card Number: 70-142797

Printed in the United States of America

*SALLY*

# *Tuning In*

RADICAL QUESTIONS engage the total quality of our life; they are questions of being. Often, they arouse large hopes: to change consciousness, to banish death from our midst. They have a radical innocence. This work may imply such questions.

I write about certain authors who give themselves to silence. The reader may choose to read some pages of this book. Clearly, we still stand in the domain of literature. Yet we must also move onward, to a personal fate closed finally by mortality, and a collective destiny unknown to children of the old earth or new moon. Literature does not suffice.

Men of letters know this. They seek to transcend themselves in a complex silence. The modern Orpheus sings on a lyre without strings. His example transforms nature, or perhaps only reveals its ancient fullness. His imagination may yet prove to be the teleological organ of evolution. Orpheus consents to dismemberment. This is the true meaning of the avant-garde.

Modern literature writes the future of mankind in an invisible hand. In this book, I develop the theme of an earlier work: I try to put before us this invisible writing. This is a special task, and I make no pretense of inclusiveness. I follow a strain till the strain loosens itself from the grasp, till it vanishes in the hints of unmade history. Perhaps my theme may find in the changing awareness of the times something to enrich its own singularity.

In the Prelude, I try to limn a certain consciousness; its

force shapes a central tradition of modern literature. The question thereafter becomes paradigmatic: whom do we choose to carry and qualify this theme?

I begin with Sade who casts his shadow on our path, an avant-gardist *manqué*. But my concerns are of this century, and I ignore the age of Novalis and Rimbaud in order to reach the present swiftly.

I choose four major figures, Hemingway, Kafka, Genet, and Beckett, who exemplify, in some hieratic order of despair, the sovereignty of the void.

In counterpoint with these chapters, I place two Interludes. These, referring mainly to Surrealism and to Existentialism, suggest a distinct yet analogous temper. In both, the destructive energy of the avant-garde seems finally redemptive; the voice of silence assumes a certain fullness of being.

The Postlude carries the dialogue of silence to some inconclusiveness. It seeks to push the terms of being and nothingness to the point where our lives meet them in terms of their own. The modern age discovers the postmodern at its center.

I need add only this: we never end by writing the book we began; nor do we write the book that others read. This is the decree of the imagination in its necessary clash with existence. We change to live, and living change still further. It is all too likely that some uneasiness in this work may betray a manner that I consider no longer my own. I dare to write only in the present.

I. H.

Milwaukee, Wisconsin
Fall 1970

# *Acknowledgments*

I AM GRATEFUL to the University of Wisconsin at Milwaukee for a summer grant which helped me to complete this work; to Wesleyan University for providing me with time, in the midst of administrative duties, to write; and to the Fulbright Commission for an award to France, which enabled me to begin my research.

The chapter on Sade appeared in briefer form in *Tri-Quarterly* (Spring 1969); and a shorter version of the Hemingway chapter appeared in *The Shaken Realist*, edited by Melvin J. Friedman and John B. Vickery (Baton Rouge: Louisiana University Press, 1970). The chapter on Beckett condenses some material in my own *The Literature of Silence: Miller and Beckett* (New York: Alfred A. Knopf, 1967). My thanks to the publishers of these three works.

In 1963, I published, in *The American Scholar*, an essay entitled "The Dismemberment of Orpheus." The essay marks the beginning of my interest in the arts of silence, but contains no material reproduced in this work.

My colleague, Melvin Friedman, has kindly read a large part of this manuscript and offered suggestions.

This work was completed in a remarkable American city: Milwaukee. My appreciation goes to Mr. and Mrs. Thomas Van Alyea, Jr. of that city.

# *Contents*

. . . and then the women
Rushed back to murder Orpheus, who stretched out
His hands in supplication, and whose voice,
For the first time, moved no one. They struck him down,
And through those lips to which the rocks had listened,
To which the hearts of savage beasts responded,
His spirit found its way to winds and air.

. . . The poet's limbs lay scattered
Where they were flung in cruelty or madness,
But Hebrus River took the head and lyre
And as they floated down the gentle current
The lyre made mournful sounds, and the tongue murmured
In mournful harmony.

Ovid, *Metamorphoses*

The decisive moment in human evolution is perpetual. That is why the revolutionary spiritual movements that declare all former things worthless are in the right, for nothing has yet happened.

Franz Kafka, *Wedding Preparations in the Country*

# The Dismemberment of *Orpheus*

# *PRELUDE:*
## *Lyre Without Strings*

### I

MEN MANAGE REALITY by their constructions, and literary history provides the most familiar construction by which scholars manage literature. How else can we force the danger or mystery of art into common parlance? Let me begin, then, with some familiar things.

We commonly believe that modern literature issues from the Symbolist Movement of the nineteenth century, as the latter issues in turn from Romanticism. Thus Edmund Wilson writes in his famous study, *Axel's Castle*: "The literary history of our time is to a great extent that of the development of Symbolism and of its fusion or conflict with Naturalism." [1] Wilson writes this in 1931, taking his title and controlling image from a drama by Villiers de l'Isle-Adam called *Axel*, 1891. At a crucial moment, the hero of that fiction, Axel, cries to his beloved: "What has the Earth ever realized, that drop of frozen mud, whose Time is only a lie in the heavens? It is the earth, dost thou not see? which has now become the illusion! Admit, Sara: we have destroyed in our strange hearts, the love of life—and it is in REALITY indeed that ourselves have become our souls. To consent, after this, to live would be but sacrilege against ourselves. Live? our servants will do that for us. . . ." [2] Axel and his Sara drink a goblet of poison and perish in the family crypt beneath the legendary castle. This seems all very extreme. But Wilson, who can scarcely abide the contortions of decadence, recounts the episode for good reason: it exudes the Symbolist mystique. The aura hangs about the great modern authors, about Valéry, Eliot, Proust, Joyce, and Gertrude Stein—Dada inhabits a narrow appendix—who, as Wilson concludes, "break down the walls of the present and wake us to the hope and exaltation of the untried, unsuspected possibilities of human thought and art." [3] This is quite valid.

But it is time, perhaps, to make a new construction of literary history. A different line has emerged *within* the tradition of the modern. It leads more directly, through the present, to a literature to come. Its authors sing on a lyre without strings. To them, Axel's credo, echoing in darker chambers of the mind, whispers prophetic truths. The Avant-Gardists at the turn of the century and the Absurdists of the sixties place these authors within a shadowy frame. Across that frame pass reflections of a changed consciousness, a radical crisis of art, language, and culture.

Perhaps Ortega sees this better than Wilson. Ortega asks: "What is behind this disgust at seeing art mixed up with life? Could it be disgust for the human sphere as such, for reality, for life? Or is it rather the opposite: respect for life and unwillingness to confuse it with art, so inferior a thing as art?" [4] The question must remain double. Art, language, and consciousness may seek transcendence in a state that we can evoke, anagogically, in the plenum of silence. But art, language, and consciousness may also seek to empty themselves as man recoils into a pure intuition of his subjectivity, recoils into a negative state of silence. "When God and the creation become objects of consciousness," J. Hillis Miller says, "man becomes a nihilist. Nihilism is the nothing of consciousness when consciousness becomes the foundation of everything." [5] Thus transcendence moves downward.

Playing their stringless lyre, modern authors enchant us with their twin melodies, and we dream of bright life or unspeakable sleep.

## II

Such doubleness may lie in the very nature of language, lie there always concealed. We recall the Orphic myth: the frenzied Maenads dismember the poet, but his head, drifting seaward in the river Hebrus, continues to sing. An abstract reading of the myth may insist on the conflict between Apollo and Dionysos, art and nature, form and energy. Orpheus, after all, serves as Apollo's priest, and rises every morning to greet the dawn on the summit of Mount Pangaeum, praising Helius, first among the gods. Ovid's version, however, gives another turn to the story. Since the death of Eurydice—why does Orpheus really glance over his shoulder and thus give his wife back to Hades? —the poet prefers the company of young men. In a fit of uncontrollable jealousy, the Maenads tear him limb from limb. We begin to suspect that the sweet maker of songs offends life in some hidden and original manner. Freud says in *Totem and Taboo*: "The theory of primal sin is of Orphic origin; it was preserved in the mysteries and thence penetrated into the philosophic schools of Greek antiquity." [6] The crime of Orpheus corresponds to the form of his atonement. Whatever that sin may be, language and form, expressions of an emergent consciousness, are complicit in it.

Yet Orpheus is surely no monster of *hubris*. The cults we associate with his name blend word and flesh into the dance of existence. Orpheus sings, and his song moves stones, trees, and beasts. The reason is simple: singing Orpheus restores himself to nature, and moves with the secret life of things. His lyre carries the music of universal harmony and eternal response. Seized by the god, he speaks in no voice of his own; possessed, he loses his self-possession. Even Apollo must reveal himself to men in poem, oracle, or trance, forms that no mortal finally controls. The mystery unites all opposites, and bursts there where being and nothingness seem to touch. This is why the pure Orphic voice always speaks as one. Elizabeth Sewell rightly notes: "Language and mind, poetry and biology meet and bear on one another in the figure of Orpheus. . . . The human organism, that body which has the gift of thought, does not have the choice of two kinds of thinking. It has only one, in which the organism as a whole is engaged all along the line." [7]

The singing body of Orpheus holds, then, a contradiction—between the dumb unity of nature and the multiple voice of consciousness—that the song itself longs to overcome. In recognition of this longing, in obedience to this contradiction, certain writers pretend to evade their destiny in words. Rilke, who understands this need, concludes one of the "Sonnets to Orpheus" thus:

> He [Orpheus] has to vanish, so you'll understand:
> Even though himself he fears this evanescence.
> For while his word surpasses this existence,
>
> He's gone alone already in the distance.
> The lyre's grating does not curb his hands.
> He is obedient, even when he transgresses.[8]

Vanishing Orpheus leaves behind a lyre without strings; the moderns inherit it. Their song of silence responds to an ancient sentence with intimations of transcendence, upward or downward. And as their voice denies sound, so their vision declines mediation. Geoffrey Hartman argues: "whereas the older poet . . . knew and acknowledged mediation, the modern either does not acknowledge or does not know a mediator for his orphic journey. He passes through experience by means of the unmediated vision. Nature, the body, and human consciousness—that is the only text." [9]

The statement may need some refinement since nature and consciousness are seldom the same. Hartman traces the unmediated vision back to Wordsworth. But what of Sade? The poet of nature and the prisoner of consciousness both disdain, in the blindness of vision, the mediations of language. Here ends the meeting of contraries. One beholds the world's body while the other stares at the mind's emptiness. They speak in different tones of silence, sacramental and demonic. Their sense and sensuality, their memory or a woman's flesh, take us worlds apart. Perhaps we need to invoke still another name: Blake. Blake and Sade live in the true antipodes, bedlamites and close contemporaries that they are.

Blake and Sade set the resonances of silence, and their contrapuntal song reveals its full range in the nineteenth century.[10] Certain early Romantics first come to mind: Coleridge, Novalis, Nerval, Poe; and others follow: Kleist, Hoffmann, Hölderlin, Büchner, Baudelaire, Leconte de Lisle, Keats, De Quincey. These authors prompt a double tendency in the literary imagination of that period. First, Romantic dream and metaphor explode words into outrageous visions. From Novalis and Nerval, through Lautréamont and Rimbaud, to the Surrealists of our century, the imagination strains toward a kind of Dionysiac frenzy. Second, Romantic irony, taking a parallel line through Heine and Mallarmé, moves the imagination toward its abolition, and persuades art of its own impossibility; we look toward Beckett. The language of the former, merging with the chaotic flux of reality, aspires to All; the language of the second, canceling reality into the pure order of number, aspires to Nothing.[11] The two languages, taken far enough, dissolve the Orphic pact between word and flesh.

Thus we rush from Romanticism to the postmodern scene. The literature of silence encloses a silence of fullness and another of vacancy. Against Blake, Rimbaud, Whitman, Lawrence, Breton, and Henry Miller, say, stand Sade, Mallarmé, Valéry, Kafka, Genet, and Beckett. (These arrays, superficial and perhaps superfluous, suggest merely this: a contrast in the effects of language rather than a discrimination of forms or themes.) It is this last line of literature, from Sade to Beckett and after, moving toward a vanishing point, that I consider here in terms of a special plea. It is the same line, with such dialectic exceptions as Rimbaud, Whitman, and Breton, that carries the mission of the avant-garde into our midst. If the construction I have made of literary history now seems too stark, it will soon blend into ambiguous hues as fact and metaphor begin to fill in the gaps of thought. Of this we can be certain: the forms of silence engage one another, and silence itself suddenly turns into speech.

## III

Where must we start? The sense of origins still haunts the critical mind though antecedents for any literary event appear mischievously in every form, in every time. Wherever I begin, I evade the nineteenth century. This historical impertinence may be excused; others have written amply to indicate the relevance of that century to the modern avant-garde.[12]

Some scholars, for instance, rightly take a contemporary stance and bend their vision toward the past. Thus Robert Martin Adams explores certain "episodes in the literary conquest of the void," and concludes: "[Nothing] . . . expresses a choked, profound hostility to the conscious mind which finds very general expression in the late nineteenth century and becomes a howling chorus in the twentieth. Consciousness comes to seem a glowing band of steel. . . ." [13] Thus also George Steiner conjectures about the "Pythagorean Genre" of various authors, past and present, with Wittgenstein's precept—"what we cannot speak about we must consign to silence"—foremost in mind.[14] And thus Michel Foucault, writing in the idiom of the new linguistic hierophants, observes of the modern tradition: ". . . each work was made to recover all the others, to consume them, to reduce them to silence, and finally to install itself beside them, beyond them, and in the midst of them (Sade and Mallarmé and their works, and The Work, are by definition the *Enfer* of Libraries.)" [15] No doubt we could plunder the entire heritage of Western thought, and call on Spinoza, Leibniz, Rousseau, Kierkegaard, Nietzsche, Hegel, Marx, Freud, Heidegger, Husserl, and Lévi-Strauss to stand in history and deliver to the silent avant-garde.

Perhaps we do better, however, to stay closer to an era wherein our sense of experience is still active. All beginnings are gratuitous, a form of faith; the real death of Hugo or fictive suicide of Axel can serve equally as a start. Roger Shattuck, no less apposite than Wilson in this matter, says of the years between Hugo's funeral in 1885 and the outbreak of the First World War: "The old coin of the realm has become worthless; the reversal of values, the *conversion* has taken place. By an evolution that only today begins to become clear, the Banquet Years yielded the arts of the twentieth century." [16] Throughout the West, the arts of modernism point to a major revolution in language. In Vienna, Prague, or Berlin, Hofmannsthal, Kafka, Morgenstern, Musil, Rilke, Kraus, and Broch discover a new space within language itself.[17] In Paris, Proust and Valéry, votaries of an art purified beyond itself, fade before the violence of Dada and Surrealism; and Jacques Rivière, questioning the very concept of literature, speaks of a general "tendency to write only as a last resort, or at least to assign extrinsic aims to writing, to literary creation. . . . Thus art . . . becomes a completely nonhuman activity, a supersensory function . . . a sort of creative astronomy." [18] And from London to Chicago, Yeats, Joyce, Lawrence, Pound, Eliot, Faulkner, Hemingway, and Williams—how many more can we name!—call attention to a vast movement characterized, as Frank Kermode says, by a kind of "formal desperation," a "schismatic" will of sweeping implications.[19]

The modernist assault on forms has, in all probability, no exact parallel in literary history. It is at once more various, reckless, and equivocal than its precedents; it challenges the idea of form itself and resolves that challenge by forcing new demands on every artistic medium. No category of space or time, order or chaos, dream or fact, action or reflection, causality or chance, syntax or metaphor, eroticism or humor remains after this upheaval of the imagination quite intact. The process of life, of oxidization as Thomas Mann suggests in *The Magic Mountain*, penetrates the artifact and questions its mode of being. The creator himself becomes, as Camus maintains in *The Myth of Sisyphus*, an "absurd creator." Disjunctive forms turn into disruptive forms, and the latter renounce their aristocratic commands, setting the audience free of the author's control. Randomness and surprise, the happiness within a happening, supersede an older teleology. Finally, forms define themselves by their absence, their felt omissions. Max Ernst's collage, entitled "The Tomb of the Muse," makes its statement by no means that we can simply adduce to the notion of form.

In this regard, we should perhaps try to discriminate between earlier and later manifestations of modernism. Such distinctions, however, may become clear only to the abstract eye of retrospection. The lines between Dada and Neo-Dada, between Expressionism and the Theatre of the Absurd, trace obscure shapes. We know, for instance, that "aesthetic distance" begins to shrink in the theatre of Strindberg and Pirandello, that the tension between stage and audience slackens early in the century. Dramatic structures unloosen; time reverses itself; mirrors throw back reflections of author and actor; masks and figures exchange their places insanely. Already, the playwright senses that his audience may be privy to "the fraud" we call theatre, and tries to exonerate himself by undermining his forms. The profound self-irony of dramatic forms develops and deepens from the modern to the postmodern era, till it becomes possible for Martin Esslin casually to say: "The time has passed when an identity was believed to exist between the structure of language, the structure of logic, and the structure of reality. That is the content expressed by the formal means of the dissolution of logical discourse in the *avant-garde* theatre." [20] But this can not mean that Genet is any less original than Pirandello.

Both schism and continuity, then, attend the dissolution of modern forms. *For the time being,* revolution has become *permanent.* We should demur, therefore, when Kermode says: ". . . the theoretical bases of neo-modernism, in so far as they show themselves in relation to form, chance, and humor . . . are not 'revolutionary!' They are marginal developments of older modernism." [21] Perhaps we should try, instead, to stand in the vanishing present and ask: what indeed is the nature of modernism in so far as hints and guesses of it may be found scattered in the life we imagine for ourselves? The answer to this question will lead us to the answer of another: what model of modernism can best serve the avant-garde of the future? The two questions cohere in our sense of the present, lacking which all predictions become exercises in retrospection.

Admittedly, these questions are hard; for the sense of the present often remains dumb. Inevitably, we seek *paradigms of innovation,* contradictions upon which the mind balances in self-renewal. The paradigm, we hope, may contain a metaphor, and thus carry within it our intuition of being.

## IV

Let us entertain some paradigms of innovation. In *The Theory of the Avant-Garde,* Renato Poggioli limns the traits of such movements as Cubism, Futurism, Dadaism, and Surrealism. These, he says, tend toward activism, an agnostic attitude toward culture. Carried far enough, the attitude leads to nihilism, the essence of which lies "in attaining non-action by acting, lies in destructive, not constructive labor." [22] Remorselessly, such movements redefine the idea of the modern, and hurtle continuously toward the future. In their iconoclastic rage, they establish a vanishing tradition of the new. Their creative energy, which may deform and even dehumanize art, ends by "transhumanizing" it. Thus the avant-garde expresses its will to transcend man and surpass the limits of nature. Poggioli proffers in sum-mary these rubrics: "activism, antagonism and nihilism, agonism and futurism, antitraditionalism and modernism, obscurity and unpopularity, dehumanization and iconoclasm, voluntarism and cerebralism, abstract and pure art. Almost all have been summed up in the central formula of alienation. . . ." [23]

It is precisely that jejune modern term, alienation, that provides us with the clue. Poggioli notes the change in the mood of alienation which "came to be felt as pathetic and tragic rather than heroic and dionysian." He continues: "By virtue of that feeling, the artist was driven to turn against himself the weapons of his own antagonism and the nihilism he had previously directed against society and the outside world." [24] From this reflexive energy, this introversion of the alienated will, emerge the arts of silence, of the void, and of death, emerge also the languages of omission, ambiguity, games, and numbers. The avant-garde conquers culture only to abolish its mission, and creates anti-art only to establish, despite itself, canons of another art; this is what Harold Rosenberg labels the "Tradition of the New." Deep in its consciousness lies still the incalculable potential of the negative. Duchamp calls his later work "delay in glass": "It's merely a way of succeeding in no longer thinking that the thing in question is a picture. . . ." [25] The object remains before us, together with our altered sense of reality.

The negative, then, informs silence; and silence is my metaphor of a language that expresses, with harsh and subtle cadences, the stress in art, culture, and consciousness. The crisis is modern and postmodern, current and continuous, though discontinuity and apocalypse are also images of it. Thus the language of silence conjoins the need both of autodestruction and self-transcendence.

Metaphors spread a net to capture unseen life; their contours ripple with each haul. Because silence is more metaphor than concept, it must need drift a little with the currents of our thought. Here are meanings, some perhaps new and some old, that I hope to gather in this metaphor of our literature:

1. Silence refers to an avant-garde tradition of literature. For our purpose, we assume that the tradition extends from Sade past Beckett. We may also wish to call that tradition anti-literature.

2. Silence implies alienation from reason, society, and history, a reduction of all engagements in the created world of men, perhaps an abrogation of any communal existence. Its radical empiricism resists and even disrupts human systems, and elicits the babble in everyday words.

3. Silence also betrays separation from nature, a perversion of vital and erotic processes. The symptoms range from misogyny to necrophilia. Man rejects the earth and abhors woman; he detaches himself from the body.

4. Silence demands the self-repudiation of art which aspires to event, dream, nonsense, or number. Art, rejoining brute matter or pure ratio, pretends to become anti-art; between these extremes, it discovers cunning equivocations.

5. Silence requires the periodic subversion of forms. At times, the resulting anti-forms feign a formlessness that nothing made or perceived by man can ever possess. Still, anti-forms oppose control, closure, stasis, telos, and historic pattern.

6. Silence creates anti-languages. Some are utterly opaque, others completely transparent. These languages transform the presence of words into semantic absence and unloosen the grammar of consciousness. They accuse common speech.

7. Silence fills the extreme states of the mind—void, madness, outrage, ecstasy, mystic trance—when ordinary discourse ceases to carry the burden of meaning.

8. Silence de-realizes the world. It encourages the metamorphosis of appearance and reality, the perpetual fusion and confusion of identities, till nothing—or so it *seems*—remains.

9. Silence turns consciousness upon itself, altering the modes of its awareness; or else condemns the mind to repetitions of the same solipsist drama of self and anti-self. Thus, the transvaluation of values or their complete devaluation ensues.

10. Silence presupposes, at times, apocalypse, the dissolution of the known world, its history and persistence, and sustains a millennial vision of non-human perfection. Thus the total accusation of life may yield to its opposite, and the affluence of being flood the abyss.

These points about negative silence may apply as well to a positive silence except where the assumptions of fullness are contradicted (points 3, 8, 9, 10). The crucial cluster in this outline of negativity refers to an autistic consciousness, imperial in its isolation, avid for the void; a corresponding language, cunning in the arts of self-abolition; and an erotic retreat from existence, from the flesh of reality, a dark prayer of transcendence under. The words that roll off the tongue include anti-art, anti-language, anti-consciousness. This is perhaps unfortunate. Obviously, we should not depend upon a prefix, "anti," to bring forth a metaphor or even a concept. Nor should we expect ten discrete definitions of silence to extend our knowledge of every author we read. The interest of the metaphor rather lies in its synergy: its power to find in disparate elements of the modern consciousness a vital pattern.

## V

The negative, acting through art, language, and consciousness, shapes the boundary state I call silence. In practice, this is a state that men may approach without ever reaching. Perhaps the negative is always implicit in consciousness, as some phenomenologists claim, a process of reduction or exclusion fundamental to the sentient self, a process that ends always by placing the self outside of Being.

Of this we can be certain: silence makes a place for itself in the intellectual ambiance of the times. The discourse of Husserl, Heidegger, Merleau-Ponty, and Sartre takes account of it as a principle of subjectivity. Wittgenstein reckons with it as the incommunicable against which language defines its rules.

Lévi-Strauss considers it as the myth of structures, the master concept of relations governing all the articulate behavior of men. Silence shifts in the perspectives of various thinkers yet remains ever at the threshold of awareness. It is a category of the intelligence of the twentieth century, and particularly of its avant-garde imagination.

It is right that John Cage, apostle of the current avant-garde, should speak to us first about silence in his original voice. Like Buckminster Fuller, Cage is really an inheritor of American Transcendentalism to which he brings the humor of Zen; he knows the wit and holiness of sound, the plenum of silence. In 1961, Cage, till then recognized only as a composer of electronic and aleatory music, publishes a work called *Silence,* and this is what he says: "I am here, and there is nothing to say. If among you are those who wish to get somewhere, let them leave at any moment. What we re-quire is silence; but what silence requires is that I go on talking;" and again he says: "Inherent silence is equivalent to denial of the will;" and again:

> nothing is accomplished by writing a piece of music
> nothing is accomplished by hearing a piece of music
> nothing is accomplished by playing a piece of music
> our ears are now in excellent condition [26]

Cage's sacramental statement on silence is a statement on attention or art, on randomness, variety, discontinuity, and purposelessness within the miraculous condition we call life. It is also a credo, as his next work, *A Year From Monday,* clearly testifies, of universal responsibility and responsiveness. "The purpose of one activity is no longer separate from the purpose of any other activity," he writes.[27] This does not imply quietism: "Our proper work now if we love mankind and the world we live in is revolution." [28] The revolution must affect language as well; thus Cage reflects: "Dealing with language (while waiting for something else than syntax) as though it's sound-source that

benefit of words. Steiner puts aside the redemptive possibilities of silence and of the new *languages* it may contain. Here Susan Sontag, attuned to the radical will of the new arts, sees the point. In her fine essay, "The Aesthetics of Silence," she says:

> As the activity of the mystic must end in a *via negativa,* a theology of God's absence, a craving for the cloud of unknowingness beyond knowledge and for the silence beyond speech, so art must tend toward anti-art, the elimination of the "subject" . . . the substitution of chance for intention, and the pursuit of silence.[38]

Miss Sontag links silence with the stringency of saints. She also perceives that it engages the fundamental premises of the modern mind and exposes the corruption of words. "In the end," she says, "the radical critique of consciousness (first delineated by the mystical tradition, now administered by unorthodox psychotherapy and high modernist art) always lays the blame on language." [39]

The blame of language and the redemption of that blame are also the concern of Elizabeth Sewell's deep studies of poetry. Her interest in silence, though never explicit, takes subtle technical turns. We already know that Miss Sewell seeks in *The Orphic Voice,* in the mystic language of things, an "affirmation of the unity of all the forms in nature, between the galaxies and the mythological lyre. . . ." [40] That affirmation leads to the fullest language of silence. But in an earlier work, *The Field of Nonsense,* Miss Sewell gives her attention to the negative side of the matter, the language of emptiness. With Edward Lear and Lewis Carroll as her main examples, she defines nonsense as "a collection of words or events which in their arrangements do not fit into some recognized system in a particular mind." [41] Nonsense is a construct, a game akin to logic and number, a method of semantic stillness; its elements exist only in abstract relations within a closed structure. "There is only one aspect of language which Nonsense can be said to disorder, and that is reference. . . ," Miss Sewell writes.[42]

Fastidious, divisible, and discrete—one and one never make two but rather zero—the language of nonsense creates its own kind of silence, to which the languages of Sade, Mallarmé, Hemingway, Kafka, or Beckett bear certain affinities.

In France, even more than in England or America, silence becomes a compelling theme of criticism. Thus Maurice Blanchot, abstruse and complex allegorist of silence, explores the theme continually in his novels as in his essays. Like the later Heidegger, Blanchot understands the authority of the negative; he dwells constantly on the limits, the impossibility of literature. His unique interpretations of the myths of Orpheus and Eurydice, Odysseus and the Sirens, Oedipus and the Sphinx, focus on the necessary failure of art. Eurydice, for instance, represents the obscure "point" toward which art, desire, death, and night seem to tend; she represents the silence that Orpheus must, and can not, attain. "Orpheus . . . forgets the work which he must accomplish," Blanchot says in *L'Espace littéraire*, "and he necessarily forgets it, for the ultimate exigency of his movement is not that there be a work, but that someone confront this 'point.' "[43] Because oblivion surrounds the "literary space" on every side, the writer knows death intimately and lives on the brinks of silence; his demon urges him to annihilate all literary forms. Indeed, negation is inherent in language itself. "In the beginning, I do not speak to say something," Blanchot writes in *La Part de feu*, "but there is a nothing which demands to speak, nothing speaks, nothing finds its being in speech and the being of speech is nothing."[44] We can predict his favorite authors: Sade, Lautréamont, Hölderlin, Rimbaud, Mallarmé, Kafka, Rilke, Artaud. In *Le Livre à venir*, however, Blanchot chooses Rousseau to inaugurate the subversion of literature, the assault by a man of letters on letters. This latter work, which may be Blanchot's richest statement on the subject, traces the modern will of literature to "disappearance," and envisages an "era without words" full of new sounds.[45] Blanchot's own movement toward the still center of art, "the original rumor," where things get said without words, qualifies him both as a theoretician and an artist of silence.[46]

Roland Barthes brings to the same theme a different sensibility, shaped in various measures by Sartre, Saussure, Lévi-Strauss, and Lacan, shaped mainly by his own original and ascetic intelligence. His first work, translated as *Writing Degree Zero,* examines the proposition: "Classical writing . . . disintegrated, and the whole of Literature, from Flaubert to the present day, became the problematics of language." [47] For Barthes, modernism begins with the seearch for "a literature no longer possible"; and literary forms are an uneasy conspiracy with solitude. "The Novel," he says, "is a Death; it transforms life into destiny, a memory into a useful act, duration into an orientated and meaningful time." [48] But writing, however stringent or desiccated, never attains the degree zero; at best, it can only maintain the paradox of its null hope. The poignant self-destruction of literature "teaches us that for some writers language, the first and last way out of the literary myth, finally restores what it hoped to avoid, that there is no writing which can be lastingly revolutionary, and that any silence of form can escape imposture only by complete abandonment of communication." [49] The author becomes "irretrievably honest" only when language becomes a pure equation or a literal silence. His work, or rather *l'écriture* as Barthes prefers to say, despite the antinomies of history, still "hastens towards a dreamed-of language whose freshness, by a kind of ideal anticipation, might portray the perfection of some new Adamic world where language would no longer be alienated." [50] This view of literature forces upon the critic a special role which Barthes elucidates in *Critique et vérité* (1966), a fine riposte to Professor Raymond Picard's attack on the "*nouvelle critique*." For Barthes, true criticism leads finally to "silence or its substitute, chatter: a pleasant *causerie,* as Roman Jakobson said in 1921, of literary history." [51] The crisis in discursive language brings to a convergence the words of author and critic, and compels a transformation in the nature of commentaries. In the end, however, criticism, which is less translation than periphrasis, can never plumb the depths of a work of art; for that depth remains "an absence." [52]

Blanchot and Barthes do not present an eccentric case for criticism; other critics also take an oblique interest in the concepts of silence. Members of the Geneva School, foreshadowed by Marcel Raymond and Albert Béguin, and including Georges Poulet, Jean Starobinsky, Jean-Pierre Richard, and Jean Rousset, tend to implicate each work into a larger field of consciousness precisely in order to overcome the inherent, the formal, limitations of literature. Poulet, for instance, says: "I am above all attracted by those for whom literature is—by definition—a spiritual activity which must be gone beyond in its own depths, or, which, in failing to be gone beyond, in being condemned to the awareness of a non-transcendence, affirms itself as the experience and verification of a fundamental defeat." [53] For him as for others of that school, the literary work is not an aesthetic object but "an act of consciousness" stemming from inner stillness. Their vocabulary often refers to "inner space," "interior distance," "transparency," "absence," "pure vacancy and latency," phrases suggesting that the metaphors of criticism have become spatial, have assumed the visual equivalent of stillness.

In this regard, criticism—and I include structuralist and phenomenological approaches as well as critiques of consciousness—may follow the broader tendency of modern literature. Joseph Frank, we recall, describes that tendency some decades earlier in his celebrated essay, "Spatial Form in Modern Literature." The essential point is made prophetically by Thomas Carlyle when he says: "Speech is of Time, Silence is of Eternity." [54] In our mind, Silence and Eternity belong to Space. Thus we may speculate that, since the nineteenth century, the trend of verbal forms denies the temporal reality of the human voice and spreads in eternal images. "We are accustomed to spatializing sound as we are to spatializing time," Walter J.

Ong says. "To bring us where we are, the word must have been transplanted from its natural habitat, sound, to a new habitat, space. Writing and print and, later, electronic devices must have reshaped man's contact with actuality through the word." [55] Language, then, which now inhabits space, calls our attention to silence, and literary forms take shape in the perpetual presence of consciousness.

Yet in the end, the speculations of critics cannot validate any particular concept of silence; they serve only to provide some theoretical frame for an emergent intuition. The intuition, I have said, pervades our sense of the intellectual present. It begins already to acquire retrospective authority. We are not surprised to hear from Jerzy Peterkiewicz that a group of Polish poets, beginning with Cyprian Novid (1821–1883), concerned themselves with the aesthetics of silence more than a century ago. Peterkiewicz entitles his work *The Other Side of Silence,* and defines its purpose thus: "to investigate the poets' desire to die with poetry and the desire to go beyond the words and whether this means the ultimate failure of poetry as a literary medium or whether, on the contrary, it suggests that poetry reaches the sublime when it ceases to be a medium." [56]

Let us conclude. Silence enters contemporary critical discourse and gives itself to various theories of culture and art. All the critics may not agree on its nature or function; nor would they all endorse the definitions that I have offered. Yet silence, as concept or metaphor, fills our place. The resistance that some academics still offer to it cannot endure. In their circle, silence will probably pass from fashion to history without ever impressing itself on the serious sense of literature. Fortunately, literature continues on its way, and hastens our presence.

## VI

The force of silence that drives through literature from its modern to postmodern phase will merely flash as personal intuition or fade as critical abstraction unless we allow it the resistance of example. In choosing these examples, we deliver ourselves of a judgment which is not wholly literary, and draw the experience of the authors into our own constructions. Thus critics finally attest to the energies they exchange with art.

I begin with the Marquis de Sade who qualifies as a modern in a typology of the void. He stands for absolute freedom, subjective creation, and is immured from reality absolutely. Unwittingly, his language echoes the hollow silence of autism. His desperate voice can still be heard in the Interlude from 'Pataphysics to Surrealism which speaks with the other voice of silence; for the experiments of the avant-garde now assume a complete as well as null universe. Thereafter, our pieties about art can never be the same. Hemingway, coming next, will seem out of place; his work harks back to a more conventional literature. The appearance may be deceptive; and I choose him over Gertrude Stein, say, because in so many simple and urgent ways his statement remains more central. Even a writer so committed to the craft of fiction as Hemingway still betrays the hold of silence on each verb. He confronts the void with valor, and ends by conveying nothing better than nothingness. Close to the margins of silence, he speaks to us of madness in rigorous measures. Kafka moves beyond Hemingway; he refuses to codify the abyss. The authority of his ambiguities absolves life of a *particular* meaning without absolving him of the quest for it. Hemingway and Kafka, progressively, carry language to the limits of absurdity. The Interlude from Existentialism to Aliterature suggests the means to accept absurdity or render it superfluous. In Sartre, humanism still persists at the edge of reason; in Robbe-Grillet, *chosisme,* denying the relevance of reason, silences the ordinary voice. Genet and Beckett go farther still. The first reveals reality in the deathly language of mirrors. The second listens endlessly to a solipsist drone. Words appear in either case on the page only to declare themselves invalid. We have crossed some invisible line; and stringless lyres now strum for a world without men. Postmodern literature moves, in nihilist play or mystic transcendence, toward the vanishing point.

CHAPTER I

# SADE:

## *The Prison of Consciousness*

He chose the imaginary.
Simone de Beauvoir, "Must We Burn Sade?"

### I

It is given to certain authors to reveal the darkness in our dreams and thus to make of history prophecy. These are not always the authors who stand highest in our esteem. They possess an extreme gift, and life blights them for their excess. Their road skirts the palace of wisdom, and their eyes behold a pile of ashes. They see only what they have already, what they have terribly seen—such is their autism. But their blindness points the way. Mysteriously, they expend themselves in the avant-garde of literature.

The Marquis de Sade is one of these authors. He was a scoundrel, a wastrel, a libertine; they also said he was mad. He may have been worse things, though his biographers doubt it. The authorities—of the French Monarchy, Republic, Terror, Consulate, First Empire, and Restoration—put him under lock and key for nearly thirty years. He comes back to us now as a cliché of language, a force in our erotic and political behavior; he comes back as a writer and even as a thinker. He writes monotonously and thinks, on the whole, equivocally; his profound duplicity delights, and finally confutes him. Yet we seek him out, behind the walls of Vincennes, the Bastille, Charenton, between the cheap yellow covers of pornography, because something in his monstrous fantasy continues to betray us to ourselves, because his judgment haunts our civilization.

## II

A writer's fantasy may take shape in the cradle, but the biography of Sade preserves its secret. On June 2, 1740, Sade is born in Paris, and on the following day he is baptized by proxy, in the absence of his godparents, at the church of Saint-Sulpice. The name he is actually given is Donatien-Alphonse-François; the name intended for him is Louis-Alphonse-Donatien. From the start, his fate is inverted. His ancient lineage recalls finer ironies: Petrarch's Laura, who married Paul de Sade in 1325, is his ancestress. He visualizes her in his prison, offering him sweetly the peace of the grave.

The Count, his father, governor-general of the provinces of Bresse, Bugey, Valromey, and Gex, seigneur of Saumane and La Coste, co-seigneur of Mazan, seems to have been grim, meticulous, and overbearing. His mother is inconsequential. Why does Sade hold women in abysmal contempt? Hatred of a mother who never had enough love to give? Jealousy of the sexual role women play? The facts of Sade's childhood are scanty and afford no answer. We only know that throughout his life his implacable enemy proves to be less his mother than his ferocious mother-in-law.

Sade is educated by his uncle, a Benedictine abbot, then by the Jesuits. He serves in various royal regiments, sees action in the war against Prussia, and is discharged, in 1763, with the rank of captain in the Cavalry Regiment of Burgundy. He seems to be engaged simultaneously to two young ladies, Mademoiselle Renée-Pélagie de Montreuil and Mademoiselle Laure de Lauris. He pretends that his heart belongs to the latter, but his father insists on an alliance with the former, who is the daughter of the President of the Board of Excise at Paris. The marriage to Renée-Pélagie, long-suffering, insipid, and loyal almost to the end, takes place by royal consent on May 17, 1763.

Marriage offers Sade no criminal distractions. A few months after the ceremony, the king commits him to Vincennes for excesses in a *petite maison*. The penalty this time is light; in two weeks Sade is set free and ordered to retire to Normandy. But the air of dungeons has seeped through his lungs; henceforth, he stands with the condemned. Sade continues to discover himself in debauch while Inspector Marais of the Paris Police shadows him. A dancer called Beauvoisin is his mistress in Paris; at La Coste, his beloved Provençal estate, he passes her off as his wife. He persuades an unemployed cotton spinner, Rose Keller, to join him at his retreat in Arcueil. There he flogs her, makes various incisions in her body, pours red and white wax on the wounds. The woman is persuaded to drop her charges for an indemnity, but Sade is detained for some months in Saumur, Pierre-Encise, the Conciergerie. The monotony, the iron cast of his need, begins to shape his days. In 1771, the Marquis is granted a commission as Colonel of Cavalry; he prefers to seduce his sister-in-law, Mlle. Anne-Prospère de Montreuil, who resides with him at La Coste. The following year, the Marseille scandal drives Sade underground, and finally into prison, till the outbreak of the French Revolution. The Marquis and his valet, Latour, are accused by five young prostitutes in Marseille brothels of heterosexual sodomy, unspecified perversions, and poisoning with Spanish fly or cantharized aniseed. Sade and Latour are executed and burned in effigy in Aix; they are caught in the flesh in Chambéry; they escape to La Coste where the Marquis, under the pious eyes of his wife, inducts various domestics into his orgies. But La Coste soon becomes too dangerous for him; for a year he masquerades through Italy as the Count de Mazan. He returns imprudently, and is arrested, in 1777, by Inspector Marais who conveys him to Vincennes with a *lettre de cachet*. The King offers him the chance to plead insanity; Sade prefers to stand trial for his crimes at Marseille. A High Court exculpates him of poisoning; he is simply convicted of libertinage, fined, and forbidden to frequent Marseille for three years. But the original *lettre de cachet* still holds; he must return to Vincennes. Sade escapes on the way to Paris; returns to La Coste; and is finally captured, in 1778, by Marais and thrown into Cell Number 6 at Vincennes. Only a revolution will set him free.

It seems an adventurous, certainly a deranged, life. Actually, Sade only begins his true life of crime behind prison bars, through fantasy, through a new kind of literature. The various public trials fail to prove or even divulge the extent of his wickedness. The "absolute writer," as Barney Rosset calls him, is born from absolute authority, a *lettre de cachet* from the King.[1] Sade, whose erotic need demands that the world divide itself between tyrants and victims, finds in Cell Number 6 a utopia swarming with the creatures of his imagination. But a complex sophistry is required to maintain the erotic excitations of this prisoner. The Marquis feigns indignation, his rhetoric swollen by appeals to Nature, Reason, and Revolt. To his wife he writes:

> My manner of thinking stems straight from my considered reflections; it holds with my existence, with the way I am made. . . . Not my manner of thinking but the manner of thinking of others has been the source of my unhappiness. . . .
>
> Let the King first correct what is vicious in the government, let him do away with its abuses, let him hang the ministers who deceive or rob him, before he sets to repressing his subjects' opinions or tastes! [2]

His favorite "tyrant," of course, is Madame la Présidente de Montreuil, his mother-in-law. With insane consistency, he writes to her: "For a long time, Madame, I have been your victim; but do not think to make me your dupe. It is sometimes interesting to be the one, always humiliating to be the other, and I flatter myself upon as much penetration as you can claim deceit." [3] At times, he forgoes the lofty tone. He whines, quarrels, wheedles, threatens, reproaches; he waxes humorous, obscene, outrageous, about the posterior of his wife, about the machinations of his enemies. His sense of detail is sharp. He constantly counts his linen or his books, and asks for more. He practices the arithmetic of despair, counting the lines, the words, even the syllables in the letters he receives, seeking therein some occult sign of his gaolers' will. The endless permutations of his ciphers are like the sexual permutations of his characters, ways of exhausting possibility and of achieving omnipotence. Yet Sade knows he is holding to reason by unreasonable means. He revenges himself on "his tyrants" by chewing on them as he eats his food; gradually, he grows into a monster of obesity.

His terrible vengeance, however, is literature itself. Much of what he writes is lost or destroyed. At Vincennes, he finishes *Dialogue Between a Priest and a Dying Man* in eight days in 1782. Transferred to the Bastille in 1784, he continues his spiteful redemption of time. He writes *The 120 Days of Sodom* in thirty-seven days in 1785; *Les Infortunes de la vertu* in fifteen days in 1787; *Eugénie de Franval* in eight days in 1788. By 1790, he can speak of fifteen octavo volumes of his works, of which roughly a quarter come down to us.

The Marquis de Sade is again transferred to Charenton in 1789, and the year after, he finally gains his freedom. France is a Republic; and Citizen Sade steps out penniless into the new world, his pale blue eyes hurting in the sun. His wife, who has been constant throughout his imprisonment, takes refuge in the Convent of Sainte-Aure. But Sade quickly forms another lasting alliance with a Madame Quesnet, born Marie-Constance Renelle. He publishes *Justine* anonymously in 1791, and enjoys the open success of his play, *The Count Oxtiern,* performed the same year at the Théâtre Molière. He becomes secretary, then chairman, of the Section des Piques, agitating, organizing, turning out political pamphlets, and almost invariably pardoning the prisoners brought before him. "He refused to judge, condemn, and witness anonymous death from afar," says Simone de Beauvoir. "The Terror, which was being carried out with a clear conscience, constituted the most radical negation of Sade's demoniacal world." [4] He is, of course, imprisoned again, and escapes the guillotine by a miracle. When the Terror comes to an end, Sade is returned to vagabondage. He cannot earn a living though both *Philosophy in the Bedroom* and *Aline and Valcour* appear in 1795. The faithful Madame Quesnet can barely support him. It is almost a relief when he is arrested in 1801 for the presumed authorship of *Justine* and *Juliette,* of which copies are found in his possession, as well as obscene hangings and engravings.

First at Sainte-Pélagie, then at Charenton Asylum, Sade spends the remainder of his days. Mme. Quesnet joins him, passing for his daughter. He writes plays and directs their performance, using the inmates of Charenton as his actors. M. de Coulmier, director of the asylum, gives Sade his protection and treats him with sympathy, though the Prefect of Police Dubois warns that Sade is "an incorrigible man," in a state of "constant licentious insanity," and of "a character hostile to any form of constraint." [5] The Minister of Interior, the Minister of Police, and Napoleon himself sitting in Privy Council agree that Sade poses an incalculable danger, and must be isolated forever from his fellow men. On December 2, 1814, Donatien-Alphonse-François de Sade expires of a pulmonary obstruction, and is buried religiously in the cemetery of Saint-Maurice.

His wish was different. In his "Last Will and Testament" he asks to be buried without ceremony in a ditch, on his property at Malmaison. "The ditch once covered over, above it acorns shall be strewn, in order that the spot become green again, and the copse grown back thick over it, the traces of my grave may disappear from the face of the earth as I trust the memory of me shall fade out of the minds of all men. . . ." [6] It is as if Sade finally understands that his true redemption lay in obliterating his fantasy of immortality. The death wish of the man is the consummation of his grisly eroticism.

## III

Paradox and duplicity riddle Sade's ideas as well as his life. His ideas are not seminal but they have the partial truth of excess, of release. They constitute a dubious myth of consciousness. We perceive the outlines of that myth as we move from his exoteric to his esoteric works, from his avowed to his underground publications. The movement, regardless of chronology, is toward total terror.

Sade's public stance is that of a novelist. In an astute essay, "Idée sur les romans" (1800), he sketches the history of the genre, paying particular tribute to the "masculine" novels of Richardson and Fielding, and declaring his admiration for Gothic fiction, especially *The Monk* of M. G. Lewis, that black fruit of European history. He also gives us his theory of fiction. The theory puts forth in respectable guise—Sade strenuously disclaims the authorship of *Justine*—his outrageous theory of life. Man has always been subject to two weaknesses, Sade argues, prayer and love; these are weaknesses that the novelist must exploit.[7] The first inspires hope mixed with terror; the second inspires tenderness; and both combine to sustain the interest of fiction. Terror and tenderness, however, create the greatest interest when virtue appears in constant jeopardy; had "the immortal" Richardson ended *Clarissa* with a conversion of Lovelace, and a happy marriage between the seducer and the seduced, no reader would have shed "delicious tears." "It is nature, therefore, rather than virtue, nature incarnate in man's heart, that the novelist must grasp." [8]

Sade speaks for the novelist and pretends to explore the business of fiction. He asks that the full ambiguity of man's nature be recognized; he rejects the sentimental and didactic rhetoric that dominate the novel. But we insult Sade's intelligence when we take him at his word. His concern is neither art nor nature but dreamful liberty. He finds that liberty in evil.

The plot of his monomyth requires villainy to remain in ascendance till the parodic resolution. In his original "Preface" to *Contes et fabliaux,* written about 1787, Sade makes this pronouncement:

The basis of nearly all tales and nearly all novels is a young woman, loved by a man who is akin to her, and crossed in her love by a rival whom she dislikes. If this rival triumphs, the heroine, they say, is extremely unfortunate. . . . This, then, is what has decided us to add an extra touch, more than age or ugliness, to the rival who crosses the heroine's loves. We have given him a tinge of vice or of libertinism to alarm truly the girls he tries to seduce. . . .

With droll duplicity Sade concludes: ". . . one has been able to lift a small corner of the veil and to say to man: this is what you have become, *mend your ways for you are repulsive.*" [9]

The formula applies rigidly to *Contes et fabliaux,* and applies, with minor variations, to *Les Crimes de l'amour* which Sade originally intended as part of his *Contes.* The crimes of love always trace a triangle. Juliette de Castelnau loves the brave Raunai but is in the power of the Duke de Guise; the Duke de Ceilcour must choose between the virtuous Dolsé and the perfidious Mme. de Nelmours; Henriette Stralson fights off the debauched Lord Granwell who ruins her betrothed, Williams. The crimes of love also culminate in incest. In *Eugénie de Franval,* for instance, the father patiently and methodically raises his daughter to be his mistress, and they both delight in torturing the mother. Everywhere, Sade focuses on the energy of evil. He varies the background: now it is the Huguenot wars of France, now eighteenth-century England (Fielding appears in one of the tales as an honest magistrate), now Spain during a Moorish invasion. But it is obvious that Sade has little interest in place, time, or person, in the concrete reality of things of human character. His myth of the battle between Vice and Virtue always takes the form of a game of sexual permutations. The necessary rules of the game define its morality.

*Dialogue Between a Priest and a Dying Man*, written in 1782, states this "morality" more explicitly. God, according to Sade, is a superfluous hypothesis; and the Redeemer of Christianity is "the most vulgar of tricksters and the most arrant of all imposters." [10] The Marquis glibly invokes cultural and religious relativism to bolster the arguments of his dying man. The only constant is Nature, and Nature is indifferent to what men call vice or virtue. It is simply a process of death and regeneration in which nothing is ever lost. Men are part of Nature and subject to instinctual necessity; they have no freedom to choose. "We are the pawns of an irresistible force, and never for an instant is it within our power to do anything but make the best of our lot and forge ahead along the path that has been traced for us." [11] The dying man ends by persuading the priest; and, needless to say, both join in an orgy with six women kept on hand for the funereal occasion.

The personal argument is hidden. Sade attacks God in the name of Nature. The idea of Christian Divinity repels him because it rests on piety and tradition, and it often serves the advantage of corrupt men. But the true cause of his revolt against Deity is double: he needs the erotic release of transgression against authority—in blasphemy, in desecration—and he resents any power that might qualify the omnipotence of the Self. These twin motifs, still implicit in the *Dialogue*, pervade his tales of sexual terror. As for Nature, it is itself Sade's largest fantasy, existing only to give substance to his wishes. Since fantasy admits all contradictions, he can claim that crime is both a necessity of Nature and the only freedom in it.

Crime, at any rate, is merely one aspect of libertinage, the politics of human freedom. This is the lesson of *Philosophy in the Bedroom* (1795). The book is a manifesto ringing as loud as Marx's: "Voluptuaries of all ages, of every sex, it is to you only that I offer this work. . . . It is only by sacrificing everything to the senses' pleasure that . . . this poor creature who goes under the name of Man, may be able to sow a smattering of roses atop the thorny path of life." [12] It is also a catechism of libertinage relieved, with deadly regularity, by practice orgies and computerized perversions. Like all Sade's works, the book is repetitious. But it is also grotesquely comic in parts, a parodic novel of manners which insists on the complaisancies of the drawing room, the school room, and the bedroom.

The assertion of Dolmancé throughout the seven dialogues is hard to miss: the end of libertinage is pleasure. To achieve this end, certain prejudices must be banished: God, Virtue, and Moderation. (Sade is one of the earliest writers to dramatize, both in life and fiction, the conflict between instinct and society.) There is no restraint in libertinage, and no limit; the sole guide is one's desires. Everything is permitted: "no exceptions as to place, to time, to partner; all the time, everywhere, every one has got to serve your pleasures. . . ." [13] The logic of this statement becomes clear when we realize that for Sade no other selves exist; the world is full only of sources of pain or pleasure. Dolmancé is therefore consistent when he says of man: "Victim he is, without doubt, when he bends before the blows of ill fortune; but criminal, never." [14] For crime presupposes the existence of others. Since each one of us is alone and for himself in the world, cruelty to others is, from one's own point of view, a matter of profound indifference—unless it can be made a source of orgasm. Dolmancé defines sadism when he says:

> . . . the reverberations that result in us when the sensation of pain is produced in others . . . will put the animal spirits more violently into circulation and these, directing themselves toward the nether regions by the retrograde motion essential to them, instantly will ignite the organs of voluptuousness and dispose them to pleasure.[15]

But the benefits of cruelty are not exhausted in orgasm, Dolmancé insists; cruelty is also "the energy in a man civilization has not yet altogether corrupted: therefore it is a *virtue,* not a *vice* [italics mine]." [16] Sade revives the terms which he has raged to obliterate. This does not prevent his heroine from learning her lesson too well. When her mother arrives to rescue her from the orgy, Eugénie helps to torture her viciously, and in a perverse re-enactment of Oedipal fantasy, plays the sexual role of a man, Eugénie's own father: "Come, dear lovely Mamma, come, let me serve you as a husband." [17]

In the middle of his fifth dialogue, Sade inserts his famous revolutionary appeal, "Yet Another Effort, Frenchmen, If You Would Become Republicans." After speaking as a libertine, he now chooses to speak as a libertarian; the two, Sade pretends, are twin aspects of the free man. His sophistry as moralist, sociologist, and legislator reaches new heights. His conclusion is predictable: "In pointing out . . . the nullity, the indifference of an infinite number of actions our ancestors, seduced by a false religion, beheld as criminal, I reduce our labor to very little. Let us create a few laws, but let them be good. . . ." [18] The libertarian makes an honorable plea which conceals the motive of the libertine; the latter offers a rationalization of the Sadian temper which further conceals a motive Sade himself does not perceive.

That motive is Manichean. Virtue and Vice are locked in eternal combat, though Vice seems to hold the upper hand. Sade poses as a naturalist who lives beyond good and evil. Yet his constant use of such terms as "degrade," "deprave," "debauch," and "pervert" indicates that his world is anything but morally neutral. It is a world in which *transgression* is real and *sacrilege* dear. "Oh, Satan!" Dolmancé cries, "one and unique god of my soul, inspire thou in me something yet more, present further perversions to my smoking heart, and then shalt thou see how I shall plunge myself into them all." [19] Can we wonder that he, like all Sade's villains, constantly applies religious imagery to sexual functions? Furthermore, Sade's world is one in which Nature must remain sterile. Copulation thrives, procreation never. He abhors the womb, and therefore sodomy, heterosexual and homosexual sodomy, rules all desire; he offers not the Lord's way but the Devil's. Though Dolmancé speaks reverently of lifting the veil off the mysteries of Nature, as a libertine he can only aggress against her, he can only impose his will, his fantasy, on life. The libertine is thus shown to be, at bottom, a desecrator of mysteries. Finally, the world of Sade is a prison of consciousness. The power of Vice and Virtue, the vitality of Nature, vanish in the dungeon of the Self. In the moment of orgasm, the Sadian Self seeks desperately to become something other than itself. Yet it cannot; it ends by incarcerating the world with itself. As a despot in its dungeon, the Self cannot tolerate pleasure in anyone else. It induces pain in order to assimilate others to its unique existence. "There is not a living man who does not wish to play the despot when he is stiff," Sade writes ". . . by an impulse of pride . . . he would like to be the only one in the world capable of experiencing what he feels. . . ." [20] The vast republic of Freudian instincts and the practical democracy of the Dionysian orgy are both toppled with this wish. The Marquis de Sade is not an aristocrat in his imaginary bedroom: he is a solipsist.

*Justine: Or Good Conduct Well Chastised* (1791), the most cherished of Sade's works, is a parody of picaresque, gothic, and sentimental fiction. (The book enjoyed an early popularity, went through six printings, and led to the arrest of both author and publisher in 1801.) It pushes the fantasies of Sade one step farther toward outrage without altering their content; it merely varies the format by accretion of horrors. The dedication to Marie-Constance Quesnet states the novel's claim to originality thus:

> But throughout to present Vice triumphant and Virtue a victim of its sacrifices, to exhibit a wretched creature wandering from one misery to the next; the toy of villainy; the target of debauch; exposed to the most barbarous, the most monstrous caprices . . . briefly, to employ the boldest scenes, the most energetic brush strokes, with the sole object of obtaining from all this one of the sublimest parables ever penned for human edification; now, such

were . . . to seek to reach one's destination by a road not much traveled heretofore.[21]

One can feel Sade's rising frenzy as he contemplates the misfortunes of the heroine of his dreams. And one can also feel his naïve relish of deception in presenting the "traitorous brilliancies of crime" as a warning to his readers. With the former, Sade manages to indulge his sadistic taste; with the latter, he gratifies his need for culpability. Thus *Justine* brings to its author a double satisfaction in the acts of living out an erotic fantasy and then perpetrating it on humanity.

The narrative is in the first person. A girl in chains, Thérèse (really Justine), charged with murder, theft, and arson, stops with her guards at a roadside inn. The Countess de Lorsange (really her sister, Juliette), who is stopping at the inn with an august personage, demands to know the story of the prisoner. Juliette had long ago discovered that "true wisdom consists infinitely more in doubling the sum of one's pleasures than in increasing the sum of one's pains." [22] But Justine was born under another star: "it was already written in Heaven that every one of the honest gestures that was to emanate from me would be answered by misfortunes," she sighs.[23] Sade employs this irony as the iron principle of his perverse picaresque. Nothing Justine ever does is too good to escape terrible chastisement, and no chastisement is too terrible to corrupt her goodness. It is a world of eternal fixity.

The assaults on Justine alternate between the sexual and the intellectual; the latter are meant to explain or justify the former. Sade sees no inconsistency in his absolute tyrants who choose to expound their views at great length to abject victims. God, Nature, Society, Sex, and Crime are exhaustingly treated. Here and there, the author introduces a bizarre or new idea. Coeur-de-fer, head of a robber gang, undertakes to refute Rousseau's doctrine of the Social Contract by arguing that it benefits only the middle class; the powerful and the deprived risk only to lose by it. Coeur-de-fer opts, therefore, for perpetual strife, radical anarchy. Another villain, the pederast Bressac, announces: "The primary and most beautiful of Nature's qualities is motion, which agitates her at all times, but this motion is simply a perpetual consequence of crimes. . . ." [24] The coprophagous monk, Clément, explains his habit by invoking the imagination:

> Extraordinary, you declare, that things decayed, noisome, and filthy are able to produce upon our senses the irritation essential to precipitate their complete delirium . . . realize, Thérèse, that objects have no value for us save that which our imagination imparts to them. . . . The human imagination is a faculty of man's mind whereupon, through the senses' agency, objects are painted, whereby they are modified, and wherein, next, ideas become formed, all in reason of the initial glimpsing of those external objects. . . . To like what others like proves organic conformity, but demonstrates nothing in favor of the beloved object. . . . It is in the mother's womb that there are fashioned the organs which must render us susceptible of such-and-such a fantasy . . . once tastes are formed nothing in the world can destroy them.[25]

This opinion is echoed by the formidable counterfeiter, Roland —*his* tastes lean toward necrophilia—when he proclaims that the libertine's mind is stirred not by a woman's beauty but by the species of crime he commits against her. All the ideas of Sade tend toward creating an absolute moral vacuum in the world, which he then proceeds to fill with his overweening consciousness.

The special effect of *Justine* derives precisely from its two correlative fantasies: the omnipotence of the Sadian tyrant-villain and the abjectness of his victim-heroine. The fantasies are sustained by various devices. Justine, for instance, insists on calling her tormentors "monster," "tyrant," "tiger"; she inflates their powers as well as their organs. For like Sade himself, she is eternally complicit in her victimization. Her mock modesty, reticence, incompetence, and meekness serve this end, as do her cries, sighs, and lamentations. There is also a clever and lascivious poignancy in the device of first-person narration which forces Justine herself to render the obscene testimony of her life. As for Sade's villains, they must all enjoy the advantages of power, wealth, or high birth. Their black eyes glint, their white teeth sparkle, their members beggar description. Their world is high-walled, wide-moated, and deep-dungeoned, hid in a dark forest or perched on a craggy peak. Their world is a veritable fortress of fantasy which reality can never breach. In that fortress, they reign supreme; their actions defy all logic, all predictions. As Justine says of her captors in the Benedictine Abbey near Auxerre, "those monsters' whimsy bursts all circumscriptions, and caprice forms the unique law by which their actions are determined." [26] The actions are disengaged from the continuum of time and history, and are accorded each the status of a superlative. The dream of omnipotence is also a vision of plenty—the latter, Steven Marcus shows, is a general characteristic of pornography.[27] But sexual abundance—rooms are awash with sperm and every orgasm seems a cataclysm—expresses a psychic rather than an economic view of the self; it is a symbol of will.

The consummation of the Sadian will is in death; the limits of an omnipotent consciousness are murder and suicide. We should not be surprised, therefore, if the villains of *Justine* serve Thanatos reverently. The gargantuan glutton with a child's penis, Count de Gernande, reaches his climax only when his wife is bled before his eyes. Roland keeps an effigy of death in a coffin in his necropolis within the bowels of the earth. He employs the noose ecstatically on his victims, and employs it even on himself. Surely no power is more absolute than in the act of annihilating a human consciousness, unless it were in the act of creating another, which Sade finds intolerable. The ultimate revenge of man who can neither kill God nor can, like God, create, is to kill His creatures. This is why, in the end, Sade must arbitrarily kill off his own fictional creations. Justine, who has survived all hazards and finally earned her peace, is suddenly transfixed by a thunderbolt as she stands idly in her room. The bolt goes through her breast, heart, and belly. Thus the Marquis succeeds where all his villains have failed: he murders Justine.

The escalation of terror continues in *The 120 Days of Sodom* (1785); the orgy is now openly conceived as a massacre.[28] Sade completes only one of the four parts of this work; the other sections remain in the form of notes and catalogues. No ideas mar the onanistic intentions of this book. Such exclamations as "Oh, incredible refinement of libertinage!" recur in order to seduce the author more than his readers. "And now, friend reader, you must prepare your heart and ready your mind for the most impure tale that has ever been told since our world was born, a book the likes of which are met with neither amongst the ancients nor among us moderns." [29] Sade, the pornographer, speaks out frankly, speaks even truly, but even as a pornographer he speaks mainly to pleasure himself.

This is why the form of *The 120 Days* is reflexive; it can only mirror, or rather echo, itself. The four master libertines listen to four historians enumerate the 150 Simple, 150 Complex, 150 Criminal, and 150 Murderous Passions, which they then put into practice. Thus story and action echo back and forth to advantage; for as Sade says: ". . . it is commonly accepted amongst thoroughbred libertines that the sensations communicated by the organs of hearing are the most flattering and those whose impressions are the liveliest. . . ." [30] The historians, in fact, serve their masters as Sade the author serves the man. The words we read turn back upon themselves; their form, repudiating an audience, becomes anti-form.

The pattern of the work justifies the rubric of anti-form in another sense: it is purely arithmetical. With demented ingenuity, Sade reduces his fantasy to an equation. There are four master libertines, four wives who are their daughters, four women historians, four duennas, eight fuckers, eight young girls, eight young boys, and six female cooks and scullery maids. The book is divided into four parts; the orgy lasts seventeen weeks, or 120 days. All the arrangements of this mathematical ménage are specified meticulously, the number of wines and dishes, the number of lashes for each punishment. The statutes which govern the progress of the orgy are as clear as they are inflexible; the schedule for the whole period is fixed. From a total of forty-six characters, precisely thirty are massacred and sixteen permitted to return to Paris. "Under no circumstances deviate from this plan," Sade enjoins himself in his notes, "everything has been worked out, the entirety several times reexamined with the greatest care and thoroughness." [31] Number and ratio, we see, rule the form of this game directed by an autoerotic computer. Sade's fiction is truly a dream of logic. In this, he prefigures the parodic dream of Beckett.

But the work is not only abstract, it is also hermetic. Nothing, absolutely nothing, must penetrate the Fortress of Silling where the action takes place, except the mind. That castle, situated somewhere on an impossible peak in the Black Forest, is impregnable because it lies within the skull. "Ah, it is not readily to be imagined how much voluptuousness, lust, fierce joy are flattered by those sureties, or what is meant when one is able to say to oneself: 'I am alone here, I am at the world's end, withheld from every gaze, here no one can reach me, there is no creature that can come nigh where I am; no limits, hence no barriers. I am free,'" Sade writes.[32] The prisoner aspires to the freedom of God. The four libertines are monstrously rich; they spend two million a year on their debauches. Furthermore, Blangis is a duke, his brother a bishop; Curval is a president, and Durcet a banker. In the real world, money and status remain at the source of their power. But at Silling, where there are no guards or jailers, forty-two people submit unconditionally to the will of four. Why? Sade wills it so. The freedom of his libertines, their limitless power, derives from one source only: the desire of the imprisoned Sadian self.

Occasionally, the Sadian self rises to metaphysical rebellion. Curval, for instance, cries: "Ah, how many times, by God, have I not longed to be able to assail the sun, snatch it out of the universe, make a general darkness, or use that star to burn the world!" [33] This is spoken in the demonic vein of Ahab. We also learn of certain libertines who poison the rivers and streams, and strive to annihilate a province. But these apocalyptic postures are always furtive, and their motive is less philosophic than sexual. Were Sade truly to recognize the rebellious imperatives of the Self, he would never tolerate four libertines to coexist on the same level: there would be only one. A society of omnipotent beings can be chartered only in pornographic fiction.

The Sadian self, I have said, finds its consummation in death, and this is nowhere more obvious than in the apocalypse of *The 120 Days* where the final authority rests with Thanatos. The first sections are dominated by cloacal fantasies; the human organism is conceived not as energy but as waste. Behind the scatological comedy and the delights of Sodom, scarcely disguised, appears the hatred of life. At Silling, the life and fecal economies of the community unite under a strict control. No birth is permitted, and elimination is reduced; therefore, life is hindered from self-renewal. Lower forms of organization, like excrement, are valued above higher forms, like food. At Silling, entropy is dominant, and annihilation the ultimate goal. This is why Sade can say: ". . . there is no libertine at least a little steeped in vice who is not aware of the great empire murder exerts over the senses and how handsomely it determines a discharge." [34] Death conquers all. Denial of others reaches a climax not in the affirmation but in the denial of self. "What can be more disturbing," Georges Bataille asks, "than the prospect of selfishness becoming the will to perish in the furnace lit by selfishness?" [35] And so the work ends with the story of the enormous nobleman, indulging his "infernal caprice, or more simply . . . the hell passion," roaring with stentorian rage and ecstasy as fifteen victims are simultaneously tortured and killed before his eyes to release his demonic orgasm. The symbolic apocalypse at the Fortress of Silling is then concluded.

We see at last the sad equation of Sade: man is orgasm, and orgasm is death. Prisoner of his consciousness, he tries to escape through the language of macabre onanism. His visions mortify, desiccate the body, and open in the flesh an abyss wherein consciousness is swallowed. The Sadian self, seeking desperately to become another, sinks back into itself. Its only release is in death.

## IV

"It was not murder that fulfilled Sade's erotic nature; it was literature," Simone de Beauvoir keenly observes.[36] His heroes speak on indefatigably, and their words adapt terror to human history. Thus Sade makes his way into the domain of letters; his dungeon opens on the present. Apollinaire and Breton, Heine and Lely, Blanchot and Camus have made him our familiar.

We see Sade, almost, as the first avant-gardist, the daemon of Romanticism and of Gothic fiction, a Surrealist before our time, and a herald of anti-literature. We imagine him as a precursor to Darwin, Freud, and Nietzsche, and as a forerunner of the anarchists, Max Stirner and Bakunin. We feel his genius in Dachau, Belsen, and Auschwitz, and in all apocalyptic politics. We accept him, at the same time, as an apostle of pornotopia, a child of the Enlightenment, and an example of metaphysical rebellion. This is all to say that we still struggle to see Sade clearly through his outrageous myth. Yet there is no doubt that his spirit moves in our culture, and defines, more than an aspect of pathology, a crucial element of our consciousness.

The element is easiest to discern in the domain of letters. Sainte-Beuve believed that Sade's great influence in the nineteenth century was as clandestine as Byron's was overt. In *The Romantic Agony*, Mario Praz sets out to redress the balance. He shows that the Divine Marquis casts his shadow on the *roman noir*, the *roman feuilleton*, the *roman charogne*, the *roman frénétique* of the period, inspires the satanism, vampirism, lycanthropy, incest, necrophilia, and cannibalism of various Romantic works, and breathes a perverse, new life into that major Richardsonian theme, the persecution of a virtuous maiden.[37] Chateaubriand, Petrus Borel, Eugène Sue, Lautréamont, Baudelaire, and even Flaubert, in France alone, are haunted by the specter of the Marquis. In America, England, and Germany, the erotic sensibility honors him secretly in the Gothic romance, the tale of terror, and the *liebestod*.

Sade's contribution to literary history does not exhaust itself in romantic decadence. It depends, rather, on his effort to supplant the sentimental novel, and to give Gothic fiction new authority. During his own lifetime, the morality of the bourgeois novel spends itself; revolutionary thought demands new values. Sade calls hell to the rescue, thinking thus to redeem the reality of fiction. He even assumes a larger task which he never quite realizes: the creation of the modern novel. The Gothic genre that Sade seeks to regenerate, Fiedler shows in *Love and Death in the American Novel*, is by its nature parricidal, opposed to the authority of Church and State, and to all middle-class pieties. It is a voice from the dungeon keep, from the unconscious, breaking all the primal taboos of civilization, hollow with guilt, frenzied with marvelous imaginings. And it tells the improbable tale of the diabolic male hero, pursuing Woman and desecrating her at every opportunity. In its deepest conception, the Gothic novel touches the rebellious motives of avant-garde literature, foreshadows its spiritual isolation, and announces its death wish.[38] In this if in nothing else, the Marquis, as Kafka says, is "the veritable patron of the modern age."

But Sade also presages anti-literature. The Surrealists, we know, claim him after Apollinaire publishes a selection of his works in 1909. Their claim, however, does not recognize the peculiarly modern problem of his language. The life of pure eroticism and the life of pure violence are equally silent. Their excesses stand outside of reason and speech; their culmination in death is mute. Yet Sade speaks volubly. As Bataille notes, "A paradox underlies his behavior. De Sade speaks, but he is the mouthpiece of a silent life, of utter and inevitably speechless solitude." [39] Language is forced to cheat in order to express annihilation, and in doing so it cheats itself. An icy awareness persists where no awareness could subsist; every whiplash is counted. The style of total terror becomes numbers, subject to obsessive additions, variations, repetitions, permutations. The style takes us out of the field of terror, expressing merely the rationalized will to violence in terms of an algebra of coitus. The style moves toward the field of nonsense.

Sade's language is further silenced by his solipsistic attitude. With whom can this author communicate? In whose ears does his speech ring? Sade stands alone as subject; all others vanish into objects of his pleasures. There is no question of genuine response. Sade's words are intelligible only as a masturbatory fantasy, taking the form of conversations between tyrant and victim. In these stylized dialogues, the characters are forced to contradict their logical destiny, immutable silence and solitude, in order to provide their author with sexual entertainment. "The enactment of the erotic scene interested him more than the actual experience," Simone de Beauvoir notes.[40] True: Sade's language serves *him* as a mirror, reflecting lewd dreams.

Certainly, the language is not intended to convey fact or truth. It is rather an organ of deceit, about which Dolmancé says:

> Without hesitation I say I know of nothing more necessary in life; one certain truth shall prove its indispensabilty: everyone employs it . . . let us behold it as the key to every grace, every favor, all reputation, all riches, and by means of the keen pleasure of acting villainously, let us placate the little twinge our conscience feels at having manufactured dupes.[41]

Language as deceit reminds us of the anti-languages of propaganda in our own century. We have now seen the extremes:

for Herr Goebbels, all official speech is truth; for William Burroughs, all speech is lying. Sade confirms the current revulsion against language by making mendacity his policy. When shall we believe him? His words remain as equivocal as those of the Cretan who declares all Cretans liars. Sade's language subverts itself, and suffers from the bad faith he shows toward his inexistent readers.

The very form of Sade's work qualifies for the term anti-literature. The conventions of Gothic fiction, the picaresque novel, the novel of manners, the philosophic dialogue, and utopian pornography make their perfunctory appearance in that work. But the function of form as control or realization of a human impulse is denied, for Sade's impulses defy all satisfaction. As Steven Marcus argues: "The ideal pornographic novel . . . would go on forever. . . . If it has no ending in the sense of completion or gratification, then it can have no form. . . . We see here one more reason for the opposition of pornography to literature." [42] It is really a question of qualitative difference. Certain modes of pornography, Susan Sontag rightly argues, should not be excluded from the realm of literature.[43] I prefer to annex these modes to anti-literature. In this as in other respects, Sade outshines the common pornographer. His works are almost wholly independent of time, place, and person, and their autistic purpose is single. Without full comprehension of his role in Western thought, Sade may thus be the first to wrench the imagination free from history, to invert the will of art, and to set language against itself.

He may also be the first to limn the modern consciousness within its void. He wants to restore man to nature, to the force of instincts. He perceives, with a rigor akin to Freudian determinism, the bizarre equivalences of mind and body, fantasy and flesh, in the pursuit of love. He has an intuition of the primal horde, the taboo against incest, the Oedipal drama we re-enact continually with our fathers and mothers, brothers and sisters. He knows that dreams extend the meaning of our waking life, and employs them in his stories accordingly. Above all, Sade complicates for us, in a tragic and irrevocable way, the image of life-giving Eros by revealing the long shadow Thanatos casts upon it. He understands that violence is a condition of vitality, and that nature revels in destruction; he brings the Enlightenment to an end. Yet he never loses the sense that love always lurks where death rules. As Brigid Brophy puts it: "The unitive purpose of Eros is never wholly defeated, because in Sade's conception the torturer and victim tend toward what Simone de Beauvoir calls a genuine couple. Sade is aware that the torturer's real crime will be not simply to inflict pain but to seduce and corrupt the victim into being his accomplice and wanting pain to be inflicted. The relation comes close to being a game. . . ." [44] This is the game that may become the apocalypse of our time.

In the end, however, Sade limits his relevance to us because he demands to be taken only on his own terms. The Sadian self permits no encounter, no negotiation. It solves the problem of evil by converting all pain, whether inflicted or received, into a source of personal pleasure. Sade can therefore experience orgasm when he hears that he has been burned in effigy. He can even look forward to the posthumous joy of being one of "those perverse writers whose corruption is so dangerous, so active, that their single aim is, by causing their appalling doctrines to be printed, to immortalize the sum of their crimes after their own lives are at an end; they themselves can do no more, but their accursed writings will instigate the commission of crimes, and they carry this sweet idea with them to their graves. . . ." [45] This is the perfect crime which perpetuates itself even when the agent has ceased to act: the crime of the imagination.

The imagination of Sade is inflamed by crime because all its energies are committed to transgression. Vice defies Virtue, against God stands the Devil. But this Manicheanism is superficial. Sade denies God vehemently, and ends by identifying himself with Omnipotence. The dialectic of transgression moves toward infinity. As Blanchot perceives: ". . . the conception of an infernal God is but a way station of the dialectic according to which Sade's superman, after having denied man in the guise of God, next advances to meet God and will in turn deny him in the name of Nature, in order finally to deny Nature by identifying it with the spirit of negation." [46] The true spirit of the Sadian self is priapic and continuous denial. This leads it *finally* to deny itself by invoking a void which may engulf even its own omnipotence. The consciousness of Sade, raised to the highest level, is anti-consciousness as his work is anti-literature. The mind and the language, caught in hatred, seek release from their own forms into a silence commensurate with outrageous vision.

There is a paradox in the attempt of the Divine Marquis to write anything, as there is a further paradox in my attempt to write about his writings. But paradoxes betray the limits of logic rather than of reality. The works of Sade prefigure the destructive element of our world, and the claims he makes upon us are hard, perhaps impossible, to meet. Yet we dare no longer ignore these claims. There can be no life for men until Sade is answered.

Wide-eyed and bodiless, Orpheus glares at the sun, waiting eternally for night.

CHAPTER II

# *INTERLUDE:*

## *From 'Pataphysics to Surrealism*

N'est-ce pas que c'était beau comme littérature?
Jarry

### I

THE SCENE is still France, almost a century after the death of the Marquis de Sade.We look back on the period marking the end of *la belle époque* and marvel at the hallucinations that a stable society can engender. Literary gangsters roam the night streets of the mind while elegant or gaudy crowds jostle gaily in theatres and cafés, on the boulevards. Europe seems at the height of its brilliant pride. Yet the time is also that of prophets from other planets. Everything becomes possible, even the denial of culture, language, and art. As Roger Shattuck says, "Like the anarchists, the artists of the avant-garde took liberties with the structure of life itself. . . ." [1]

The avant-garde, in a technical literary sense, comes into being with 'Pathaphysics, Futurism, Dadaism, and Surrealism. Sade, Lautréamont, Rimbaud, a whole century of Romantic metaphor, countless years of human error, and man's search for the Absolute—all these prepare its way. In a larger sense, the avant-garde merely follows the logic of Western history. Yet following or leading, its spirit creates those vanishing forms that intrude upon us still, demanding a reckoning.

## II

Alfred Jarry (1873–1907) invents 'Pataphysics. He also dedicates his life to a career that denies both art and life. In his world, paradox and triviality rule the waning day. He believes the soul is a tic, and love a form of perpetual motion. He ends as a prophet of otherness, standing beside himself, Ubuesque. He also ends as a humorist of the infinite. André Breton notes, in his *Anthologie de l'humour noir*, that the distinction between art and life explodes with Jarry who carries revolvers, discharging them freely into the world, and so unites himself to its facts.[2] The explosion of each bullet seems a note in his laughter.

Jarry is born in Laval, near Brittany. His father is an artisan, his mother a romantic woman with aristocratic pretensions. Jarry, brilliant, shy, intransigent, capable of limitless effrontery, holds great affection for his mother; for his father he has only contempt. At the Lycée de Rennes, which he attends from 1888 to 1891, he finds the prototype of all objects of his disgust. M. Hébert is a teacher, incompetent, obese, and monstrously banal, who speaks of "my science of phisics"; Hebé, or Père Héb, becomes Père Ubu, and his science becomes the anti-science, 'Pataphysics. Jarry goes to Paris in 1891 to study at the Lycée Henri IV with Henri Bergson, thinking to prepare for the École Normale. He chooses, instead, a life more consistent with relentless self-dispossession; he chooses the literary life.

Haughty, buffoonish, formidably witty and erudite, Jarry crashes into bohemian Paris. His diminutive stature and glinting black eyes soon become familiar in the cafés; so do his various affectations: the metallic voice, the outlandish costumes with stove-pipe hats, the menacing armaments. His friends include Léon-Paul Fargue, Marcel Schwob, Octave Mirbeau, Catulle Mendès, and particularly Alfred Vallette, editor of the *Mercure de France*, and his beautiful wife, Madame Rachilde, a novelist. Through the *Mercure*, Jarry meets many of the poets and critics of the Symbolist Movement; he even attends, as a newcomer, Mallarmé's Tuesday soirées. But his style, once lyrical, becomes more and more rasping; the demon of parody begins to possess him. Jarry drinks wine, absinthe, and even ether, prodigiously. His sordid lairs become legendary. He calls them "Dead Man's Calvary," "Our Grand Chasublerie"; he ornaments them with a stone phallus, a stuffed owl, censers, crucifixes. Jarry still likes to fish and to bicycle through the country; his affection for bicycles, which he calls our "external skeleton," will remind us of Beckett's heroes cycling absurdly through the mind. But Jarry, who now speaks and acts entirely as Ubu, has wrenched himself from life. His pride matches his excesses; both are equal to his poverty. When his friends break through the door of his room, no larger than a large closet, on the second and a half floor of 7, rue Cassette, they find him paralyzed. He dies in the hospital; his last wish is for a toothpick. "His life," Shattuck writes, "and his work united in a single threat to the equilibrium of human nature." [3]

It is more than a threat; Jarry perfects the act, the art, of human denaturalization. He carries Romantic self-assertion, beyond alienation of the Self, to the limits of self-dissolution. This is implicit in Sade whose presence lurks in Jarry's science fantasy, *Le Surmâle*, (1902). The hero of that work, André Marcueil, lives on Perpetual Motion Food; races a train across Asia, riding on his vélo; copulates indefinitely under experimental conditions; and with sheer brain energy, overwhelms an 11,000-volt machine designed to inspire love. At the end, the machine "falls in love" with Marcueil as they "embrace" in a shower of sparks and destruction. Jarry asks the central question: "Who are you, Man?" [4] And he answers: both God and Machine. The dehumanization of man, we see, is also his apotheosis. It is no wonder that to young André Gide, Jarry seems to speak with the voice of a nutcracker.

In converting man into machine and life into artifice, Jarry obeys the Absurd, and therein lies his freedom. The principle of universal convertibility, on which 'Pathaphysics is founded, also denies fixed valence and discrete identity. Fact is equivalent to dream, past to present, reason to madness, space to time, and self to other. There are no limits, no contradictions. Parody, paradox, and hallucination are techniques of veracity. Humor depends on a continual reversal of terms. Style takes the form of radical ambiguity. As Jarry himself puts it: ". . . the relation of the verbal sentence to every meaning that can be found in it is constant . . . ;" from which Shattuck concludes: "All interpretations are on a par, are equivalent. . . . A text means all things equivocally . . . writing is a slip of the tongue." [5] The silence of Jarry is precise and consistent.

But what, precisely, is the science of 'Pataphysics, of which Ubu is a Doctor? In *Gestes et opinions du docteur Faustroll*, 1911, Jarry explains:

> 'Pataphysics is the science of the realm beyond metaphysics. . . . It will study the laws which govern exceptions and will explain the universe supplementary to this one. . . .
>
> Definition: 'Pataphysics is the science of imaginary solutions, which symbolically attributes the properties of objects, described by their virtuality, to their lineaments.[6]

In short, 'Pataphysics is the science of Nonsense. It assumes the absolute futility of thought. It implies both equivalence and reduction, and functions as a parodic myth. In that "myth," God is the shortest distance between zero and infinity, as Dr. Faustroll claims. Dr. Faustroll babbles on, and his monkey, Bosse-de-Nage (Bottom-Face), punctuates his master's learning with scatological events, crying always: "Ha, ha." The science has a gay and desperate side. We can understand why it inspires a number of free spirits to found, in 1949, a Collège de 'Pataphysique.

Like Sade, Beckett, or Burroughs, Jarry suffers from a reductive rage; he belittles our world. At times, there is something almost sacramental about his peculiar nihilism. But the ferocity of his deadpan humor betrays his animus against the condition of man. Great-souled, Jarry's person is small; and he dwells in burrows or caves. A misanthropist, he gallantly evades the complications of love. The little we know about his sexual life suggests that he feels horror for woman, *mater generatrix*. The world's body remains alien to him, and the "adipose tissue" of motherhood is "odious because it has a function—it produces *milk*." [7] The most famous expression of Ubu remains "Shitter"! Reduction leads finally to waste; this is the essential joke of life.

The literary joke, however, is more ample, and its form rather more cunning. *Ubu Roi* is staged at the Théâtre de l'Oeuvre by Lugné-Poe in 1896; decors, costumes, and masks are designed by Bonnard, Toulouse-Lautrec, and Vuillard among others. On opening night, the author makes a clipped speech, in accents of repressed arrogance, to all the writers and critics assembled. Then Ubu appears on stage, huge, pear-shaped, and unavoidable. His first word, uttered loudly, is "Merdre." The audience goes berserk; fistfights and catcalls continue through the evening. William Butler Yeats sits in the audience and struggles to understand, with the help of Rhymer, Jarry's French. He understands enough to comment in his *Autobiographies:* "After us the Savage God." [8] The objective mask of comedy conceals the horrors and disfigurations still to come.

The horror of *Ubu Roi* is that it happens Everywhere; actually, its setting is Poland which, as Jarry pedantically explains, is Nowhere. The action is childish, cruel, bestial, funny, and absurd; the hero is gross, deadly, stupid, rapacious, and wholly without scruples. Ignoble as he may be, Ubu endures, a brutish Everyman who resembles us all *because* he is nature, a canny union of id and ugly ego. His concerns are three: "physique," by which he means matter, "phynance," by which he means money and status, and "merdre," which subsumes all his concerns. Ubu is the all-gut gutless wonder, the bulging monument of bourgeois clichés, the end of history. He embodies the banality. He poisons his guests with a dirty broom, murders his master, the King of Poland, to usurp his throne, massacres the nobility to empty their coffers, and flees from the battlefield. The play which begins arbitrarily with obscenity must end, as Père and Mère Ubu make their way to France, with nonsense. "Ah, gentlemen!" Père Ubu says, "however beautiful it [France] may be, it can never equal Poland. If there weren't any Poland, there wouldn't be any Poles!" [9] Existence is farce. Yet the play grimly denounces the corruptions of man and society, and its humor explodes in violence and sudden death. At bottom, *Ubu Roi* is an assault on the audience, on the reality they think to possess. Its proper coda is "The Song of Disembraining" in which we are all Rentiers of Reality:

> Look, look at the machinery revolving,
> Look, look at the brain flying,
> Look, look at the Rentiers trembling!
> (Chorus) Hurrah, arce-horns, long live Père Ubu! [10]

But the assault of the play is also on language. Ubu speaks his own debased argot, mispronouncing words and making up others of his own: "merdre," "oneille," etc. The speeches are brief, truculent, jocular, and entirely otiose. It is as if language were constantly searching for its lowest common denominator in slang, obscenities, oaths, expletives, and clichés. Elegance is banished and poetry appears fleetingly in the form of rude popular ditties. Words express nothing, change nothing. The action of the play is an outrage, neither comic nor tragic, its structure is that of chaos disguised as slapstick; its style denies its own powers. Jarry parodies himself in Ubu, and parodies art in his writings. Once, in "real life," he fires his revolver at a sculptor and then exclaims: "N'est-ce pas que c'était beau comme littérature?" [11] The expression remains with him throughout his career, a clarion of contempt.

Jarry's contempt for art, however, is not simple. He admires Maeterlinck, for instance, and some aspects of the Symbolist aesthetic. He requires simplicity of design in the theatre, heraldic decors, masks and costumes that represent "effigies of character," a particular statement of the universal. He requires stylization, as in a marionette show or a Japanese play. He insists on a theatre for elite audiences, a theatre of *action* in which the elite participate in the genuine act of creation—let the masses copulate! [12] In such a theatre, the proper applause is silence. Speaking of *Ubu Roi*, Jarry says: "It is not surprising that the public should have been aghast at the sight of its ignoble other-self, which it had never before been shown completely." [13] The work of art, then, is an act of vicarious creation for the elect; for the rest, it is only insult and affront.

With time, however, even the act of creation loses its special authority. Jarry's parody deepens; his art becomes more gratuitous. *Almanach du Père Ubu*, (1899), is pastiche, a collection of dates, figures, tables, drawings, letters, catalogues, necrologies, etc. In *Ubu enchaîné* (1900), the destructive spirit consumes itself: Ubu chooses self-enslavement, slaughtering everyone who stands between him and his aim. "*Cornegidouille!*" he exclaims, ". . . we will not have demolished all if we do not demolish also the ruins!" [14] Nonsense attains its apocalyptic end. Why not ask for a toothpick on one's deathbed?

Alfred Jarry believes that the mind functions after death, and that its dreams are all we ever know of paradise.[15] We do not see the dreams of that mind in his work; we only see the splattered brain:

> Soon we were white with brain, my loving wife and I.
> The brats were eating it up, and we were merry as hell.[16]

Like Sade, like Lautréamont, Jarry carries his revolt against life to the seat of consciousness, and substitutes his dream for what men call reality. Like them, he strikes in the crotch. Laughingly, he crushes love into a bloody thing; the blood itself turns into excrement. This "sublime debauchee" is also a master of modernity. "With Alfred Jarry," Apollinaire writes in "The New Spirit and the Poets," ". . . we have seen laughter rise from the lower regions where it was writhing, to furnish the poet with a totally new lyricism." [17]

## III

Guillaume Apollinaire (1880–1918) is himself a more subtle apostle of "the new lyricism." For a time, he affects the accents of Jarry and his gruffness. But Apollinaire lacks the metaphysical truculence of his senior; eclectic, expansive, equivocal, his temperament wavers between outrage and nostalgia. The modern movement in art, music, and literature, struggles around him, making its way from the haunts of Montmartre and Montparnasse toward the light. Apollinaire finds himself in the midst of things, mediating between the past and the future, an advocate of the creative present. He gives the avant-garde a language and a name in history. Cubism, Futurism, Dadaism, and Surrealism owe him a debt of oblique definition.

Apollinaire is born in Rome, Guillaume Albert Wladimir Alexandre Apollinaire de Kostrowitzky, one of two illegitimate sons of Angélique de Kostrowitzky, of Polish nobility, and Francesco Flugi d'Aspermont, a dashing military figure. (For many years, Apollinaire encourages the rumor that his father is a Roman prelate, and allows his friends to paint his own portrait with miter and crosier.) When the liaison between his parents comes to a discreet end in 1885, Mme. Kostrowitzky settles with her two children on the French Riviera. Young Kostro, as he is called, studies at schools in Cannes and Monaco; he grows up under the Mediterranean sun. Later, he travels north, through the Ardennes and Germany; their gothic marvels blend into his classic temper.

In 1898, Apollinaire leaves school, goes to Paris to seek his fortune. He drifts naturally toward *la vie bohème*. Together with André Salmon, he claims Jarry as his idol. Apollinaire works as a bank clerk, a journalist, a ghost writer, a researcher in the Bibliothèque Nationale which he ransacks, and even as a pornographer. He edits various periodicals, such as *Le Festin d'Ésope* and later the *Soirées de Paris.* He publishes in the *Mercure de France.* The group of painters and writers who frequent the *bateau lavoir* of the Rue Ravignan in Montmartre are his intimates; they include Picasso, Gris, Braque, Jacob, Reverdy. He also knows Vlaminck and Derain who live in the suburb of Le Vésinet where his mother has taken up residence. By 1910—the year is also that of Jean Metzinger's famous portrait of Apollinaire—he establishes himself chief theoretician of Cubism in art and literature.

The ebullience of Apollinaire recedes a little when he finds himself, in 1911, in the Santé prison. The Mona Lisa has been stolen from the Louvre, and the police suspect him of complicity. The experience is humiliating, even terrifying. Six days later, Apollinaire is discharged, a hurt and bewildered man, his sense of disorder deepened. The authority of social as of artistic forms rests on sand; the world is all contingency. But Apollinaire in resilient and soon recovers. He discovers Chirico and Chagall; he follows the experiments of Delaunay with the color spectrum. He publishes *Alcools* in 1913. And when the war breaks out, he joins the army exuberantly, rising to the rank of second lieutenant before a shell wounds him in the head while reading a copy of the *Mercure* in the trenches. A huge banquet celebrates the return of the bandaged hero to Paris. Apollinaire settles in Saint-Germain-des-Prés with Jacqueline Kolb, "la jolie rousse." He seems a little more irritable than his friends can recall. Still, *Nord-Sud,* publishing Tzara and Breton, honors him, in 1917, as patron of the New Spirit. That same year, Apollinaire completes his play, *Les Mamelles de Tirésias,* using the term "*drame surréaliste*" to describe it. The future rushes to meet the present. But the health of Apollinaire breaks down. He marries Jacqueline in 1918. Some months later, he dies of influenza, two days before the Armistice. His mother appears briefly at the funeral and silently carries off his officer's cap.

In his life, Apollinaire never outreaches himself. He likes the world too much; his plastic intelligence refuses to place itself in jeopardy. He remains a mediator and a gentle judge. As he says of himself in "La Jolie Rousse": "I judge this long quarrel of tradition and invention, of Order and Adventure." [18] His last testament, "The New Spirit and the Poets," is predictably a mixture of prophecy and platitude. His poetry, sly and elegiac, is at heart a poetry of sentiment. The English governess, Annie Playden, the paintress Marie Laurencin, his wife "Ruby," receive, among others, the erotic tributes of a man attuned to the reciprocities of matter and spirit. His desire requires no apocalypse for its fulfillment. By comparison with *Ubu Roi, Les Mamelles de Tirésias* is a lovable skit, set in Zanzibar, about the repopulation of France.

Yet Apollinaire also understands the perversity of the modern. His interest in pornography—he writes it as well as edits its classics—is not motivated solely by lucre. He senses that mutations in human values always revert to sexual fantasies, to obscenity and violence. In the introduction to his edition of Sade, he writes: ". . . this man, who appeared to be of no importance through the whole of the nineteenth century, may well dominate the twentieth." [19] The "spiritual pus" which Sade injects into literature circulates through the works of Laclos, Poe, Baudelaire; and according to Apollinaire, the same toxic serves as necessary irritant to modernity. His own sketch, "The False Messiah, Amphion," combines decorous sadism with gratuitous crime, pointing vaguely to the obsessions of an age to come.

Apollinaire, we note, yearns to engage the future. "The poets wish to master prophecy, that spirited mare that has never been tamed," he writes. "And finally they want, one day, to mechanize poetry as the world has been mechanized." [20] He champions the Futurists in his "manifeste-synthèse," *L'Antitradition futuriste* (1913). His faith in the machine—its rhythms affect his poetry—is often naïve. But he predicts correctly its influence on art, and hails both still and moving pictures as the medium of the twentieth century. His calligrams strain for the presence of the ideogram; his "simultaneism" suggests the collages of Dada. In his own poetry, dislocation, surprise, and ambiguity suspend the logical functions of words. The syntax is free and the punctuation absent. Apollinaire senses that chance and inspiration may mingle; he senses the retreat from organized discourse. Cubism has taught him that the world of appearances can speak an original language. He now opens a way for Surrealism.

As early as 1908, he experiments with the style of Surrealism in a piece called "Oneirocriticism":

> The coals of the sky were so near that I was afraid of their heat. They were on the point of burning me. But I was conscious of the different eternities of man and woman. Two animals of different species were coupling, and rose-vines covered the trellises which moons weighed down with grapes. From the monkey's throat came flames which made the world blossom like a lily.[21]

This falls short of Surrealist techniques, vivid dreams and automatic writing. Still, Apollinaire playfully entertains, in *Le Poète assassiné* (1916), the end of poetry. The hero, Croniamantal, is martyred with knives as St. Sebastian was shot full of arrows. His followers dig a hole in the earth, carve his features into its walls, line them with concrete. The hole is filled with earth again. Beside this invisible sculpture of the Poet, a laurel tree grows. The parable of Orpheus's dismemberment is thus bequeathed to posterity.

## IV

The influence of Apollinaire remains ambiguous. He writes lasting verse while encouraging disciples to deride Art. Tristan Tzara seeks his approval. Apollinaire answers him in 1916: "I have liked your talent for a long time and like it even more since you have honored me by directing it toward a path in which I precede you but do not surpass you at all."[22] Apollinaire also casts a spell on young Breton, Aragon, Soupault, and reveals to them the secret of their city. His lines,

> Perdre
> Mais perdre vraiment
> Pour laisser place à la trouvaille
>
> ("Toujours")

whisper to them the hope of the new poetry. But there are others, like Jacques Vaché, who recall the pure intransigence of Jarry. Apollinaire, after all, serves as a French officer; he even covets the Legion of Honor. When Apollinaire dies, Vaché writes: "HE MARKS AN EPOCH. The wonderful things that we will be able to do—NOW!"[23] When the time comes for the Dadaists to rank their heroes, Apollinaire shows twelfth on the list, behind Chaplin, Lautréamont, Rimbaud, and Jarry.

For if Dada allows contradiction, it never permits compromise. Its challenge to the Western consciousness is meant to be complete. Dada taunts the world with its enormous talent, especially in the visual arts, then shows the world that talent can as easily taunt itself. No piety escapes its contempt. But contempt is also the style of its hope. Tzara and Lenin play chess in Zurich and each leaves that haven to start a revolution. Revolutions, we know, beget purges or squabbles. Petty betrayals mark the path of Dada and vanity remains one of its avatars. The critics say Dada is futile, is sterile, it leads nowhere. It leads to the nervous present. In 1936, Alfred Barr's anthology, *Fantastic Art, Dada, Surrealism* proves the currency of the movement. In 1968, William S. Rubin's *Dada, Surrealism, and Their Heritage* proves the same point again. Eager young crowds still flock to Dada "retrospectives" everywhere, seeking in its zany language some vision to confirm their own. Dada speaks best when it speaks without words, as children and psychopaths do in their art, or as an insane culture may express itself in its daily facts.

There is probably no beginning to Dada; suddenly it is there.

Above the noise of the big guns, the babble of Dada makes itself heard. Zurich lies in the peaceful dead-center of World War I. On February 1, 1916, a German called Hugo Ball, amateur novelist, mystic, and performer, founds the Cabaret Voltaire; his mistress, Emmy Hennings, helps with song; beer and sausage are plentiful. The Voltaire attracts artists and writers. These include Tristan Tzara, Marcel Janco, Richard Huelsenbeck, and Hans Arp. Posters, collages, and readings of "simultaneist verse" are their specialty; also readings from Apollinaire, Jarry, and Rimbaud, balalaika folk-songs and Negro music. As Arp puts it in Hans Richter's excellent study, *Dada: Art and Anti-Art*, "while the guns rumbled in the distance, we sang, painted, made collages and wrote poems with all our might. We were seeking an art based on fundamentals, to cure the madness of the age, and a new order of things that would restore the balance between heaven and hell." [24] Arp speaks for the constructive impulse of Dada which Tzara later assimilates to his insolent, jocose, and anarchic temper. After the single issue of Ball's *Cabaret Voltaire* (1916), Tzara takes over the editorship of *Dada* (1917–1920); his influence becomes paramount. He acts as if no men ever lived before him. But the Futurists precede him, of course. Richter, himself an early Dadaist, admits:

> The youthful élan, the aggressively direct approach to the public, the provocations, were products of Futurism, as were the literary forms in which they were clothed: the manifesto and its visual format. The free use of typography, in which the compositor moves over the page vertically, horizontally and diagonally, jumbles his type faces and makes liberal use of his stock of pictorial blocks—all this can be found in Futurism years before Dada. Bruitistic poems, in which words alternated with noises, had shocked audiences under the Futurist motto that a new dynamic age had dawned.[25]

But Dada, under Tzara's riotous leadership, knows how to advertize itself. Its home is the street, the café, the newspaper page, the art gallery, the music hall. It enlists, somehow, the genius of Picasso, Kandinsky, Klee, Chirico. It lives on the breath of insult, of scandal. Contradiction is its *mana:* Dada is Anti-Dada! But its energy soon diffuses itself. Ball vanishes from the scene, and later dies among the peasants of the Ticino, a holy man. Arp and Richter default, obeying their deeper allegiance to art. Huelsenbeck leaves for Berlin. Tzara continues on his way to chaos, cheered by the "Andalusian bull," Francis Picabia, editor of 391 (1917–1924), recently come from Barcelona. "Every page must explode," Picabia declares, "whether through seriousness, profundity, turbulence, nausea, the new, the eternal, annihilating nonsense, enthusiasm for principles, or the way it is printed. Art must be unaesthetic in the extreme, useless and impossible to justify." [26] The proper climax of Dada Zurich takes place in the pandemonium of the Saal zur Kaufleuten, on April 9, 1919. An audience of peaceful citizens is enraged by the performance, turning into a mob as savage as the armies just returned from the front. Thus Dada makes its point.

There may have been premonitions of Dada in the New World. We know that Edward Steichen experiments with photography as early as 1902, and Alfred Stieglitz edits an avant-garde magazine of the arts, 291 (1915–1916). Both men influence the visual techniques of Dada. And Marcel Duchamp, whose "Nude Descending the Staircase" dominates the famous Armory Show of 1913, already incorporates "found objects" into his art. "As early as 1913 I had the happy idea to fasten a bicycle wheel to a kitchen stool and watch it turn," Duchamp writes. "A point that I want very much to establish is that the choice of these 'ready-mades' was never dictated by aesthetic delectation. The choice was based on a reaction of *visual indifference* with a total absence of good or bad taste . . . in fact a complete anaesthesia." [27] Duchamp remains an anchorite of the void, a geometer thereof, like Kafka and Beckett. He consecrates his life to holy chess. His great chess opponent, Man Ray, also transforms useful objects into dead ones. With mathematical correctness, both attest to the disintegration of reality. So does Arthur Cravan in his madcap existence. He travels through wartime Europe on forged passports, challenges the world heavyweight champion, Jack Johnson, to a fight in Madrid, flouts all the literary and social conventions of his time, and vanishes one day in the Caribbean, a fitting end to his absurd "career." But Dada spreads from Zurich mainly into Germany and France. In defeated Germany, its character is often bitter, apocalyptic; it becomes a means of hastening the end. Huelsenbeck, Raoul Hausmann, and the Oberdada, Johannes Baader, stand at its center: Franz Jung, George Grosz, and Kurt Schwitters, founder of Merzism, stand close by. Baader vanishes periodically into a sanatorium to maintain his police certification of criminal irresponsibility. Huelsenbeck pretends to write his manifestoes with a revolver. And Hausmann declares German Dada irrevocably opposed to everything Teutonic, especially the "spirit of Weimar." Only Achim von Arnim, they all agree, can touch Lautréamont from afar.

It is in France, however, that Dada moves into the mainstream of Western literature. Cravan's *Maintenant* (1913–1915), printed on butcher paper, and Reverdy's *Nord-Sud* (1917–1918), foreshadow the event. Tzara also corresponds with Breton, Aragon, Soupault, and Ribbemont-Dessaignes. When he arrives in Paris in 1919, they greet him as a hero. His magnetic presence quickly asserts itself, and the journal of Breton, Aragon, and Soupault, *Littérature* (1919–1924), falls under the Dadaist influence until 1922. Dada reaches new heights of arrogance. Picabia issues a "Manifeste cannibale Dada." Max Ernst shows his first works, "Beyond Painting":

> The setting was the cellar. All the lights were out, and groans came from a trapdoor in the floor. Another joker, hidden behind a cupboard, was insulting those present . . . André Breton was striking matches. G. Ribbemont-Dessaignes was shouting over and over again, "It is raining on to a skull." Aragon was mewing. Ph. Sou-

pault was playing hide-and-seek with Tzara, while Benjamin Péret and Charcoune were shaking hands over and over again.[28]

The temper of Dada Paris, however, seems mainly *literary*; it pretends to concern itself with language. At heart, its concern is antic. This begins to pall on Breton. A mock trial of Maurice Barrès, admired by many Dadaists in their youth, reveals the growing rift between Breton and Tzara. The former wants to move beyond cynicism, beyond nihilism; he is even willing to accept certain forms of authority. Dissent leads to accusation and acrimony; slander and insult follow. In 1922, Tzara convenes the "Congress of Paris" to decide "whether a railway-engine was more modern than a top-hat"; the event marks the end of a unified front for Dada. Breton feels free to found a new theory, a new school: Surrealism. The funeral oration of Dada is delivered at Weimar, in May 1922, by Tzara himself:

> Dada marches on, destroying more and more, not in extension but in itself. . . .
>
> Dada is a state of mind. This is why it transforms itself according to the races and the events it encounters. Dada applies itself to everything, and yet it is nothing; it is the point at which Yes and No, and all opposites, meet; not solemnly, in the palaces of human philosophy, but quite simply, at street corners, like dogs and grasshoppers.[29]

Dada lives! Sensing the moment of satiety, it gives itself to nothingness. No sober definition of Dada can hold. The movement affects artists as diverse as Arp, Janco, Hausmann, Picasso, Giacometti, Ernst, Duchamp, Picabia, Richter, Grosz, Ray, Schwitters, Chagall, Chirico, Magritte, Kandinsky, Klee, Braques, Baargeld, Dali, Villon, Cornell, Miro, Masson, and Tanguy. It embraces such writers as Tzara, Breton, Eluard, Cendrars, Huelsenbeck, Péret, Soupault, Ribbemont-Dessaignes, Vaché, and Aragon. This is a formidable array of talent, more impressive finally in its plastic than in its literary contribution. Obviously, the virulent revolt against art proves to the immense advantage of what we still call art. But Dadaism is also polemic; the manifesto is its favored form. Despite itself, it creates a new consciousness. We should be mistaken to disregard one as the other.

The Dadaists speak well for themselves. Tzara, for instance, says in *Sept Manifestes dada:*

> Dada is our intensity: which erects bayonets without consequence on the Sumatran head of the German infant; Dada is life without slippers or parallels. . . .
>
> Dada is not folly, nor wisdom, nor irony, look at me, nice bourgeois. . . .
>
> We tear, furious wind, the sheets of clouds and of prayers, and prepare the great spectacle of disaster. . . .
>
> I call *jem'enfoutisme* the state of life wherein everyone observes his own conditions, knowing, meanwhile, how to respect other individualities. . . .
>
> Liberty: DADA DADA DADA, howling of shuddering pains, interlacement of opposites and of all contradictions, of grotesques, of inconsequences: LIFE. . . .
>
> What we now want is *spontaneity*. Not because it is more beautiful or better than all other things. But because all that issues freely from ourselves . . . represents us. . . .
>
> Simplicity calls itself dada. . . .
>
> Dada, after calling the attention of the whole world to *death*, to its constant presence amongst us, proceeds by destruction. . . .[30]

Others testify according to their humor or need, and continue to supply Dada with their vitality:

> *Huelsenbeck:* We had no time to lose; we wanted to incite our opponents to resistance, and, if necessary, to create new opponents for ourselves. We hated nothing so much as romantic silence and the search for a soul: we were convinced that the soul could only show itself in our own actions.[31]
>
> *Baader:* A Dadaist is someone who loves life in all its unaccountable forms, and who knows, and says that, "Life is not here alone, but also there, there, there (*da, da, da*)."[32]

*Hausmann:* . . . our disgust of civilization, of the organized *copro-cosmos.*

Dada is the germ of a new type of man.

The word Dada symbolizes the most primitive relation to circumambient reality. . . .[33]

*Arp:* Dada was a revolt of unbelievers against believers.[34]

*Aragon:* The DD system makes you free: break through everything, flattened faces. You are the masters of everything you will destroy.[35]

*Picabia:* Dada itself wants nothing, nothing, nothing. . . . Dadaists are nothing, nothing, nothing, certainly they will achieve nothing, nothing, nothing. . . .[36]

*Breton:* Leave everything
Leave Dada
Leave your wife, your mistress
. . . . . . . .
Take to the roads.[37]

*Ribbemont-Dessaignes:* What is beautiful? What is ugly? What is great, strong, weak? . . . Don't know. What is myself? Don't know, don't know, don't know.[38]

Dada seeks to transform consciousness without admitting its purpose. Its stance is paradoxical but also agonistic. It revels in denunciations of Family, Country, Virtue, Religion, History, Reason, Civilization, and Art. Dada seems to foreshadow the famous statement of Lt. Henry, in Hemingway's *A Farewell to Arms:* "I was always embarrassed by the words sacred, glorious, and sacrifice and the expression in vain. We had heard them. . . . There were many words that you could not stand to hear and finally only the names of places had dignity." [39] Dada dares not hope loudly for a new order; it can only insist on freedom, passion, and surprise.

The same paradox underlies the Dadaist aesthetic. Dada is never more vicious than when it attacks Art, exposing the greed, vanity, and hypocrisy that surround it. Even such avant-garde movements as Futurism, Cubism, Abstractionism are anathema to it. "For the first time Dadaism does not present itself in an aesthetic mode before life," Hausmann cries.[40] When Tzara arrives in Paris, the first question he puts to the eager young writers of *Littérature* is: "Why do you write?" Art is error, childishness, Tzara asserts in his *La Première Aventure céleste de M. Antipyrine* (1916). The others agree enthusiastically, and write and paint to prove their assent.

Yet the literature of Dada is of a special kind; it is an anti-literature. "NO MORE WORDS!" Tzara proposes. Of literary works, nothing ever needs to be said. Aragon writes a poem, "Le Mouvement perpetuel," renouncing language: "But the words / Now what exactly were the words saying / Idiot." [41] Breton goes farther: "A monstrous aberration makes people believe that language was born to facilitate their mutual relations." [42] The anti-forms of Dada defy sense and expectation, permanence and harmony. Ideally, they present themselves as a gratuitous action. Each "work" refuses to preserve its ontological character, and opens itself to free improvisation: ". . . it belongs in its innumerable variations to the spectator. For its creator, it is without cause and without theory." [43]

The work, we see, composes itself in order to undermine its authority. The "simultaneist poem" requires the reading of several statements at the same time. The "bruitist poem" employs sheer noise, loud and raucous. The "abstract phonetic poem" creates patterns of pure sound, devoid of sense; it fulfills Mallarmé's dream of poetry, a musical echo. The "static poem" manages letters and typography as a painter manages form and color; the alphabet becomes a principle of visual design. The work also confuses the traditional categories of aesthetics. It blends various genres, superimposes different media in the forms of collages and montages. It wants to realize, perversely, the idea of the *Gesamtkunstwerk* which haunted Romantic and Symbolist writers. And it refuses to recognize the distinction between life and art, the found and the created object. Abstractions become sensuous, and concrete things fly from their concreteness. As Hausmann puts it, "The doll discarded by a child or the colored rag are expressions more necessary than that of any soul whatsoever. . . ." [44] Thus Kurt Schwitters and Max Ernst, magicians of banality, turn bric-a-brac into blood, laughter, and mystery. Furthermore, the work opens itself to chance. It desiccates words, inverts them, invents them. Tzara devises the technique that William Burroughs calls, forty years later, the "cut-up method":

> To make a dadaist poem
> Take a newspaper
> Take scissors
> Choose in the newspaper an article as long as
> the poem you intend
> Cut out the article.[45]

The cosmos reveals itself, after all, in a design of "acausal orderedness." Why, then, shouldn't a "work of literature" suspend its telos? Finally, the work undercuts itself in radical irony, denounces itself. Tzara's assertion in "Monsieur AA l'anti-philosophe nous envoie ce manifeste" often serves as a paradigm of Dadaist works:

> I close, I open, I spit. Beware! This is the time to tell you that I have lied. If there is a system in the lack of system—that of my proportions—I never apply it. Which is to say that I lie.[46]

Anti-literaure requires anti-forms of expression. But what audience does that literature require? When language avers its mendacity, communication rests solely on mystery or paradox. The tacit pact between the writer and his audience is broken. A new sense of the literary act begins to emerge. It emerges, for instance, in Dadaist meetings where language asserts its oral presence; as Ball insists, the "simultaneist poem" enhances the value of the human voice. For him too, the "phonetic poem" is a means of escaping the ordinary corruptions of language. "We must return to the deepest alchemy of the Word, and leave even that behind us, in order to keep safe for poetry its holiest sanctuary," he writes.[47] Schwitters, who wants to discover the central myth of his age, seeks to release words from their associations and thus open a window on infinity. Werner Haftmann is partly right when he says: "The Dadaist claimed Genius, as the term was understood by the Romantics, as his natural prerogative. He saw himself as an individual outside all bounds. . . ."[48] But we also need to add that the Dadaist creates a post-Romantic aesthetic, an ambivalent and catatonic semantic.[49] Tzara, as usual, makes a larger claim: ". . . art for cosmic diversity, for totality, for the universal, is innate in the slow life that moves and even sleeps in what we habitually call death."[50] The aesthetic of Dada indeed tends toward the silence that divides life from death, the line at which creation and destruction finally meet.

But the true voice of Dada, uniting its moral and aesthetic sense, speaks through its humor. The Mona Lisa painted with a moustache, the urinal displayed as sculpture, the fur-lined teacup are now notorious: innumerable antics make up the history of the movement. The word Dada itself is conceived as a synonym of Humor. How else could Nothingness masquerade in public, and Absurdity disport itself before our eyes? Dada takes humor seriously, as it does violence and pandemonium. The explosive response, George Hugnet says, is a way of recognizing the virtual quality of things, their radical contingency.[51] The humor is neither black nor white. It is the laughter of an outlaw and a Zen master, a visionary clown choking on outrage, a machine clanking in its nightmare.

In the end, the antics of Dada are perhaps more arresting than its theories, its manifestoes more exciting than its verse. This is in keeping with the spirit of anti-literature; the work is no "better" than the act. Tzara gives us, in "Mr. Antipyrine," a funny and obscene coda.:

LA PAROLE

si l'on peut demander à une vielle dame
l'address d'un bordel
oi oi oi oi oi oi oi oiseau[52]

## V

Literary movements have a curious life; they do not end when we expect them decently to do so. Tzara survives Dadaism, but the spirit of the latter survives its hero. For a time, it seems that the original power of Dada must dissipate itself in Surrealism. Tzara himself claims that he never revises his vision. Yet his *L'Homme approximatif* (1931) is hailed by many as a Surrealist work; and *Midis gagnés* (1939), *Phases* (1949), and *De Mémoire d'homme* (1950), reveal a new sense of universal acceptance, a heightened credibility of image and idea. During the thirties, literature responds to the political conscience of the times; the shadow of the Spanish Civil War lengthens to meet the Second World War. Like other writers, Tzara feels the heavier mood. He still maintains that poetry is an activity of the mind, not a means of expression. But in *Le Surréalisme et l'après-guerre* (1947), he explains: "It [poetry] is itself a reality. . . . But to become valid, it must be part of a larger reality, that of the living." [53] In this statement we are close to the motives of Breton's revolt against Dadaism a quarter of a century earlier.

André Breton can never accept the nihilist's view of reality. Throughout his life, he chooses eroticism over obscenity; he prefers the affirmative. Born on February 18, 1896, in Tinchebray, he shows force and literary brilliance from the start. Baudelaire, Mallarmé, Huysmans, and Barrès are among the idols of his boyhood. In Paris, he studies medicine and neuropsychiatry, and reads the major works of Freud. Incongruously, he chooses Paul Valéry as his first patron; later, he attaches himself to Apollinaire. But it is that extraordinary young man, Jacques Vaché, who makes the deepest impression on Breton. They meet in Nantes in 1916, both wearing army uniforms. Thereafter, Vaché represents the rebel buried in Breton's unconscious, and the very principle of humor. "Sterility at the finger tips, the spirit of humor itself rises, walking on egg shells during the years of the 'last' war, body squared forward and face in profile," Breton describes him.[54] Revolver in hand, Vaché threatens to fire into the first-night audience of *Les Mamelles de Tirésias*. The spirit of extremism recalls Jarry and helps to make Dadaism rife for a period. Then comes the break with Tzara, presumably over the "affair" of Maurice Barrès, May 13, 1921. For Breton, this is a turning point; turbulent life lies ahead of him.

Some claim that Dadaism and Surrealism are, in the beginning, like two peas in a pod; others differ violently. In retrospect, Huelsenbeck can say: "Surrealism has undertaken to realize, through an artistic movement, the spiritual intentions of Dadaism. It struggled for magic reality, which we the Dadaists, had first unveiled. . . ." [55] Hans Richter puts it simply: "Surrealism gave Dada significance and sense, Dada gave Surrealism life." [56] But the polemics of hope and the promptings of vanity continue to move hand in hand for thirty years.

Breton designates *Les Champs magnétique*, (1921), as the first Surrealist work. Co-authored by Soupault and himself, the work makes bold use of dream, hypnosis, and automatic writing. These buried activities of the psyche provide a focus of exploration and dissent for writers as different in temperament as Aragon, Éluard, Crevel, Desnos, Péret, and for such painters as Ernst, Picabia, Chirico. In 1924, Breton publishes the first *Manifeste du surréalisme*. A Bureau of Surrealist Research is founded the same year, at 15, rue Grenelle, and the official organ of the movement, *La Révolution surréaliste*, is published under the direction of Pierre Naville and Benjamin Péret. On its cover appears the brave rubric: "We must formulate a new declaration of the rights of man." This is in accordance with Breton's famous statement: " 'Transform the world,' Marx said; 'change life,' Rimbaud said. The two watchwords are one for us." [57]

The ambiguities of the Surrealist revolution in the mental and physical, in the poetic and political, spheres are never resolved. Breton opposes Communist interference with the inner life, and moves unsteadily toward a form of utopianism that permits him, in later years, to include Trotsky among the elect: Marx, Freud, Lautréamont, and Rimbaud. Aragon drifts in the opposite direction; increasingly, he yields to the Stalinist leadership of Moscow. The Communist group associated with *Clarté* can tolerate the Surrealists so long as the latter proclaim, in their *Déclaration du 27 janvier 1925*:

> We are specialists in Revolt. There is no means of action we are not capable of using if the need arises. . . .
>
> Surrealism is not poetic form.
>
> It is a cry of the mind turning toward itself and determined in desperation to crush its fetters.
>
> And, if need be, by material hammers.[58]

But the Surrealist revolution is ultimately grounded on a mysticism of the subconscious. Collaboration with the Communists becomes quarrelsome. Breton's *Second Manifeste du surréalisme* (1930), exacerbates the difficulties; defections and excommunications become the order of the day. Vitrac, Masson, Soupault, and Desnos no longer stand in the Surrealist ranks. In 1930, Breton founds a new magazine, *Le Surréalisme au service de la révolution,* in an effort to mediate bitter differences. But newcomers—Dali, Buñuel, Tanguy, Man Ray—amplify the strains of discord. It is almost a relief when Breton, Éluard, and Crevel are expelled from the Communist Party in 1933. Surrealism can now pursue its revolutionary ideal without benefit of party or government.

Breton becomes a tireless spokesman for the movement. He organizes exhibitions, he lectures throughout Europe. In 1938, he visits Mexico, meets Diego Rivera and Leon Trotsky, who warmly approve of his work. In 1941 he takes refuge from the Nazis in America, and publishes, with Max Ernst, Marcel Duchamp, and David Hare, the revue VVV. (Dali, espousing the cause of Church and State in Spain, is no longer in Breton's favor; he nicknames Dali "Avida Dollars.") After the war, Breton returns to Paris and becomes an adherent of the movement called "Citoyens du Monde." He dies in 1966. Surrealism, which has sought to remake creation, also remakes itself from a process of poetic birth into a project of universal transformation. It remains a deep act of faith in man and in his metamorphoses.

It is not difficult to see the antecedents of the movement, its historical assumptions. Sade, Baudelaire, Rimbaud, Jarry, all beckon to the Surrealists darkly, though none excite their furious admiration more than the author of *Chants de Maldoror.* "We oppose, we continue to oppose, the placing of Lautréamont in history, his assignment to a place between This figure and That one. . . ," they cry.[59] In taking Lautréamont out of history, they save him from their condemnation of Western civilization:

> We shall triumph over everything. And first of all we'll destroy this civilization that is so dear to you, in which you are caught like fossils in shale. Western world, you are condemned to death.[60]

Again, the philosophic call of Surrealism sounds in its manifestoes. The Romantic ideas of genius, madness, and imagination define the basis of liberty in Surrealism, the total freedom of thought. With Freud, the unconscious is finally acknowledged as a larger part of mind, and dreams join the waking state to make what Breton chooses to call "surreality." His first manifesto provides the slogan: "SURREALISM, n. Psychic automatism . . . the actual functioning of thought. . . . ENCYCLOPEDIA. *Philosophy.* Surrealism is based on the belief in the superior reality of certain forms of previously neglected associations, in the omnipotence of dream, in the distinterested play of thought." [61] Implicit in the slogan is a magical view of the universe and of its invisible correspondences. Breton's second manifesto identifies the quest of the Surrealist poet with that of the alchemist; the search for the philosopher's stone gives the human imagination a dazzling victory over the world of things. In their common quest, men stand equal in the democracy of the subconscious and recover, each and everyone, the forgotten language, the subliminal message.

But the tension between inner freedom and public action continues to strain the Surrealists. "The poet of the future," Breton declares, "will surmount the despressing notion of the irreparable divorce of action and dream." [62] The cause of art, at bottom, is the same as the cause of human liberty. Breton is particularly anxious in his second manifesto to aver the revolutionary force of Surrealism. The motive of social action, he argues, is simply part of a larger motive, that of human expression in all its forms. Beneath language lies a sunken continent, the true domain of men. Breton can therefore say without self-contradiction: "The simplest Surrealist act consists of dashing down into the street, pistol in hand, and firing blindly, as fast as you can pull the trigger, into the crowd. . . . The justification of such an act is, to my mind, in no way incompatible with the belief in that gleam of light that Surrealism seeks to detect deep within us." [63] The act is not morally simple; its simplicity is formal. As an expression of disgust, it compels us to focus on the point where chance and necessity, dream and act, irrevocably meet.

But a meeting of dream and act does not assure their unity, or even their balance. The Surrealists fail outside their art. Their victory is not in history but in a virtual history. Their thematic contradictions can be resolved only in a central area of the mind. Three visions converge on that area: an Orphic, an Erotic, and a Comic vision.

The Orphic vision is one of mystic participation. In his lecture at Yale University, December 10, 1942, Breton defines certain Surrealist propositions. To automatism and laughter, he adds the Orphic unity of man and nature, life and death, the antinomies of human consciousness. Quoting an earlier text, he says:

Everything leads us to believe that there exists, in the mind, a certain point from which life and death, the real and the imaginary, past and future, the communicable and the incommunicable, above and below, cease to be perceived as contradictions.[64]

In this belief, Surrealism never wavers. It goes so far as to assert the esoteric quality of its knowledge, and place a malediction on its works in order to frighten away profane souls. As above, so below; as outside, so inside. These are the ancient truths by which the tyranny of the rational, the habitual, or the illusory world may be opposed. The Surrealist intuition, Breton writes, " . . . alone provides the thread that can put us back on the road of Gnosis as knowledge of suprasensible Reality, 'invisibly visible in an eternal mystery.' "[65] Occult in its insights, Surrealism still denies that the world eludes all sensuous apprehension. Turning toward the East for inspiration—the third issue of *La Révolution surréaliste* contains addresses to the Buddhist schools of the world and to the Dalai Lama—Surrealism still searches for a new science of relativity, a unified view of existence. Marcel Raymond sums up the Orphic impulse among Surrealists when he says: "There is in them a deep nostalgia, and a desperate regret at the impossibility of going back to the 'source' where potentialities exist side by side without excluding one another, to the chaos preceding all determination, to the central, anonymous, and infinite focus of the universe. . . ."[66]

It is but a small step to the Magna Mater, the great female principle cast into oblivion by the efficient West. The Romantics reclaim Woman from mythic consciousness; the Surrealists restore her to the psychic life of men. Love is primal, the source of unity and release. It is the ground of liberty; it allows each to identify his truth in the flesh. Nadeau is right; for the Surrealists, the true revolution is "victory of desire." *Amour fou* and *amour unique*, dissolving the self and recovering it as a single creation in another: such is the aim of the Surrealists in their lives as in their art. "Men can no longer love, after Breton and Éluard, as they did before them. . . ," Nadeau concludes.[67] Advocating sexual freedom, they still find their inspiration in a single woman. Breton chides a corrupt world for believing that Eros must pall or wither: "To feel the need to vary . . .

is to testify that one . . . has doubtless forfeited *innocence*." [68] In *Les Vases communicants* (1932), Breton further attempts to show that dream and waking are as two vessels communicating the substance of desire. And in his manifestoes he traces the "ligne de coeur" back to Heloïse, and further back even to "the *primordial Androgyne* that all traditions tell us of, and its . . . incarnation within ourselves." [69] Despite their lip-service to Sade, the Surrealists refute his autism. Perhaps alone among avant-gardists of the period, they celebrate the sacrament of love; Breton's *Nadja* (1928), Éluard's *L'Amour, la poésie* (1929), and Péret's *Anthologie de l'amour sublime* (1957), unveil different faces of that love.

But the Surrealists also know the force of the actual. In a harsh world, love sometimes frees itself in laughter. Their comic vision breaks with things as they are and reconstitutes them on a deeper level of awareness. As early as 1927, in an editorial entitled "Hands Off Love," they side with "Charlot" against a puritannical system dedicated to thwart love and laughter; the occasion is Chaplin's first divorce suit. Earlier still, they recognize in the bitter humor of Lautréamont, Jarry, and Vaché, a revenge on creation. But the Surrealist image, in the catachresis of its poetic language, represents an effort of redemption rather than of revenge. Certainly, Breton includes in his *Anthologie de l'humour noir* (1947), such grim wits as Swift, Sade, Poe, and Kafka, a profound sense of desperate comedy. It is nonetheless significant that the anthology includes few Surrealists proper. The latter, assuming life as a given, cannot give themselves fully to the blackness of laughter. Their humor, though touched by Sade or Masoch, remains an expression of playful liberty.

The philosophic call of Surrealism may sound in its manifestoes; its works, however, still grace our museums and libraries. The artists who respond to the call range from Masson and Miro, pure painters of line and color, to Magritte, Tanguy, and Dali, image-makers of our dreams. In between, Ernst, Chirico, Ray, Arp, Duchamp, Picabia, and Klee evolve their individual styles as they leave Dadaism behind. Visionary and erotic subjects and biomorphic shapes dominate the mood, as do great silences and empty time-spaces. Occasionally, collages, *frottages*, found objects, or *peintures-poésies* appear. More often, artists work toward an interior image, a mystic scape. With characteristic fustian, Dali describes his "paranoiac-critical method" as "a spontaneous assimilation of irrational knowledge based upon the critical and systematic objectification of delirious phenomena"; elsewhere, he explains: "My whole ambition in the pictorial domain is to materialize the images of concrete irrationality with the most imperialist fury of precision." [70]

Dali's pictures suggest forgeries of the unconscious. This is precisely the literary weakness of Surrealism. In their resolve to rescue art from the destructive frenzy of Dada, the Surrealists endorsed the equivocal practice of "automatic writing." "Step right up, here is where the kingdoms of the instantaneous begin. . . ," Aragon shouts.[71] In chance as in spontaneous creation, the Surrealists believe, a new relation between freedom and necessity may develop. Defending dream narratives and automatic composition, Breton warns, however, that these methods offer no aesthetic panacea; indeed, their conversion into an aesthetic may bring a fall from grace.[72] Joyce is therefore no Surrealist; he simply mines a deeper vein of language, and the result is still a *literary* work. "It is not at all a question for us of awakening words and submitting them to a learned manipulation in order to make them serve the creation of a style, however interesting," Breton protests.[73] "A poem must be a debacle of the intellect," he says again. "Poetry is the opposite of literature." [74] The power of the poetic image derives from the marvellous, which is inexplicable; it depends on the degree of its arbitrariness, of its untranslatability. The conclusion of Breton about beauty is predictable: "Convulsive beauty will be erotic-veiled, explosive-fixed, magic-circumstantial or will not be at all." [75]

The Surrealist theory of language, of creativity, accords, then, with its poetic mysticism. Its applications, however, are equivocal. Aragon, for instance, confesses that Surrealism entails *prac-*

*ticed* inspiration; Éluard gives himself to automatic writing very little. Even Breton ends by admitting that pure automatism is never more than an ideal or hyperbole. Though the Surrealists want to believe that poetry lives in images of direct revelation, neither their verse nor their prose depends entirely on images. They still argue and still exhort. Their immense hope is to create, through objective chance, sleep, automatism, a new kind of language, a new consciousness, something larger than art or literature. Their hope breaks on the surface of reality into poetic hues, into many-colored refractions.

Breton's *Nadja* (1928) catches some of these refractions. Random meditations, recollections, coincidences, and dreams compose a work that opens with the ancient query: "Who am I?" We are taken into a world of transparencies, an enchanted universe of glass where the visible and invisible melt: "I rest at night on a glass bed with glass sheets, where *who I am* will appear to me, sooner or later, graven in diamond." [76] Into that world drifts a strange, visionary creature, Nadja, who is the wandering soul. Her agony is the agony of love and terror in a realm of perpetual contingencies. Subject becomes object; the author blends into his creature; the reader dreams and is the dream of *anima mundi*. Breton asks: What are the hidden laws of the universe, its occult powers, its correspondences? We move in "the kingdom of silence." Word and act seem to exchange a meaning none has previously understood. Beauty shudders as the self meets itself walking down the street. Yet the reader of *Nadja* finally feels constricted. He emerges from a claustral realm, over-determined by unknown forces, in which psychotics obey dark compulsions. In denying the norms of "Literature" and the limits of existence, Breton ends by enforcing the strict rules of the invisible.

The same may be said of *L'Immaculée conception* (1930), which Breton writes in collaboration with Éluard. Mythic, erotic, oneiric images attempt to render the mysterious life of man, from conception to death. "Has anyone heard the birds near four in the afternoon in April? These birds are mad. It is I." [77] Love and laughter attest to the protean transformations of the soul: "Love multiplies our problems. A furious liberty takes hold of lovers more devoted to one another than lungs to the air." [78] But the poetic play of word and flesh can not finally exempt the poets from their common burden: "Eyes lowered, we carry the burden of silence since eternity and forever." [79] Silence beckons the Surrealists; it promises unspeakable freedom. But as their imagination moves beyond itself, it also encounters the sudden density of silence, its hardness.

Perhaps the difficulty is implicit in their mentalism, their belief in the omnipotence of mind, of spirit, as a pure and undirected activity. Unlike Sade, the Surrealists save themselves from autism by a genuine eroticism. And Breton, particularly, never ceases to thrust upon his acolytes the obduracy of the actual. Yet Sartre is right to perceive in Surrealist works—the limp watches of Dali and the marble suger lumps of Duchamp—an attempt to destroy the solid or material world without actual violence. "Quite the contrary. . . ," Sartre challenges, "by the symbolic annulment of language by producing aberrant meanings, by the destruction of painting by painting and of literature by literature, surrealism pursues this curious enterprise of realising nothingness by too much fullness of being. . . . And the *esprit* which the surrealists wish to attain on the ruins of subjectivity, this *espirit* of which it is not possible to have an inkling otherwise than by the accumulation of self-destructive objects, also sparkles and flickers in the reciprocal and congealed annihilation of things." [80] Caught between their affirmation of dream and act, collective unconscious and singular sentience, hidden law and manifest freedom, the Surrealists, nonetheless, bring to a climax the impossible search for a vanishing form.

## VI

After Sade, everything becomes possible—in the mind. After Lautréamont, after Rimbaud, everything becomes possible in literature, including the ritual murder of language. The body of the world can be torn; Orpheus can be dismembered; consciousness can be inverted. Suicide, symbolic or acutal, becomes the consummation of the avant-garde. We know the fate of Sade behind prison walls. Lautréamont vanishes at the age of twenty-four, and Rimbaud ceases to write after nineteen. Jarry wills his death; Vaché, Rigaut, Crevel, Artaud kill themselves; Cravan disappears in the Carribean. Seeking death, they deliver the ultimate verdict on creation. They suspect mediating forms, and proudly condemn themselves to the Self. "From Mallarmé to Breton," Anna Balakian writes, "the poet will prefer silence to the risk of misrepresenting his newly found surreality." [81] The silence, at times, finds expression in anti-literature; at times, it probes the heart of the universe. Even humor can be pushed to the point of mystic negation. Even matter can be spiritualized, and spirit made to deny or bestill itself.

Yet from 'Pataphysics to Surrealism we can also trace a bold creative force, intact in destruction. Language acquires new concreteness and reveals, at the same time, new dimensions of the Absolute. It opens itself to the unknown, to dream, chance, and absurdity, and in so doing creates mental space for the artist, an altered perception. The forms of art expand their definition, their function. "When the distinctions of art and reality have broken down, we are ourselves incorporated into the structure of a work of art. Its very *form* importunes us to enter an expanded community of creation which now includes artist and spectator, art and reality"; so Shattuck summarizes the effort of the avant-garde.[82] From 'Pataphysics to Surrealism, the imagination, haunted by revolution, ends by revolutionizing our concepts of radical change. Perhaps that is the crux of all creative effort, a metamorphosis of Orphic gods.

CHAPTER III

# *HEMINGWAY:*

## *Valor Against the Void*

Hail nothing, full of nothing, nothing is with thee.
Hemingway, "A Clean Well-Lighted Place"

### I

THE WORK of Ernest Hemingway may prove, above Faulkner's, Eliot's, or O'Neill's, above the work of any other American of that generation, closest to our consciousness, our blankness and rage. Familiar as it may now seem, the work engages modernism on the deepest levels, and its experience occupies the time and space we inhabit. Indeed, Hemingway's fiction makes for itself a place in the tradition of silence that extends from Sade, through Kafka, Genet, and Beckett, to the inverted literary imagination of our own day.

Generations come and go, each carrying the banner of a shabby or brilliant despair. Hemingway understands the constancy of death better. With the phrase of Gertrude Stein humming in his youthful ears, and the statue of Marshall Ney rising against the Paris sky, he senses "that all generations were lost by something and always had been and always would be. . . ." [1] Sharing little with the Dadaists and Surrealists who prowl about him on the Left Bank, he knows the void separately, and summons his own resources of valor against it. His life, his style, morality, and vision, derive from that lone encounter and enlarge its definition.

## II

The encounter becomes part of an American legend. It is easy to see how the legend invades Hemingway's life until the closing act which, in its abysmal ironies, reinstates the man's freedom. It is harder to see how the biography of Hemingway conforms to the European myth of the avant-garde.

He is born in Oak Park, Illinois, a suburb of Chicago, on July 21, 1899. His father is a doctor, a man of the Michigan outdoors, sharper in sight than a bird of prey; he will commit suicide. The mother is a musical and rather pious woman; her sensibility is narrow. Hemingway loves his father, whom later he accuses of cowardice, and detests his mother, who becomes later his example of the "American bitch." Between them and the unfelled woods of America, he plays out the drama of childhood; between their quarrels he strikes the bargains of manhood and old age. The boy hunts and fishes, and learns what he must learn of right action, of nature, and of human betrayal. The stories of Nick Adams tell the artists's version of that story. Is it strange that bravery and misogyny should haunt Hemingway through the years, through wars and legendary exploits, through four marriages, to the final atonement with a shotgun fired at point-blank range?

At high school, Hemingway establishes a reputation in writing, athletics, and solitude. He writes sketches and stories, edits the school weekly, displays Latin and wit. He swims, plays right guard on the football team, and boxes belligerently. He is taciturn, and runs away from home twice, performing odd jobs as laborer or sparring partner. He graduates in 1917 as "Class Prophet" while the guns are rumbling in Europe. No college can absorb his interests, his energies. He joins the *Kansas City Star*, and the apprenticeship of the author begins in earnest. But for Hemingway, literature must always find its truth in the knowledge of death.

In 1918, Hemingway serves as a lieutenant in the Red Cross Ambulance Corps on the Italian front; on July 18 of that year, he is hit by a large mortar shell at Fossalta, and 237 fragments of steel are extracted from his right leg alone. This is what Philip Young calls "the big wound." [2] Hemingway, who has seen death before, now becomes its familiar. "I can remember just thinking that we were the home team and the Austrians were the visiting team," he recollects a quarter of a century after.[3] It happens otherwise. Carlos Baker describes the event thus:

> They all heard it coming—the far cough as it left the muzzle, and the strange "chuh-chuh-chuh" sound as it arched and descended. "Then there was a flash, as when a blast-furnace door is swung open, and a roar that started white and went red." It was like a hurricane of such force that it tore the eardrums and snatched away the breath. "I tried to breathe," wrote Ernest afterwards, "but my breath would not come. . . . The ground was torn up and in front of my head there was a splintered beam of wood. In the jolt of my head I heard somebody crying. . . . I tried to move but I could not move. I heard the machine guns and rifles firing across the river."
>
> His legs felt as if he were wearing rubber boots filled with warm water. Beside him was a man who made no sound. Just beyond him was another, badly hurt and crying piteously. Ernest groped for his neck and legs, heaved him up in a fireman's carry, and began to stagger back towards the command post. He had covered fifty yards when a round from a heavy machine gun tore into his right leg at the knee. It felt like an icy snowball. He stumbled and fell with the man on his shoulder. He never afterwards remembered how he had covered the final hundred yards. But he made it, delivered his man, and lost consciousness.[4]

In *A Farewell to Arms*, Lieutenant Frederic Henry describes the same event with the sharp edge of art: "I went out swiftly, all of myself, and I knew I was dead and that it had all been a mistake to think you just died. Then I floated, and instead of going on I felt myself slide back." [5]

Hemingway will be hit many times again, in fist fights and in military combat, in car accidents and in plane crashes; skylights will splinter on his head, and pistol bullets—fired accidentally by himself!—rip through both his legs. Prone always to violence as to accident, his large and powerful frame will come to seem like a battered fortress. He will face the bull, the lion, the African buffalo; he will harpoon a whale and haul in the giant marlin. He will kill, as the critics say, to live, to keep sane; and he will also write: "I expected, always, to be killed by one thing or another and I, truly, did not mind that any more." [6] But it is probable that Hemingway experiences at Fossalta, for the first time, nothingness—endures that radical metaphor of the modern world both as a biological fact and as a personal destiny. Like the authors of silence, he develops an intuition of the great emptiness behind the meticulous shape of things.

The young hero, however, seems to recuperate nicely in a military hospital in Milan. There, the first American to be wounded on the Italian front meets a beautiful nurse, Agnes von Kurowsky. The idyll ends when Agnes falls in love with an Italian nobleman. Back at Oak Park, Hemingway discovers that the pastoral world of his youth has vanished. Is this not the gravid theme of an entire phase of American letters? He meets Sherwood Anderson and admires his literary manner, the voice of America speaking bitter-sweetly after the virile voice of Mark Twain. Hemingway's own inspiration, however, is more taut, tragic; its form will be purer. He gives himself to sports, seeking in action, in a tensed muscle or a graceful line of life, a shape for his vision. In 1920, he hires out as roving reporter for the *Toronto Star;* and the next year, newly married to Hadley Richardson, he sails with her to Europe.

The reporter covers a land torn from Spain to Turkey. (His sardonic dispatches now fill *The Wild Years,* 1962.) The artist settles in Paris, and enters literary history under the rubric of The Lost Generation. Hemingway meets Gertrude Stein and outgrows her tutelage. He knows Pound, Eliot, Ford, Joyce; he borrows books, and sometimes money, from Sylvia Beach at Shakespeare and Company. The expatriate gives his portrait of the young artist in *A Moveable Feast* (1964). But cycling, horse racing, boxing, more than the chatter of the avant-garde, consume his interest. He fishes in Cortina, skis in Schruns, swims in Hendaye, and teases the bulls of Pamplona. He also drinks with the best matadors, Ordoñez or Niño de la Palma. "Artist, art, artistic!" he cries to one of his friends. "Can't we ever hear the last of that stuff." [7] Hemingway, nevertheless, writes, and writing sets a new trend for fiction. His books begin to appear: *In Our Time* (1924), *The Sun Also Rises* (1926), *Men Without Women* (1927), *A Farewell to Arms* (1929). A major author emerges on the glittering scene of the twenties; the Hemingway code achieves renown. He divorces Hadley and marries Pauline Pfeiffer.

Codes are sometimes obscured in the glitter. What happens to Hemingway thereafter can be known only to his struggling soul. The rich surround him, and the legend drives out the life. The vultures of self-destruction smell out death, as they do in "The Snows of Kilimanjaro," and circle ever closer. Hemingway writes *Winner Take Nothing* (1933), and hunts in *Green Hills of Africa* (1935). He witnesses *Death in the Afternoon* (1932) in the bull rings of Spain. The titles speak for themselves. He makes his home in Key West and uses his beloved boat, *Pilar*, to kill in the Gulf Stream. The politics of the thirties catch his ear distantly. He says: "Writers are forged in injustice as a sword is forged," and for a few years behaves as if this were true of himself.[8] He even gives a speech before the Second Congress of the leftist League of American Writers, in 1937, denouncing fascism as a "lie told by bullies." "A writer who will not lie cannot live and work under fascism," he concludes.[9] His own *To Have and Have Not* appears the same year, in awkward testimony to the spirit of the times. More authentic, because it expresses a loyalty more deep, *For Whom the Bell*

*Tolls* (1940), draws on his love for Spain, to which he returns as foreign correspondent during the Civil War. Together with his old friend, John Dos Passos, Hemingway witnesses the last bitter battles before the collapse of the Republic while trying to complete a script for a film, *The Spanish Earth.* The politics of death sweep across the fierce landscape as Hemingway attempts, once again, to regain mastery over his memory of inevitable darkness.

After the Spanish Civil War, Hemingway begins to frequent Cuba. Martha Gellhorn, a writer and journalist who had been with him in Spain, joins him there. She discovers and remodels La Finca, a villa outside Havana, which becomes the home of his late years. Hemingway divorces Pauline to marry Martha; she will remain the most recalcitrant of his wives. By now, however, the legend of Hemingway can withstand all contradictions. The rich, the famous, the beautiful, the brave, and perhaps simply the hopeful, descend on La Finca, or on the Hotel Floridita where Hemingway holds court among frozen daiquiris. His boasts, more often than not, are made good. With the approval of the American Embassy, he organizes a loose network of "spies" which he calls the Crook Factory; he conceives "Operation Friendless" and transforms the *Pilar* into a Q-boat, searching for German submarines.[10] Martha spends a good deal of her time covering the war in Europe.

For reasons of his own, Hemingway hangs back until the spring of 1944; then he throws himself into the middle of things. In England, he flies with Group Captain Peter Wykeham-Barnes on dangerous missions, bombing V-1 launching sites. He follows the invasion of Normandy, and participates in the fighting around Chartres and Rambouillet. He jeopardizes his status of foreign correspondent as he races with a company of irregulars past General Leclerc to "liberate" the Ritz in Paris; vintage champagne flows. With Colonel Buck Lanham's 22nd Regiment, 4th Infantry Division, he engages in the vicious fighting of the Ardennes and the Hürtgen Forest. He seems never calmer, perhaps never happier, than when the soundless wings of the German 88s pass over his head.

The war ends. Hemingway had met Mary Welsh in London the previous summer; she becomes his last wife. The Hemingways return to Cuba where Ernest receives, at the American Embassy, his Bronze Star. The feats of his heroism are genuine in spirit if not in every fact. The figure that begins to emerge, however, is that of A. E. Hotchner's *Papa Hemingway* who calls Ava Gardner "daughter" and Marlene Dietrich "The Kraut." There are always accidents, always mishaps. Mary fights off death on an operating table, somewhere in Montana, while Hemingway supervises the work of the frightened intern by his side. For once, a bearded Orpheus reclaims his Eurydice from Hades. The Hemingways sail for Italy, shoot ducks in the marshes around Venice, dine with aristocracy at the Gritti Palace, or drink at Harry's Bar. The beautiful young Venetian, Adriana Ivancich, and her sportsman brother lighten their company. But spring succeeds winter without redeeming time. The hidden bitterness, the black wound of Hemingway shockingly reveals itself in his next novel, *Across the River and into the Trees* (1950). The "champion" still asks the world, "And how do you like it now, gentlemen?" without knowing that all champions conspire in their end.

Two years later, back in Cuba, Hemingway wages his last heroic fight, makes his stand with Santiago, in *The Old Man and the Sea* (1952). The work demands a certain generosity of response and in this demand confesses its weakness. The news of the Nobel Prize comes to him in 1954; it might have come a quarter of a century earlier. What follows is what no Hemingway hero, bearing everything else, knowing how to last and how to endure, could ever bear: physical and mental decay compounded, the void within life. On his last safaris, in 1954, Hemingway's plane crashes in the African veldt; he reads his obituaries in the newspapers; his plane crashes once again. The damages to his body are lasting; the damages to his spirit are nothing new. For seven years, Hemingway and steadfast "Miss Mary" pick their way through dream, terror, and hope. The dreams become steadily uglier. Toward the end, he secretly undergoes electro-therapy at the Mayo clinic. His moments of lucidity now contain but one hope. Early in the morning of July 2, 1961, he shoots himself at his ranch near Ketchum, Idaho. Mary can only believe it is an accident. There is some truth in her belief: Hemingway always felt that death was "just another whore." [11]

No doubt, the legend of Hemingway looms larger than his detractors can allow, larger in some ways than life itself. Biographers know that he does not come near perfection. He can be cruel, a veritable bully, turning suddenly, savagely, against friends. He can boast, invite flattery, and strain all credibility. He can indulge in malice as in self-pity. At times, he barely conceals his misogyny; contempt for his mother gives him an exaggerated need to dominate women.[12] His black humor, controlled strictly in art, betrays him on less formal occasions: "There are no subjects I would not jest about if the jest was funny enough . . . just as, liking wing shooting, I would shoot my own mother if she went in coveys and had a good strong flight." [13] The details of darkness accrue; for spite always finds a scope in human affairs, drawing a tight circle around heroic men. Hemingway seeks to engage existence on its heroic level. He knows how crucial, in his case at least, "lived experience" is to an artist who must challenge Tolstoy and Shakespeare.[14] The black strain that mars his life links him strangely with the desperadoes of silence.

## III

Wherein lies the man's achievement in literature, and how does he participate in the life of the avant-garde? Like the Symbolist poets, Hemingway wants to purify the language of the tribe; like the Dadaists and Surrealists, he disdains "literature." He values the rigor of art; he abhors untruth. Hemingway suspects the power of literature to falsify experience, its readiness to mediate vitality and concreteness. "I used to wish. . . ," he writes, "that I lived in the old days before all the books had been written and all the stories told for the first time. In those days it was no disgrace to drink and fight and be a writer too." [15] Superficially, Hemingway objects to gentility. On a deeper level, he distrusts the accretions of language.

Hemingway's distrust of language has many guises. His vocabulary is perhaps the smallest of any major novelist. To speak is to lie, Burroughs avers; this is fanatic. Hemingway is merely taciturn; he advises curtness in feeling, in action. He emulates the clipped speech of the English upper classes and of the laconic Westerner. The few words he imports from foreign languages tend to be simple, even obscene; the essential task is to confront *nada* with *cojones*. For Hemingway, true obscenity is something else. It can be described as "unsoundness in abstract conversation or, indeed, any other metaphysical tendency in speech." [16] Knowing that the currency of words has been inflated by fustian or mendacity, that the connotations or words have been counterfeited, he seeks new values for language in slang, in fact, in understatement.

Slang is a colorful form of reticence. It is metaphor in the process of becoming cliché. Alive, it refers to concrete situations; dead, it serves as impersonal response. Moreover, slang shuns sophistication as it shuns loquacity. It is not only metaphor or cliché, but also protest. It issues from the underground of fiction. Fact, on the other hand, speaks on behalf of reality, and challenges the imagination to a keener effort. In his interview with George Plimpton, Hemingway states that the *Racing Form* represents "the true Art of Fiction." [17] This statement, which may suggest the current technique of the "non-fiction novel," actually pleads for constructionism. Hemingway makes his point clear:

From things that have happened and from things as they exist and from all things that you know and those you cannot know, you make something through your invention that is not a representation but a whole new thing truer than anything true and alive, and you make it alive, and if you make it well enough, you give it immortality.[18]

On fact, the house of fiction stands; without it, the house collapses in a rubble of sentiment. Understatement, by refusing to exceed the authority of language to interpret fact, helps to keep the edifice spare. Hemingway's understatement stems from a private conviction that good things deserve to remain unexpressed; it ends by serving an artistic purpose. Understatement requires omission, and the art of omission is one that he learns from the great Impressionist painters, Cézanne particularly. Referring to his early years in Paris, Hemingway speaks of his "new theory that you could omit anything if you knew that you omitted and the omitted part would strengthen the story and make people feel something more than they understood." [19] Omission compels participation. Thus the house of fiction, with its empty spaces, is finally inhabited.

But slang, fact, and understatement, as verbal modes, are equivocal. They appear to harden the surface of language; at first, they seem techniques of semantic restraint or even absence. They produce a stillness. Yet their end is to create meaning; they finally function as techniques of semantic presence. Such is the duplicity of silence in Hemingway's fiction. Literature creates itself in self-opposition, and style evolves into a pure anti-style.

The mannerisms of Hemingway's anti-style are only too memorable. Repetitions of word and phrase, suggested by the rhythmic experiments of Gertrude Stein, insinuate their significance precisely because they avoid expansion and customary elaboration. Substantives carry the burden of his statements, and make all analysis superfluous. The conjunctive "and," strung on end, gives equal weight to different parts of a period that moves without syntactic modulation. The little that stands before us stands sharply, brilliantly present; the rest is ruthlessly banished. Often, action replaces speech; thought and feeling remain implicit. As Harry Levin puts it, ". . . the act, no sooner done than said, becomes simultaneous with the word, no sooner said than felt." [20] We are in the huge and abrupt present, given to us without connectives or transitions. If judgments must be made, they can be made ironically, and Hemingway's irony can be cruel and bitter.

These celebrated traits are seldom viewed in the perspective of anti-literature. The clue comes from Sartre who saw in the chopped-up, discontinuous style of Camus's *The Stranger* the form of an absurd vision. The same may be said of Sartre's own *Nausea* as of Hemingway's *In Our Time*. The simple accretion of invariable units, the succession of discrete events, defy synthesis. We are indeed close to the assumption of nonsense. For nonsense depends on verbal distinctness and precision. "Nonsense. . . ," Elizabeth Sewell says, "will have to concentrate on the divisibility of its material into ones, units from which a universe can be built. This universe, however, must never be more than the sum of its parts, and must never fuse into some all-embracing whole which cannot be broken down again into the original ones." [21] Fastidious and disjunctive, nonsense devises its own structures, abolishing reference, approaching number. Toward these structures, the anti-style of Hemingway often moves without forfeiting its tragic reference. Its rigor, terseness, and repetitions, its intractable concreteness and vast omissions, resist rhetoric, resist even statement, and discourage the mind from habitual closures. The style emerges from silence and tends toward it again by a process of exclusion; in between, it defies insanity.

Style engages human conduct, and conduct engages fate. Hemingway, we know, abhors the cant of ideology; his ethic is elementary. If you "feel good" after an action, you have acted morally. Morality, then, is a subjective response; but it is the response of one who accepts a code of skill and courage, and knows that death exposes the shabbiness of human endeavor.

This difficult code offers few comforts and relies on fewer presuppositions. It leaves out much of what history has bequeathed to us of philosophy and religion. The radical skepticism of Hemingway is backed only by what a man truly possesses: his flesh, the home of his morality. As a result of this reductive ethic, the characters of Hemingway are forced to be tough; they avoid all unnecessary responses to the world around them. But they also exact from themselves the extreme response when circumstances warrant it: speechless violence. In the moment of violence, Frederick J. Hoffman shows in *The Mortal No,* men function neither as rational nor as historical creatures; they put themselves beyond humanity.

This is why the ethic of Hemingway's characters is not only reductive but also solitary. What they endure, they can never share with others. Existentially, they remain alone; they find momentary communion only in a dangerous ritual. Always, they disengage themselves from the complexities of human relations, and simplify their social existence to the primary functions of the body. "The only thing that could spoil a day was people . . . ," Hemingway writes. "People were always the limiters of happiness except for the very few that were as good as spring itself." [22] In eating and drinking, in love-making, in combat, his heroes silence the shrill demands of civilization, and elude the mind's perversity and the heart's deceit. Their epicureanism is a search for truth, and truth in their day has a withering touch. Truth finds itself by exclusion though in Rabelais's lustier day it offered to devour the world entire.

When we exclude enough, we are left with nothing, *nada.* This, and not physical death, is the destiny of Hemingway's heroes. As a symbol of non-being, of the void, of life's ineluctable emptiness, death chills the spine of the bravest: there is no answer to it but suicide. The old fisherman, Santiago, thinks that "man can be destroyed but not defeated." [23] Yet man can indeed be defeated, as the earlier work of Hemingway repeatedly shows. The defeated are not merely tough; they are embodiments of oblivion. Still, even the defeated may possess dignity. The old man in "A Clean Well-Lighted Place" has failed in his attempt at suicide, but remains a "clean old man." The old waiter who parodies the Lord's Prayer by reciting "Our nada who art in nada, nada be thy name. . . ," understands his client; for he too has excluded all but light and cleanliness from his life.[24] Exclusion is a principle of negation, and as Freud has taught us, the very words "No" and "Not" serve the powers of Thanatos in subtle ways. Exclusion finally leads to death-in-life, the fate of Hemingway's unredeemed. Theirs is the stillness we hear beneath the finicky language.

Yet it is perverse to see only the emptiness of Hemingway's world. In its lucid spaces, a vision of archetypal unity reigns. Opposite forces obey a common destiny; enemies discover their deeper identity; the hunter and the hunted merge. The matador plunges his sword, and for an instant in eternity, man and beast are the same. This is the moment of truth, and it serves Hemingway as symbol of the unity which underlies both love and death. His fatalism, his tolerance of bloodshed, his stoical reserve before the malice of creation, betray a sacramental attitude that transcends any personal fate. Though man is doomed to stand and struggle alone, he may carry his initiative, "push his luck," too far; he may transgress by ignoring the tacit harmonies of the universe. The process of nature continues, heedless of human effort, like the Gulf Stream: ". . . the palm fronds of our victories, the worn light bulbs of our discoveries and the empty condoms of our great loves float with no significance against one single, lasting thing—the stream."[25] Suddenly, we understand those innumerable, small ceremonies of magical penance and propitiation that Hemingway's heroes constantly perform: they are secret invocations of Being at its source. His redeemed characters know that the universe is not Naught but One. And they all cast, like one man, a single shadow across death, the unifier of all our tales. Hemingway himself says: ". . . all stories, if continued far enough, end in death, and he is no true storyteller who would keep that from you." [26] The story rests in silence.

## IV

Silence serves as a metaphor of Hemingway's fiction though his fiction is unsilent. In 1926, Hemingway says to Samuel Putnam that he wants to "strip language clean, to lay it bare down to the bone." [27] A year earlier, he realizes that aim in *In Our Time.*

The collection begins with a scream: "The strange thing was, he said, how they screamed every night at midnight. I do not know why they screamed at that time. We were in the harbor and they were all on the pier and at midnight they started screaming. We used to turn the searchlight on them to quiet them." [28] The scream and the beam, darkness and clarity: therein lies the achievement of Hemingway's style. The same sketch ends with the image of mules, their forelegs broken, dumped in the shallow bay. The author remarks, "It was all a pleasant business. My word yes a most pleasant business." Then comes the story "Indian Camp." Young Nick Adams watches his father perform a caesarian operation on an Indian woman, and sees the body of her husband in the upper bunk, razor still in hand, his throat cut from ear to ear. The story resolves itself in an incantation of repeated sounds in distinct images.

> They were seated in the boat, Nick in the stern, his father rowing. The sun was coming up over the hills. As bass jumped, making a circle in the water, Nick trailed his hand in the water. It felt warm in the sharp chill of the morning.
>
> In the early morning on the lake sitting in the stern of the boat with his father rowing, he felt quite sure that he would never die.[29]

The initiation to birth and death, the vitality of nature, the reliance on the father, the deceptions of the self, remain purely implicit in discrete sensations, and in the magic reiteration of certain words, "boat," "father," "morning," "water." This is the Hemingway scene.

The pointillism of the scene can be more obvious. In "Cat in the Rain," for instance, Hemingway writes:

Italians came from a long way off to look at the war monument. It was made of bronze and glistened in the rain. It was raining. The rain dripped from the palm trees. Water stood in pools on the gravel paths. The sea broke in a long line in the rain and slipped back down the beach to come up and break again in a long line in the rain. The motor cars were gone from the square by the war monument. Across the square in the doorway of the cafe a waiter stood looking out at the empty square.[30]

This is a scene painted by an Impressionist. The eye provides the frame; the mind provides the transitions; the beholder interprets the pattern. Hemingway controls our perceptions by a careful disposition of lacunae. Each event seems to occur independently; each seems coeval with all other events. The effect is abrupt because it is pristine; a great blankness lies behind it.

Brusqueness also conveys the rush of action. "The Battler" begins with a breakman throwing Nick Adams off a moving freight train. Nick walks up to a solitary figure huddled by a camp fire:

"Hello!" Nick said.
The man looked up.
"Where did you get the shiner?" he said.[31]

This is how people meet in a world where violence seldom has antecedents. The slang term is apt; the speaker is a mad prize fighter whose life may be read in his face: "It was like putty in color. Dead looking in the firelight." [32] Ravaged by publicity more than by blows, the battler roams no-man's land, loathing everyone. His sole attendant is a mannerly Negro who hits him with a blackjack whenever he turns dangerous. This emptiness, common to so many characters of Hemingway, affects another battler, Krebs, the veteran in "Soldier's Home." "Krebs acquired the nausea in regard to experience that is the result of untruth. . . ," the author succinctly explains.[33] Krebs loves no one, not even his mother; his single passion is to avoid complications. Both battlers are anomic creatures, their lives delimited at one end by violence and at the other by the void.

Even in that perfect idyl, "Big Two-Hearted River," the hero constantly senses the contingencies of the void. Nick feels happy in the ritual simplifications of his fishing trip, and he is alone. "He felt he had left everything behind, the need for thinking, the need to write, other needs. It was all back of him." [34] He makes camp:

> Now things were done. There had been this to do. Now it was done. It had been a hard trip. He was very tired. That was done. He had made his camp. He was settled. Nothing could touch him. It was a good place to camp. He was there, in the good place.[35]

These rhythms suggest a ceremony of exorcism, as Malcolm Cowley has noted; they are the feelings of a happy man hanging on to happiness by the skin of his teeth.[36] A strange threat chokes the mind, discovering thereby its verbal equivalent of silence. But the specific nature of the threat is deleted from the story; the powers of darkness emerge only in a symbol of the greatest reticence, the swamp.

> In the swamp the banks were bare, the big cedars came together overhead, the sun did not come through, except in patches; in the fast deep water, in the half light, the fishing would be tragic. In the swamp fishing was a tragic adventure. Nick did not want it. He did not want to go down the stream any further today.[37]

The cold swamp encircles *In Our Time.* Yet the stories have the ring of a bell heard over the frozen air. Between their pure sound, the vignettes flash across the eye once and are never forgotten. The garden at Mons where the Germans get potted as they climb over the wall; the absolutely perfect barricade jammed across an enemy bridge; the six cabinet ministers shot at half past six; Maera lying still, face in the sand, while the bull's horn gores him repeatedly; and Nick, hit in the spine, propped against a church—all represent the same awful moment. Story and vignette, sound and sight, blend perfectly, enclosed by the same deep stillness. It is the stillness of terrible truth, and it helps to make the collection the best written by an American in our century.

## V

Hemingway sees life as he sees art: a process of laying bare to the bone. Men strip their illusions as they must shed their flesh. The boy who learns of the death, and of the dishonesty, of his father in "My Old Man," concludes: "Seems like when they get started they don't leave a guy nothing." [38] "They" are agents of the withering truth, and their influence prevails in Hemingway's two best novels, *The Sun Also Rises* and *A Farewell to Arms.*

*The Sun Also Rises* persists as our paradigm of radical loss. The sun rises on characters, like Jake Barnes, who need to sleep with electric lights switched on six months of the year, rises and sets and rises again without dispelling the dark. In this wasteland, the Fisher King is fated. Were his physical wound to heal miraculously, nothing would really change. "Oh Jake . . . we could have had such a damned good time together," Brett says at the end, and Jake, who knows better, replies, "Yes. . . . Isn't it pretty to think so?" [39] Hemingway compresses the terror of his novel into that ironic question. The terror has no reason and no name; it is simply the presence of an absence; and the only recourse of the characters is to discover a rhythm, a style, of endurance. For the best among them, like Romero, there is grace under pressure, which may be the only grace man can ever know.

The novel is predictably circular in structure; we end to begin again. The characters also form themselves in a circle about the hollow center, Lady Brett Ashley, her slouched hat hiding an exquisite despair. The contrast is between Robert Cohn, shabby romantic in a purple land (W. H. Hudson's), and Jake Barnes, maimed stoic and ironist of the night. In this parable of modern love, whores dance with homosexuals, and the impotence of the hero matches the heroine's nymphomania. The quality of Book One is the quality of a nightmare barely kept in abeyance. "It is awfully easy to be hard-boiled about everything in the day time, but at night is another thing," Barnes says in a cold sweat.[40]

In Book Two, fishing and bull-fighting deflect the dread. Brett goes off to San Sebastian with Cohn; Barnes and Bill Gorton go off fishing in the Burguete. The intricacies of love are hushed, the urgencies of worship muted. Barnes tries to pray in a Spanish church: ". . . and as all the time I was kneeling with my forehead on the wood in front of me . . . I was a little ashamed, and regretted that I was such a rotten Catholic, but realized there was nothing I could do about it. . . ."[41] The cold high country near Roncevaux, where Roland once gave his life for God and Emperor and the Twelve Peers, beckons; there the trout swim in clear streams. "I shut my eyes," Jake says. "It felt good lying on the ground."[42]

Down on the lower ground, at Pamplona, the society of spiritual cripples waits to receive life from the Feria of San Fermin. The passion they lack they hope to find as *aficionados* (*afición* also means passion) of the ring. By the time the feria is over, Brett has robbed all the men around her of their manhood. Romero stands alone. Can she redeem herself in him? Will she only bring his ruin? Romero has innocence, courage, and grace. His knowledge is from another time, another place. He understands that the bull is his equal, perhaps his other self: ". . . his left shoulder went forward between the horns as the sword went through it, and for just an instant he and the bull were one. . . . Then the figure was broken."[43] He can pay homage to Brett, in the ring, without diminishing himself. But when he offers her the bull's ear, she forgets it in the drawer of a bed-table. There can be no true meeting of Brett and Romero, as there can be none between Brett and Barnes. The feria turns into a bad dream; the characters disperse.

The reducing cycle nears completion in Book three. Brett decides "not to be a bitch," and releases Romero. "It's a sort of what we have instead of God," she explains to Jake who has hurried to her side in Madrid.[44] In his view, Brett's sacrifice is genuine because she has paid. "You paid some way for everything that was any good. . . . Either you paid by learning about them, or by experience, or by taking chances, or by money," Jake believes.[45] Everyone pays. Some, like old Count Mippipopolous, pay gallantly; others pay badly. But payment is always reduction, divestment; at the end, the skin shrinks tighter on the skeleton. The best lay down their life against death, and no one can offer to pay more. Such is Romero who functions in the novel more as a symbol than as a character. His existence incarnates the crucial insight of *The Sun Also Rises:* only in confrontation with death does life acquire meaning and lose its terror. In this stark paradox, terror is transcended.

The keynote of *A Farewell to Arms* is not terror but doom. The world breaks everyone impartially, and death falls on the earth like a steady rain. Death comes in war, "suddenly and unreasonably"; and it comes in peace to those who would give birth: "Poor, poor dear Cat. And this was the price you paid for sleeping together. . . . This is what people got for loving each other." [46] Nature finds its final unity in decay.

But there is also the unity of love. Within the great circle of decay, two lovers strive to keep intact: ". . . there's only us two and in the world there's all the rest of them. If anything comes between us we're gone and then they have us," Catherine says to Frederic Henry.[47] There are not two, there is only one. For as Catherine goes on to say: "There isn't any me any more. Just what you want. . . ." [48] But the circle of decay tightens. There is no place really "to drop the war," as Catherine reminds Frederic; their "separate peace" in Switzerland is only part of a greater biological war. "You'll fight before you'll marry," Nurse Fergus tells the lovers. "You'll die then. Fight or die. That's what people do. They don't marry." [49] Catherine, of course, dies. Love also finds its unity in doom.

In the Italian mountains, "the picturesque front," the war seems to mark an end to history. "Perhaps wars weren't won any more," Henry wonders. "Maybe they went on forever." [50] It is more certain that the war confutes the collective experience of mankind. In a famous passage, Henry says:

I was always embarrassed by the words sacred, glorious, and sacrifice and the expression in vain. . . . There were many words that you could not stand to hear and finally only the names of places had dignity. Certain numbers were the same way and certain dates and these with the names of places were all you could say and have them mean anything. Abstract words such as glory, honor, courage, or hallow were obscene beside the concrete names of villages, the numbers of roads, the names of rivers, the numbers of regiments and the dates.[51]

Universal violence compels language to be mute; the public and the private fates of characters converge. The novel ends fittingly with an apocalyptic image. Frederic Henry recalls a log crawling with ants that he had thrown into a camp fire. "I remember thinking at the time," he says, "that it was the end of the world and a splendid chance to be a messiah and lift the log off the fire and throw it out where the ants could get off on to the ground." [52] But the messiah only steams the ants with whiskey and they perish.

Yet *A Farewell to Arms* is richer than its macabre insistencies. Rinaldi, Ferguson, the army priest, the barman at Stresa, all move with stringent, with stubborn life. Catherine Barkley, who appears stilted, oddly unreal, finally forces her hidden hysteria upon our consciousness, and in death acquires dignity. Henry remains the Hemingway hero, laconic and inevitable as tragedy. But the novel reminds us that, for Hemingway, country is more ample than people. The novel breathes the seasons; it gives the firm touch of places. We see the pebbles white in the sun, and the blue water moving swiftly in the channels. We shiver when the weather turns cold at night and the rain commences to fall the next day. Still, the narrowness of death ends by pinching our response. Like Frederic Henry, lying wounded in an ambulance, we feel the blood of a dead soldier drip as "from an icicle after the sun has gone." It drips always on the same spot of our skin.

The great phase of Hemingway's art closes with *A Farewell to Arms*. The stories of *Men Without Women*, unlike some earlier pieces, cannot be charged with "the kinetographic fallacy" which Carlos Baker defines as "the supposition that we can get the best art by an absolutely true description of what takes place in observed action." [53] But their depth is sometimes attained at a price: Hemingway loses the rigor of omission and exposes his sentimentality. The collection, nevertheless, contains such classic fictions as "The Undefeated." Hemingway still knows that words belong to the public domain; the hidden world requires a subliminal language. This is the language that conveys evil in "The Killers." It is also the language of the death of love in "Hills like White Elephants":

> "They look like white elephants," she said.
> "I've never seen one," the man drank his beer.
> "No, you wouldn't have." [54]

This dialogue may have been composed by Samuel Beckett. Here it is again, in the incredible opening sentence of "In Another Country": "In the fall the war was always there, but we did not go to it any more." [55] The threat of oblivion presses syntax into ineluctable shape. The narrator of "Now I Lay Me" lies in the dark listening to silk-worms chewing; he dares not close his eyes lest his soul depart. The predicament of Hemingway is much the same: he dare no more ignore than articulate the dark. The tension of the void bestills his art.

## VI

Silence is not only a metaphor of Hemingway's work; it is also the source of its formal excellence, its integrity. He begins to lose his virtue, his *areté*, in the thirties and never recovers it completely. Edmund Wilson is probably right in saying that Hemingway succumbs to "deliberate self-drugging" in the period.[56] The opium of the people may be identified as sex, bread, or religion, as Mr. Frazer bitterly reflects in "The Nun, the Gambler, and the Radio." But what is the opium of Mr. Frazer himself who suffers from "the horrors"? In lieu of the gambler's courage or the nun's faith, it is a radio whispering thoughtlessness in the dark.

*Winner Take Nothing*, which contains that story, contains others that reveal the grotesqueness of American life. The huge whores in "The Light of the World," the religious fanatic who asks to be castrated in "God Rest You, Merry Gentlemen," the absurd tourists in "Homage to Switzerland," the old French couple struggling through Prohibition in "Wine of Wyoming," express the dislocations of spirit when the times are out of joint. Hemingway forces himself to acknowledge the social fact, and admits reluctantly the sense of community. A new poignancy, foreign to his best work, unsettles the stories; a kind of disgust wavers between society and self. When Hemingway returns to his true form in "A Clean Well-Lighted Place" or "A Way You'll Never Be," the style contracts again and sings madly. The latter story portrays Nick Adams in a state of shell shock; he "can't sleep without a light of some sort." "That's all I have now," he explains to a fellow officer.[57] The next moment, Nick rants about locusts, and silently babbles: "And there was Gaby Delys, oddly enough, with feathers on; you called me baby doll a year ago tadada you said that I was rather nice to know tadada with feathers on, with feathers off. . . ." [58] This is Hemingway still inward with his terror, a terror he can still overcome, artistically, in the unflawed "The Short, Happy Life of Francis Macomber."

But the embarrassing evidence against him accrues. When *To Have and Have Not* appears in 1937, critics on the Left hail it as proof of Hemingway's conversion to the gospel according to Marx. The social question implied by the main narrative is this: how does a brave man, Harry Morgan, come to be an outlaw? The subplots of the novel are glutinous, and they concern a number of sordid and arbitrary figures from the worlds of politics, finance, entertainment, and literature, whose soft corruption contrasts with the hero's violence. Needless to say, the reader sees only Harry Morgan.

Morgan fits D. H. Lawrence's image of the American, "hard, isolate, stoic, and a killer." [59] His big blonde wife, Marie, can also testify to his ithyphallic character. Morgan relates to no one though he remains an excellent provider for his family. He acts swiftly, and his actions are part of no moral or political scheme. It is a question of survival, and of *cojones*. Mean, pitiless to others as he is toward himself, he stands in nature rather than in civilization. The fact that men are deprived of their dignity by the Depression, or that the Conchs are starved out of the Florida Keys to make room for tourists, or that the veterans are abandoned by the government to perish in a hurricane, hardly seems relevant to his buccaneer's outlook.

Hemingway evades these implications of his character. Throughout the novel, the reader feels that Morgan struggles heroically to escape from an image imposed on him by the ethos of the times. "They don't give you any choice *now* [italics mine]," Morgan says.[60] Hemingway knows very well "they" never did. And Morgan knows it too. When one of the Cuban gangsters lectures him on the necessity of terrorism in the revolution, Morgan silently fumes:

> F--- his revolution. To help the working man he robs a bank and kills a fellow works with him and then kills that poor damned Albert that never did any harm. That's a working man he kills. With a family. . . . The hell with their revolutions.[61]

The inevitable showdown comes. The Cubans are all killed single-handedly; Harry Morgan lies on the cockpit floor in a pool of his own blood. He mutters in delirium the famous lines: "One man alone ain't got. No man alone now. . . . No matter how a man alone ain't got no bloody f – – – ing chance." Hemingway adds: "He shut his eyes. It had taken him a long time to get it out and it had taken him all his life to learn it." [62] It may also take the reader a lifetime to believe it. Morgan's bloody conversion seems less convincing than contrition wrested from the jaws of death in some obscure Jacobean play. What Morgan lacks at the end is not the strength of "mortal interdebtedness," but simply the use of both his arms. *To Have and Have Not* fails because the essential vision of Hemingway clashes in it with an ideology felt merely as sentiment. The form of the novel reflects the strain as the narrative attempts to expand its focus, change its ground, and alter its point of view egregiously.

The same clash is wilfully resolved in the play, *The Fifth Column;* its hero chooses justice rather than love. As a counter-espionage agent, Philip Rawlings is barely credible, and his girl, Dorothy, develops merely as a type. What can she offer but love and sex, and that, as Philip states, is "a commodity you shouldn't pay too high a price for." [63] Philip himself enjoys a dual personality. During the day he is hard, breezy, or efficient, as the Loyalist cause may require. At night he is tender, vulnerable, and suffers from the "horrororous," or "super-horrors." At bottom, he is still the hysterical Hemingway hero, holding on to himself for dear sanity. But the tension in Philip's life is external. He confronts no real choices, and his mistress serves mainly as an idea, a fleshless seduction. As Hemingway himself puts it in the preface, "There is a girl in it [the play] named Dorothy but her name might also have been Nostalgia." [64] Thus melodrama resolves itself in allegory.

*For Whom the Bell Tolls* can be read more seriously. It is the most traditional of Hemingway's novels, the most novelistic. It seeks to give violence a context, assign to it a public motive.

From the title, which argues after John Donne that no man is an island entire of itself, to the ending, which denies Jordan the relief of suicide so long as he possesses enough life to serve others, the book declares itself for human solidarity. In war, men rid themselves of the self. Even the renegade Pablo ends his desertion because his loneliness becomes insupportable. Love itself ceases to be entirely personal; Jordan says to Maria, "I love thee as I love liberty and dignity and the rights of all men to work and not to be hungry." [65] And at the headquarters of the International Brigade in Madrid, Jordan recalls the feeling of light coming through the great windows of Chartres Cathedral.

Yet, once again, the action of the novel complicates, even undercuts, its avowed theme. The Communists who gossip and wrangle at Gaylord's stymie the military efforts of the Republic. The most terrifying scene in the novel shows Pablo at work, forcing the village fascists to run a gauntlet of drunken peasants armed with hooks and flails. And Jordan—who wonders how many true fascists are among all the men he has killed—is left at the end of the novel with Lieutenant Berrendo, a careful and humane officer, in the sights of his machine gun. The bridge is destroyed, but the fascists win the war.

Indeed, the closer we move to the center of the novel, the more familiar becomes the Hemingway pattern. Jordan is no Marxist. "You believe in Life, Liberty, and the Pursuit of Happiness. Don't ever kid yourself with too much dialectics," he admonishes himself.[66] He believes that people ought to be left alone. He wants love to clear the mind of revolutionary and patriotic clichés. "Continence is the foe of heresy," he concludes.[67] He is chary of thought: "Turn off the thinking now," he says; "Don't lie to yourself. . . . Nor make up literature about it. You have been tainted with it for a long time now." [68] In the face of danger, Jordan calls on his grandfather, a guerrilla hero of the American Civil War—the father is a "coward" who shoots himself! Gradually, the personal motive displaces the rest; we are again alone, in the noisome presence of death which Pilar describes so that none can ever forget.

At the very center of the novel, love and death fuse in the timeless present. Maria becomes indistinguishable from Robert. "Can you not feel my heart be your heart?" she asks him, and he replies, "Yes, there is no difference." [69] The life of both is always "Now, *ahora, maintenant, heute.*" [70] The present, created by love and death, devours all memory and circumstance. The present explodes in orgasm:

> They were having now and before and always and now and now and now. Oh, now, now, now, the only now, and above all now, and there is no other now but thou now and now is thy prophet . . . one only one, there is no other one but now, one, going now, rising now, leaving now, wheeling now, soaring now, away now, all the way now, all of all the way now; one and one is one, is one, is one, is one, is still one, is still one. . . .[71]

In this passage, which expresses purely, absurdly, the unitary vision of Hemingway, style moves toward anti-style, toward silence, toward the point around which the novel turns and turns and turns again. The first and last sentences of the novel circle and meet on the pine-needled floor of the forest on which Robert Jordan loves and dies.

Despite its amplitude of character, of incident, despite its earthy setting and available reference, *For Whom the Bell Tolls* clings to Hemingway's original vision. Jordan has conquered his nightmares and can sleep under the stars. But his word still owes fealty to death. If he moves in that world with a confidence, a naïveté, that Barnes or Henry might envy, it is because Jordan can act: he can kill. The novel becomes trivial or prolix whenever it becomes explicit; the thoughts of Jordan can be ludicrous. Yet there is no contradiction in the art of this fiction, only redundance, only sentimental superfluity.

## VII

*Across the River and into the Trees* usually sends the critics howling. It is a bitter novel, sadly and bitterly uncontrolled. The obsessions of Hemingway's life now disrupt his art, and his reductive tendencies frankly reveal themselves in a preparation for death. Colonel Cantwell waits for a fatal heart attack as his experience contracts around him. "Everything is much smaller when you are older," he says.[72] He can only care for those mutilated by life: ". . . you only felt true tenderness and love for those who had been there and had received the castigation that everyone receives who goes there long enough."[73] The cutting edge can still be felt. "Every day is a disillusion," Renata says; and Cantwell answers: "No. Every day is a new and fine illusion. But you can cut out everything phony about the illusion as though you would cut it with a straight-edge razor."[74] And so Cantwell mocks and rails against the world with his angry and shriveled heart, and seeks in vain to purge his anger in love. But his true solace is the void. As he lies in bed beside Renata, he tries to think of nothing, "as he had thought of nothing so many times in so many places."[75] Instead of ecstasy, he finally draws "sleep's other brother." Everything Hemingway knows about silence appears in the novel, defaced by self-pity and shoddy rage. The language buckles under pathology.

The last stand of Hemingway, in *The Old Man and the Sea,* takes the form of a parable, a fantasy really, of old age. Santiago is a gaunt old man, deprived, alone. The sail of his skiff is patched with flour sacks and looks like a "flag of permanent defeat."[76] His inner life is limited to stark dreams: "He only dreamed of places now and of the lions on the beach."[77] Eating bores him; a water bottle sustains him. Talking is superfluous at sea and Santiago respects the code, talking rarely to himself. *La mar* stands as the original, fertile silence. Reduction now leads to this: a "strange old man," an image of the Self which does not think but only endures.

Santiago has a single fate, and it is the big fish, his Other Self. He pities the great marlin, he joins it:

> His [the marlin's] choice had been to stay in the deep dark water far out beyond all snares and traps and treacheries. My choice was to go there to find him beyond all people. Beyond all people in the world. Now we are joined together and have been since noon. And no one to help either of us.[78]

The fish and Santiago's two lacerated hands make three brothers, a trinity of one. Three sunrises witness the unendurable struggle. "Come on and kill me," Santiago breathes at the end. "I do not care who kills who." [79] The fish is finally strapped to the skiff, its dead eye like the eye of a "saint in a procession," and the passion of the fish is shared by the man as the sharks begin to hit its noble body. Santiago returns to his hut alone, shouldering the mast uphill; he sleeps on his face, arms outstretched, palms turned up. There is only the boy, Manolin, to cry over the bleeding hands of Santiago asleep. A woman tourist, looking at the great skeleton on the beach, says: "I didn't know sharks had such beautifully formed tails." [80] Irony within irony: sharks are a spineless specie.

The fable is elemental, the scene stripped. A single, heroic protagonist stands before us. His tragedy seems to be the classic tragedy of transgression. Santiago fears that he has gone out too far and violated his "luck." His sacramental sense prompts him to confess: "I am glad we do not have to try to kill the stars." [81] Clearly, Hemingway assays the simplest, the most universal, statement of the human condition. Where, then, is his error?

Is it not rather a failure of nerve? Hemingway retracts from a limit of experience he had previously attained, from a deeper knowledge of violence and evil. He composes a noble fantasy of old age after tasting from the bitter cup of Lear. The sharks devour the fish and defeat Santiago—the sharks out there in the sea. Their evil seems entirely external. Yet Hemingway knows that sharks also inhabit the mind. If the agents of destruction are merely adventitious, the fate of man is merely absurd. Yet Hemingway knows that violence engages both freedom and necessity, that true terror corresponds to a void within. There is only a hint of this in *The Old Man and the Sea.* Here is how the first shark, a terrifying Mako, appears:

> The shark was no accident. He had come up from deep down in the water as the dark cloud of blood had settled and dispersed in the mile deep sea. He had come up so fast and absolutely without caution that he broke the surface of the blue water and was in the sun.[82]

Hemingway, however, loses the hint. The language falters, and instead of the ineluctable recognition, we get words such as these:

> It is silly to hope, he thought. Besides, I believe it is a sin. Do not think about sin, he thought. There are enough problems now without sin. Also I have no understanding of it.
>
> I have no understanding of it and I am not sure that I believe in it. Perhaps it was a sin to kill the fish. I suppose it was even though I did it to keep me alive and feed many people. But then everything is a sin. Do not think about sin. It is much too late for that and there are people who are paid to do it. Let them think about it.

And later, when the fish is half-ravaged:

> "Half-fish," he said. "Fish that you were. I am sorry that I went too far out. I ruined us both. But we have killed many sharks, you and I, and ruined many others. How many did you ever kill, old fish? You do not have that spear on you for nothing." [83]

Language becomes a mannerism; silence becomes a parody of itself. The condition of the old Cuban fisherman, splendid as he is, fails to carry the symbolic burden of the human condition. The style still holds back, though it has little to withold.

## VIII

The black paradox of Ernest Hemingway remains the same: he can never stray far from the reticence of death, madness, and the void without betraying his vision. Critics have speculated about the "fourth" and "fifth" dimensions that Hemingway believes can be given to prose fiction.[84] They have suggested the dimensions of death, transcendence, and the mystic present. Silence, which bears some relation to these topics, may be conceived as an added dimension to his prose. In that dimension, the exclusive rage and unitary obsession of Hemingway find their best expression.

Yet there is some infirmity, perhaps, in that silence, and it must be acknowledged. It disguises a deliberate restriction of feelings, the tightness of holding tight. Philip Young, we know, relates this attitude to the trauma of Hemingway's wound at Fossalta and to a subsequent neurosis identified by Fenichel as "primitivation."[85] Everything must be simplified. Everything must be simplified and repeated. During his life span, Hemingway doubles up on his tracks across three continents to conquer the fright of being. His compulsion to repeat turns the later work into a parody of the earlier.

We need not speculate on the disease of genius. Whatever ravages Hemingway's life, whatever insanity finds its way to the end, he still manages to create a unique literary style, and manages to create a style of survival that compels envy and emulation the world over. He offers also a parable of the literary imagination nearing the end of its tether, of consciousness struggling against the nihilism that consciousness alone can engender. In his work, literary statement approaches the edge; language implies the abolition of statement. A minimal assertion holds the world of Hemingway together against madness. We are prepared for Kafka. We can see how literature begins to purify itself valiantly in modern acknowledgement of an old void. Naked, Orpheus enters the great, empty spaces of violence.

CHAPTER IV

# *KAFKA:*

## *The Authority of Ambiguity*

All these parables really set out to say merely that the incomprehensible is incomprehensible, and we know that already.
Franz Kafka, "On Parables"

### I

FRANZ KAFKA provides us with the secret emblem of our literature. He dies in 1924, fifteen years before the world cracks open for the second time in a century, before his race experiences the worst pogroms of its history. Yet we only begin now to feel the weight, the authority, of his ambiguities. We return continually to his work. Camus says, "The whole art of Kafka consists in forcing the reader to reread." [1] Perhaps we also return to the work in order to redeem it from earlier obscurity. No adequate edition appears until 1946. Reprinted in New York that year, the German edition confronts the world at last with its terrible image. Kafka enters modern literature as a rumor and maintains himself in it as a mystery.

Born sixteen years before Hemingway, Kafka belongs, nonetheless, to a later stage of literary discontinuity. Though no two writers could be less similar in character or in biography, the American and the Czech reveal common tendencies: a mastery of dramatic economy, a precise genius of omission. Both make their home in the void. It is Kafka, however, who gives us the starker form of indeterminacy, and expresses the disjunction of the modern sensibility on a deeper level. In this, he precedes Surrealists and Existentialists alike, and prepares us for Genet and Beckett. Georg Lukács, the Marxist critic, saw in Kafka the end of realism, and the doom of the West. Images of doom can unlock the doors of destiny.

## II

"If there is a transmigration of souls then I am not yet on the bottom rung," Kafka notes in his *Diaries*. "My life is a hesitation before birth." [2] He is born, nevertheless, in Prague on July 3, 1883, the eldest of five children. Two brothers die in their infancy, leaving him to bear the brunt of parental authority; his three sisters are much younger. The mother is a Löwy, a descendant of scholars and dreamers. "In Hebrew my name is Amschel, like my mother's maternal grandfather," Kafka apologizes with a trace of pride.[3] The father, a butcher's son, is a practical, overbearing, and self-vaunting man. Hermann establishes a prosperous business in ladies' garments, and embosses a jackdaw—in Czech, the meaning of *kavka*—on the firm's stationery.

The father may be Kafka's most awful invention. We see him through the son's eyes in that extraordinary "letter" that Kafka writes in 1919, and delivers to his mother instead. *Dearest Father* proves to be an exercise in memory, reproach, and self-refutation. The author recalls his banishment, for a minor misdeed, out onto the balcony in a night shirt. He remembers the tall, broad, naked figure of the father towering above him in a bathing hut. He writes: "For me as a child everything you called out at me was positively a heavenly commandment." [4] The mother appears to him in league with the heavens; she offers no succour. Little Franz exchanges his self-confidence for a boundless sense of guilt. Thus the exigencies of childhood become eternal myth.

Franz attends the strict German schools in the Old Town of Prague. Every failure redounds to his guilt. He keeps his literary sketches a secret. In 1902 he attends the German university and begins to study law. Kafka professes a deep distaste for the subject though his temper seems almost Talmudic. "Absolute truthfulness was one of the most important and distinctive features of his character," the benign Max Brod, friend, biographer, and executor, writes. "Another distinguishing feature was his unimaginably precise conscientiousness." [5] Kafka steeps himself in Goethe, Flaubert, Dickens; already, he knows and resists the pain of Hölderlin, Kleist, Grillparzer, Strindberg, and Kierkegaard. In 1906, he receives his doctorate in jurisprudence.

The Workers' Accident Insurance Institute for the Kingdom of Bohemia employs him. His gray day in bureaucracy ends at two in the afternoon—time enough to write. But Kafka suffers constantly from headaches, from constipation, from insomnia; his lungs are weak. In the office, he becomes witness to human misery and injustice, the pervasive signs of the state. At home, he feels dependence, uncertainty, and the rare release of creation. Always, he seems torn between the desire to embrace mankind and the need to keep aloof.

But he cannot remain entirely aloof. Max Brod, Oskar Pollak, Franz Werfel, Martin Buber, Willy Haas, introduce him to the intelligentsia of Prague. He joins the discussions at the salon of Frau Bertha Franta. He knows the art and theories of the *Kunstwart*, attends the passionate performances of Isak Löwy in the Jewish theatre of his day. He hears the lectures of Rudolf Steiner, the theosophist, and wonders if he may not be clairvoyant himself. He goes to the mass meetings of Czech patriots, and listens with sympathy to their debates. He hikes, swims, rides, travels to Paris, Zurich, and Venice. He even manages the workers in his father's business and takes their side in disputes.

Above all, Kafka writes. In 1909, he shows a manuscript entitled "Preparation for a Wedding in the Country" to Max Brod. Kafka dislikes to publish his work; he prefers to read it among friends. The breakthrough comes three years later. In the nights of September 22 and 23, 1912, Kafka writes "The Judgment." "I was hardly able to pull my legs out from under the desk, they got so stiff from sitting," he notes in the *Diaries.* "The fearful strain and joy, how the story developed before me, as if I were advancing over water. Several times during this night I heaved my own weight on my back. . . . Only *in this way* can writing be done, only with such coherence, with such a complete opening out of the body and the soul." [6] That same year he begins *Amerika.* But few works satisfy him. Typically, he considers "The Metamorphosis" badly flawed. His publisher, Kurt Wolff, pleads for manuscripts. Only short pieces appear in magazines. He begins *The Trial* in 1914 and fails to complete it. He begins *The Castle* eight years later and dies before finishing his longest work. He receives but one literary honor, the Fontane Prize, during his lifetime. The greatest prize comes to him posthumously when Brod disobeys Kafka's instructions to burn all his writings, and gives them to the world instead. But Kafka himself never feels easy in this world. He seeks in literature a threefold retreat: from love, doubt, and disease.

Love comes to him, strangely, the same year he writes "The Judgment." Kafka meets in Max Brod's house Fräulein "F.B." (Felice Bauer) from Berlin. Thus Kafka lists all the points for and against his marriage, and summarizes all the arguments once again:

| | |
|---|---|
| To remain chaste. | To get married. |
| Bachelor. | Married man. |
| I remain chaste. | Chaste? |
| I preserve all my powers in coherence | You will remain without your coherence; you will become an idiot, will follow every wind, but will never get any forwarder. I draw from the blood circulation of human life all the power that is available for me |

| | |
|---|---|
| Responsibility only for myself | The more infatuated with yourself. (Grillparzer, Flaubert.) |
| No worries, concentration on work | As I grow in strength I shall stand more. But there is a certain kernel of truth in this.[7] |

The conclusion is always the same: "Miserable me!" In 1917, the couple break their engagement for the last time. (The story of Kierkegaard and his Regina seems to repeat itself in cruel parody.) Later, Kafka meets a gifted woman, Milena Jesenska, in Vienna. He is tubercular; she is married to a sinister personage from whom she cannot tear herself. Four days in Vienna, in 1920, and a last encounter in Gmünd, in 1922, frame their anguished correspondence. "I knew his terror before I knew him," Milena says, revealing the nature of their communion.[8] At last, Kafka finds some happiness in the shadow of death. At Müritz, on the Baltic Sea, he meets young Dora Dymant in 1923. She is a Zionist, an excellent student of Hebrew. Kafka severs all his ties and rejoins her in Berlin where he attends the Institute of Jewish Studies. Their life seems idyllic—for almost a year.

"The category of sacredness (and not really that of literature), is the only right category under which Kafka's life and work can be viewed," Brod states.[9] From the beginning, Kafka never ceases to doubt, and never ceases to believe. The heritage of Jewry surrounds him; the wisdom and hope of Israel hang in the air he breathes. But the Judaism of Hermann Kafka is what we might expect of him: practical and crude. Franz understands Job and Kierkegaard better. At times, he reflects darkly: "We are nihilistic thoughts that come into God's head."[10] More often, he simply struggles against his Jewish fate. He holds out against Zionism almost to the end; and in *The Castle*, he meets the Cabbala with a mystery greater than its own. He cannot finally marry Dora because his orthodoxy remains in doubt.

The flesh seldom forgives the quarrels of the spirit. Kafka, always delicate as child and youth, drives himself to write into the small hours of the morning. The sanatoria of Central Europe await him. In 1917, he learns the diagnosis: tuberculosis. He coughs blood. "My head has made an appointment with my lungs behind my back," he says wryly.[11] The disease stalks him throughout the rest of his life. Toward the end, the doctors send him back home from Berlin. In the company of Dora and faithful Dr. Klopstock, Kafka moves from one terminal clinic to another. He dies serenely, on June 3, 1924, in a sanatorium outside of Vienna. They return the wasted body to Prague, and bury it in the Jewish cemetery of Straschnitz.

The biography of Kafka may conceal traits of weakness and even of petulance. It easily reveals a will, a tenacity of suffering, akin to saintliness. At the center of Kafka's life one almost hears the silence of the stars. A stranger in his family, a German Jew among Czech Jews, a Jew in the midst of Czechs, a Czech beneath the Austro-Hungarian Empire, and an invalid among men, Kafka seems to exist in hermetic space; this is the argument of Pevel Eisner's *Franz Kafka in Prague*. But captives often shake the heavens from their prison houses. Kafka, who all his life reads biographies to find in the existence of others proof of his own, creates a unique paradigm of being. "What is laid upon us is to accomplish the negative," he writes in one of his aphorisms; "the positive is already given." [12] He achieves a negative transcendence.

## III

Erich Heller notes: "Kafka represents the absolute reversal of German idealism. If it is Hegel's final belief that in the Absolute truth and existence are one, for Kafka it is precisely through the Absolute that they are for ever divided." [13] The demon of nullity rules his life and haunts his imagination.

We feel it in Kafka's attitude toward his own body. "I write this very decidedly out of despair over my body and over any future with this body," he says in the *Diaries*.[14] He attributes his physical weakness to guilt, the strain of struggling with the father. But he also seeks himself to further mortify "His Majesty the Body." In *Letters to Milena,* he confesses the periodic desire of his flesh for some specific abomination, "some small nasty smell, some sulphur, some hell." [15] The very substance of Kafka seems to accuse itself, as does his spirit. "Nothing, nothing, nothing. Weakness, self-destruction, tip of a flame of hell piercing the floor." [16] His consciousness empties itself; he knows the calm terror of Robinson Crusoe. The negative forbids all connections, and smashes the marriage bed before it can be ever set up.

Like comfort or health, woman is an enemy. "Women are snares, which lie in wait for men on all sides in order to drag them into the merely finite," Kafka says to Janouch.[17] He speaks of some early sexual experiences in Riva, in Zuckmantel, in Prague, and Max Brod mentions a certain lady, "M. M.," who bore Kafka, without his knowledge, an illegitimate son. But Kafka does not conceal his distaste: "Coitus as punishment for the happiness of being together." [18] His love always lies buried under fear or self-reproach. He cannot become a father and so refute Hermann on his own grounds. His nausea is lucid. To F. B. he writes:

> Sometimes this bond of blood too is the target of my hatred; the sight of the double bed at home, the used sheets, the nightshirts carefully laid out, can exasperate me to the point of nausea, can turn me inside out; it is as if I had not been definitively born, were continually born anew into the world out of the stale life in that stale room, had constantly to seek confirmation of myself there, were indissolubly joined with all that loathesomeness, in part if not entirely, at least it still clogs my feet which want to run, they are still stuck fast in the original shapeless pulp.[19]

Kafka dares us to call him a masochist. He knows Freud's work and rejects the psychoanalytic theory of disease. "All these so-called diseases, pitiful as they look, are beliefs, the attempts of a human being in distress to cast his anchor in some mother soil . . . ," he counters.[20] Still, the images of Kafka's distress betray a dream of immolation:

November 2. This morning, for the first time in a long time, the joy again of imagining a knife twisted in my heart.

May 4. Always the image of a pork butcher's broad knife that quickly and with mechanical regularity chops into me from the side and cuts off very thin slices which fly off almost like shavings because of the speed of the action.

It is enough that the arrows fit exactly in the wounds that they have made.

Now I realized that it [the vulture] had understood everything; it took wing, leaned far back to gain impetus, and then, like a javelin thrower, thrust its beak through my mouth, deep into me. Falling back, I was relieved to feel him drowning irretrievably in my blood, which was filling every depth, flooding every shore.[21]

Transfixion assures no transfiguration; Kafka knows this. He also believes that man has no recourse but to turn the weapon against himself. His love letters thus become pleas for desertion. He gives himself to fear, to guilt, with certain devotion. To Milena he says: "Nowadays I don't wait to scream until the screws for the confession are applied. . . "; yet his hope once more overtakes the scream, and he says: "No people sing with such pure voices as those who live in deepest hell; what we take for the song of angels is their song." [22]

We sense behind Kafka's work a baneful metaphysic. His aphorisms refer explicitly to the infinite cunning of the Evil One and to the versatility of his devils. This leads some critics to consider Kafka a Gnostic who sees the universe ruled by some demiurge from whom human souls rarely escape to heaven. "Gnostic and Manichean," Erich Heller says, "is, above all, 'the face that is filled with loathing and hate' at the sight of physical reality. Kafka refrains from any dealings with nature. . . . Within the human sphere everything that is of the flesh is treated with a sense of nausea and disgust." [23] This is true. But Kafka also views sinful matter as the form of human "impatience," an illusion created by man's desire for certainty, a product of the Tree of Knowledge. "Because of impatience we were driven out [of Paradise], because of impatience we cannot return." [24] If the spiritual world seems at times a demonocracy, this is because man has not yet learned to *wait*. Kafka expresses his religious intuition thus: "Whoever has faith cannot define it, and whoever has none can only give a definition which lies under the shadow of grace withheld"; and so concludes: "I try to be a true attendant upon grace. Perhaps it will come—perhaps it will not come. Perhaps this quiet yet unquiet waiting is the harbinger of grace, or perhaps it is grace itself." [25]

Perhaps and perhaps. Here, at the dubious center, the work and the man meet. True patience demands incertitude; the attendant upon grace becomes the author of indeterminacy. Kafka transforms his prayers into ambiguous fictions. Therein lies the authority of his art.

Superficially, the fiction seems to unmake itself. Kafka pretends that his stories are merely "scribblings," an attempt to "escape from father." He resists publication; he wants to leave no work behind. For him, the artist is merely a bird of bright plumage flapping in the cage of existence, himself merely a jackdaw. He abhors the "noise" in modern literature, and cocks his ear at silence. The writer and the man, we see, adopt the same stance of self-rejection. But rejection often moves dialectically. In his *Diaries*, Kafka also speaks of his "literary mission"; and like Flaubert, he confesses that art consumes his life: "What will be my fate as a writer is very simple. My talent for portraying my dreamlike inner life has thrust all other matters into the background; my life has dwindled dreadfully, nor will it cease to dwindle." [26]

We begin to understand: Kafka finds no human fulfillment possible outside of paradox. He affirms to deny, and makes self-contradiction a statement. Above all, he raises the conflict between faith and doubt, sense and absurdity, positive and negative, to the highest level. This requires patience. Patience is a kind of refusal; it resists accommodation in a world of easy meanings. Perhaps we can call it simply doubt. "My doubts stand in a circle around every word, I see them before I see the word, but what then! I do not see the word at all, I invent it," Kafka says.[27] This is the language of silence, echoing in the void. Parable and paradox, allegory and symbolism, all share the mode of radical ambiguity. Blanchot is right: "The more Kafka writes, the less certain he is in writing . . . the more he writes, the closer he comes to that extreme point toward which the work tends as toward its origin." [28] There are no definite closures in this writing, no graven images in Kafka's temple. The diaries and letters, the sketches, the major fiction, expose the same theme over and over again, giving it various forms, observing it from every angle, until the theme disappears in the infinite perspectives of Kafka's mind, until the very objects of reality dissolve in pure consciousness. The rage for absurd analysis leaves no unity intact; all things multiply and are multiple. The concrete detail, the grain of sand, expands into a universal question. Kafka never revises a sentence in *The Trial* or *The Castle* but to give it the precise mystery of the Absolute.

Patience requires doubt, disunity, profusion, and indeterminacy. But patience requires more; it also demands mystery. Like Diogenes, Kafka stands within three concentric circles:

> The core A explains to B why this man must torment and mistrust himself, why he must renounce, why he must not live. . . . To C, the active man, no explanations are given, he is merely terribly ordered about by B; C acts under the most severe pressure, but more in fear than in understanding; he trusts, he believes, that A explains everything to B and that B has understood everything rightly.[29]

This is a parable not of division or confusion but of incommunicability. Kafka insists on a certain epistemological duplicity. The commentators on the crucial parable of *The Trial,* "Before the Law," conclude: "The right perception of any matter and a misunderstanding of the same matter do not wholly exclude each other." [30] The myth of "Prometheus" ends inexplicably:

> The gods grew weary, the eagles grew weary, the wound closed wearily.
>
> There remained the inexplicable mass of rock.—The legend tried to explain the inexplicable. As it came out of a substratum of truth it had in turn to end in the inexplicable.[31]

The Hunter Gracchus, condemned to wander between life and death, thus sums up his fate:

> Nobody will read what I say here, no one will come to help me. . . . And there is sense in that, for nobody knows me, and if anyone knew he would not know where I could be found, and if he knew where I could be found, he would not know how to deal with me, he would not know how to help me.[32]

"The Problem of Our Laws" shows that the laws must, inevitably, remain unknown. And in "Couriers," the human race appears as "couriers who hurry about the world, shouting to each other—since there are no kings—messages that have become meaningless." [33] The art of Kafka, like the theology of Kierkegaard, maintains the secrecy of the Absolute, and honors its concealment.

In the end, Kafka's art delimits the country of hope by exhausting the terrain of despair. Committed to self-destruction, he declares his faith in the Indestructible. Dada revolts him. "Dada is—a crime," he says to Janouch. "The spine of the soul has been broken. Faith has collapsed." [34] Kafka shares with Israel the sense of Emunah, spiritual perserverance in history. "The course of the world is depicted in more gloomy colors than ever before," Martin Buber writes of Kafka, "and yet Emunah is proclaimed anew, with a still deepened 'in spite of all this,' quite soft and shy, but unambiguous."[35] The proof of perseverance is in the fiction.

## IV

Kafka's fiction madly provokes the exegete in us. We all feel the need to place it in some perspective. At times, we view it as a symbol of man's struggle with the Absolute, and discover its parallels with Kierkegaard's thought. (The ideas of infinite resignation, teleological suspension of the ethical, belief by virtue of the absurd, concealment of God, and particularity of man's relation to the Unknowable, in *Fear and Trembling*, first come to mind.) At times, we read it as a black family romance, a terror tale of guilt and incest through which looms the figure of the archetypal father. We consider it, else, a parable of the modern state and its enforced dehumanization; or consider it in the ashen glow of Jewish experience as a parable of man's captivity in history. But man is also captive of his flesh, subject to disease and mortality. We interpret Kafka's fiction as a protest of spirit against matter, against nature; we hear in it the eternal prayer of self-transcendence.

These perspectives do not exclude one another, for Kafka's art opens all perspectives. If his art stands for anything, it may be this: the dark and clarity of consciousness, the impossible quest for self-apprehension. It is a quest that men neither abandon nor fully attain. Increasing their consciousness of existence, they manage only to intensify the predicament of consciousness.

He could have resigned himself to a prison. To end as a prisoner—that could be a life's ambition. But it was a barred cage that he was in. Calmly and insolently, as if at home, the din of the world streamed out and in through the bars, the prisoner was really free, he could take part in everything, nothing that went on outside escaped him, he could simply have left the cage, the bars were yards apart, he was not even a prisoner.[36]

All the perspectives on Kafka's fiction blur into a numinous emptiness. "The *un-*, the dark, the void, are the only designations Kafka could find for the mystery at the center of the tale," Politzer says.[37]

The short stories, collected mainly in *The Penal Colony* (1948) and *The Great Wall of China* (1948), span his career. We do well to begin with them.

The early efforts are tentative. In "Conversation with the Supplicant," however, Kafka already despairs over the otherness of reality. His supplicant wants to see things as they must be before they reveal themselves to his senses. The terror of the banal invades the story; the surface of life crumbles. The hero requires an invisible balustrade to cross the town square. We are prepared for surrealist intrusions, judgments from another realm. This is precisely what Kafka conveys in "The Judgment." Despite the sly autobiographical references—Georg has the same number of letters as Franz, his fiancée has the initials of Felice Bauer, the portrait of the father suggests Kafka's own, etc.—the story convinces us that the judgment of the father on his son, death by drowning, corresponds to a legitimate need of the son, and that the latter corresponds again to a metaphysical verdict. "So now you know what else there was in the world besides yourself, till now you've known only about yourself!" the father roars.[38] But neither the raging father nor the son who blindly complies with the sentence, neither friend nor mistress—no, neither author nor reader—can finally understand a judgment that derives its sole authority from itself.

"The Metamorphosis" goes farther. "As Gregor Samsa awoke one morning from uneasy dreams he found himself transformed in his bed into a gigantic insect." [39] Thus begin all enormities, and their explanation rests on their presence. The metamorphosis of Gregor is downward, toward formlessness, toward silence, yet his awareness remains human, obdurately so. Even enormity fails to alter the consciousness of man: this is the desperate irony of the story. Gregor pleads to remain a traveling salesman in the shape of a hideous insect. The family assumes that the insect must be Gregor simply because it appears in his room, and they reject that assumption only when their self-interest exceeds their obtuseness. The self and its delusions persist, making for outrageous comedy, the comedy of error and misunderstanding, the comedy of radical imperfection. The sexual element vaguely confirms that persistence. Gregor clings to the picture of a fur-clad woman in his room and entertains fantasies of love with his sister, Grete. (In the *Diaries,* Kafka speaks of "indiscretions" in the story.) But the essential movement is toward reduction. Gregor eats less and less; mother and sister strip his room of furniture; an apple, hurled by the angry father, festers in his back. From his dark place, the creature looks sadly upon the family, sitting in a circle of light. Gregor wilts while the family, after its initial setback, acquires new life. The old father gains in vigor, the young sister matures. It is Grete, his kindly caretaker, who finally suggests that they rid themselves of a nuisance no longer called Gregor. When the insect dies, the charwoman disposes of it without ceremony, and the family ignores the event. The story ends: "And it was like a confirmation of their new dreams and excellent intentions that at the end of their journey their daughter sprang to her feet first and stretched her young body." [40] Perhaps the true metamorphosis is that of Grete. Perhaps the loathsome transformation of Gregor contains the hope of some rebirth. On the first day, we recall, Gregor finds himself jammed into the doorway to his room, "when from behind his father gave him a strong push which was literally a deliverance and he flew far into the room, bleeding freely. The door was slammed behind him with the stick, and then at last there was silence." [41] Perhaps deliverance, after all, comes as an inverse birth, a loss of human form.

The same question applies to the officer, in "The Penal Colony," who ends on the Harrow of an infernal machine. As an executioner, he had witnessed the torture of countless others, their faces radiant in the sixth hour as they begin to understand the inscription drilled into their dying bodies. "Be Just," he instructs the Designer to drill into his own, as the explorer, the condemned man, and the soldier watch uncomprehendingly. But the machine, which functions more smoothly than it has since the days of the old Commandant, suddenly goes berserk. It disgorges its parts, destroys itself like a Tinguely machine; and it kills the officer outright, with a spike through the head. Perhaps justice can never be inscribed or understood. Perhaps the old dispensation has simply come to an end, leaving the new Commandant to the influence of his women, leaving the explorer, an outsider, free to return whence he came. Perhaps, too, the officer finds atonement in his absurd apparatus precisely because "no sign was visible of the promised redemption; what the others had found in the machine he had not found; the lips were firmly pressed together, the eyes were open, with the same expression as in life, the look was calm and convinced, through the forehead went the point of the great iron spike." [42] Though guilt can never be doubted, the officer says, redemption can never be known. In Kafka's work, this statement holds as well in reverse: though guilt is never understood, redemption is never uncertain. We may interpret the tale in terms of God and the Devil, the Old Testament and the New, the religious mind and the secular sensibility. We end only with the feeling that victims and executioners are, as in "Jackals and Arabs," complicit. We also suspect that if outrage demands nothing less than a transformation of consciousness, art demands that transformation to remain hidden.

With certain exceptions—"The Country Doctor," for instance—Kafka seldom permits his techniques of semantic evasion to become purely hallucinatory. He prefers the precise illogic of the creature Odradek—Politzer finds in the etymology of the word suggestions of "the little dissuader"—which turns "The Cares of a Family Man" into epistemological comedy.[43] He employs apes, horses, or mice as protagonists who cast disbelief on human endeavor. He resorts to the meaningless enumerations and permutations of "A Visit to a Mine" or

"Eleven Sons." He applies rigorous logic, pure analysis, to define lacunae of meaning, to survey the field of non-sense. He forces the syntax to qualify each phrase, contradict it, forces the sentence to delay its sense to the end. He omits, eliminates, and so puts before us urgent words without a context:

> Coal spent; the bucket empty; the shovel useless; the stove breathing out cold; the room freezing; the leaves outside the window rigid, covered with rime; the sky a silver shield against any one who looks for help from it. I must have coal; I cannot freeze to death; behind me is the pitiless stove, before me the pitiless sky, so I must ride out between them and on my journey seek aid from the coal dealer.[44]

So begins the journey of "The Bucket Rider." Where? When? Why? There is no context; everything is therefore permitted. An invisible suppliant rides a bucket and vanishes into the icy mountains. The parable perpetuates the mystery; it does not explain it. Art assuages nothing.

Toward the end of his life, Kafka chooses the Artist as an embodiment of human perplexities. On the surface, the mood appears serene; the ambiguities writhe underneath. In "The Hunger Artist," for instance, the hero attains perfection only in death. The artist breaks all fasting records though no one knows or cares; the world makes itself felt as "non-understanding." In the end, the artist shrivels into a bundle of straw and in his place a leaping panther is caged. Art may be a wasting compulsion—the hunger artist fasts because he dislikes all food —or a diminishment of life. But the discipline of artists is like the rage of saints: both declare the heavens unjust.

Two of the major stories in *The Great Wall of China* pursue this theme to its end in silence. "Investigations of a Dog" calls art and science, the human race itself, into question. With bland raillery, with insane cogency, Kafka's dog goes farther than Dostoevsky's Underground Man; the dog proves a greater master of futility. "Whence does the earth procure the food it gives us?" The dog asks though he knows that "we survive all questions, even our own, bulwarks of silence that we are." [45] Vaster than music, which prompts the dog's investigation into the nature of things, is the oppressive stillness. "We are the dogs who are crushed by the silence . . . the others seem to thrive on silence," he cries.[46] The labor of consciousness ends always in entombment, "deeper and deeper in silence, it seems, so deep that one can never be dragged out of it again by anybody." [47] Dog and man—man remains conspicuous by his absence in the story—have no colleagues in their curiosity, in the wakeful superfluity of their mind.

The metaphor of the artist, of human consciousness really, becomes unspeakable in "The Burrow." The speaker, in the eternal fussiness of his self-regard, suggests the introspective maker, the builder of all imaginary labyrinths. He seeks safety, isolation, and perfection. Yet the contingencies of danger, intrusion, and failure affect his most scrupulous plans. The hush of his abode is broken by faint scratchings and whistles, and by the sinister burrowings of another beast. His cherished Castle Keep sems both a fortress and prison, the seat of his guilt. The animal can neither leave his dark construction behind nor yet reconcile himself to its hollow maze. The burrow remains an insane artifact and a natural grave. The other beast—is it both Self and Other?—burrows closer into the speaker's silence without giving sign of recognition: ". . . if it had heard me I must have noticed some sign of it, the beast must at least have stopped its work every now and then to listen. But all remained unchanged." [48] The voice simply ceases, the soft earth crumbles in the passageways. The story, full of autobiographical allusions, prompts Politzer to say: "The image of Kafka's work at the moment of his dying is "The Burrow." [49]

## V

The novels of Kafka, though unfinished and posthumous, reveal on a deeper level the authority of his ambiguity.

*Amerika* (1946) receives its title from Max Brod. (Some critics prefer to call it *Der Verschollene*, "the lost one.") The story begins to take shape in Kafka's mind as early as 1912, and the first chapter, "The Stoker," appears in an anthology published by Kurt Wolff in 1913. Kafka, sensing perhaps the uncertainties of his novel, compares its hero with the hero of *The Trial*: "Rossmann and K., the innocent and the guilty, both executed without distinction in the end, the guilty one with a gentler hand, more pushed aside than struck down." [50] But Rossmann is not executed; Kafka decides on the more enigmatic ending of "The Nature Theatre of Oklahoma." The affinities that Kafka himself sees between his work and Dickens' fade as the novel presses toward its metaphysical inconclusiveness. The critiques of capitalism, industrialism, and revolution, of America as dream and nightmare, give way to unanswerable questions. The barbarisms of a society in which the Statue of Liberty brandishes a sword suggest absurdities of another order. This ironic novel of initiation or *bildungsroman*, this parodic picaresque, this bitter farce, still awkward in its art, finally evades the assumptions of every genre.

Certain features of *Amerika*, however, betray Kafka's purpose. Karl Rossmann moves from bad to worse as the novel reduces his hopes, his circumstances. His dramatic encounters take the form of trial scenes. Women initiate his downfall, and persist to confute him with the power of their actuality; unconsciously, they thwart his efforts of transcendence. The world closes on Karl, terrifying, arbitrary, comic in its irrelevance, without ever disclosing to him the secret of its authority or the source of his guilt. The classic quest for maturity, identity, and connection ends as a myterious denial of innocence.

As Karl Rossmann, a poor boy of sixteen who had been packed off to America by his parents because a servant girl had seduced him and got herself a child by him, stood on the liner slowly entering the harbor of New York, a sudden burst of sunshine seemed to illumine the Statue of Liberty so that he saw it in a new light, although he had sighted it long before. The arm with the sword rose up as if newly stretched aloft, and round the figure blew the free winds of heaven.[51]

The very first sentence evokes memory and hope, blame and innocence, and conjoins the sword with the free winds of heaven. The subtle pattern of the novel confutes all our expectations. New York offers itself to Karl as a spectacle of motion and restlessness; its harbor seethes with random energy. He begins his new life by meddling with the fate of a stranger, a stoker, and only makes things worse for him. Karl cries and kisses the stoker's hand. An influential Senator appears from nowhere, bamboo stick in hand, and declares himself to Karl as his Uncle Jacob, ready to safeguard his destiny. But destiny is much like the huge "American writing-desk" in Karl's room, a structure of absurd intricacies. We are not surprised that Jacob suddenly decides to expel his nephew by a letter delivered exactly at midnight. The comic pretext of dismissal is really the pretext of life itself.

With a picture of the family and some Veronese salami packed in his box, Karl takes to the road, and the road leads to the Hotel Occidental in Rameses. Two petty adventurers, Robinson and Delamarche, join him, use him, compromise his work in the hotel where he serves as a lift boy, and rescue him from a policeman. The oblique sexual byplay with Clara and assorted waitresses continues with the manageress of the hotel, her assistant, Therese, and the fat singer, Brunelda. Against the kind or obscene distractions of women, the masculine authority of the Head Waiter and the Head Porter, of Uncle Jacob and Delamarche, reminds Karl of his radical insecurity. "Yes, I'm free," Karl says in a rare moment of self-knowledge, ". . . and nothing seemed more worthless than his freedom."[52] Karl slowly learns and quickly forgets that "the verdict was determined by the first words that happened to fall from the judge's lips in an impulse of fury."[53] Perhaps Karl never really learns anything. When Brunelda puts the opera glasses before his eyes, he sees nothing through them, and feels that her "insupportable whims were now being wreaked on him." [54] To every humiliation or blessing he can only bring the obstinacy of human responses.

In *Amerika,* Kafka presents under the aspect of comedy a cruel world wherein all clues, all hints of behavior, are garbled. It is almost irrelevant that the novel remains unfinished. Its last chapter, "The Nature Theatre of Oklahoma," promises to give the errant hero a place in nature and society, a role and a name. But the promises are quietly, insanely, denied. Women dressed in white robes pose as angels, and devils stand by their side. Karl asks to be recognized as an engineer; he is accepted only as a technician; and the record reads: "Negro, a European intermediate pupil." [55] Secretly, he wants to be known as an artist. There are booths for every profession in the "theatre," including a special box for the President of the United States, but everyone is known only as an "actor." Perhaps the only possible response to this scene is one of abysmal platitude. A man says to Karl on learning of his acceptance in the theatre: "Then I congratulate you. We have been taken on too. It seems to be a good thing, though you can't get used to everything all at once; but it's like that everywhere." [56] Perhaps the only response is one that platitude conceals: abysmal uncertainty. Like the Information Giver in the Hotel Occidental, Kafka gives "an almost imperceptible shake of the head to indicate that he did not intend to answer this question and it was the questioner's business to recognize his error and formulate the question more correctly." [57]

## VI

The questioner loses himself in the question in *The Trial;* the self, struggling to the last, vanishes from the scene, leaving only the other. " 'Like a dog!' he said; it was as if the shame of it must outlive him," K. thinks as he falls, stabbed by a butcher's knife.[58] But the "shame of it" is merely an echo of the expiring self, the final "as if" of the mind. The real sentence of *The Trial* is its silence.

We know this: K. submits to wanton arrest one fine morning, and a year later two strangers execute him. We search for an explanation. Kafka and K. seem contemporaries. The author, we recall, writes in the midst of a world at war; his engagement to Felice Bauer torments him; tuberculosis tears at his lungs. But such extraneous reasoning will not penetrate the novel until both author and reader consent to meet within the same frame of indeterminacy. For the central achievement of *The Trial* is a kind of unity. All things belong to the Court, and all people, precisely because the Law remains inexplicable. The trial itself is a metaphor of human effort, an effort doomed to failure because it is a product of human consciousness. The central achievement of *The Trial* is a kind of unity that requires from us a new consciousness.

Kafka creates that consciousness by denying all our expectations. The meaning of each event depends upon the perspective in which it is seen, and the perspectives are infinite; this is the lesson of "The Parable of the Doorkeeper." Contradictions lead to ambiguities; the latter fade into vast omissions. Comedy underlies the contingency of things, the gratuitousness of actions. The real becomes sur-real without becoming more logical. The lucidity of each part refutes not only the clarity of the whole but also the final possibility of lucidity. We are free to believe that Man and Court, Innocence and Guilt, Freedom and Authority, Reason and Grace, caught in mutual reproach, will also meet within the mysterious network of associations at the point where a new consciousness begins to emerge. " 'The right perception of any matter and a misundertanding of the same matter do not wholly exclude each other,' " the priest, quoting certain commentators on "The Parable of the Doorkeeper," says to K. in an effort to alter his view of his predicament.[59] The statement is even more equivocal than it seems; for it is a quotation, and the priest himself turns out to be a prison chaplain. K. has no chance. Unlike K., however, we retain a crucial option: we can suuspend the need for a normative definition of experience.

We always see more than quibbling K. sees though our perceptions are created by his outrage. As the trial takes over his life, the focus of the novel narrows, and our perplexity deepens; the form forces upon us a confrontation with the essential mystery of the Court. All other interests of K. appear merely as distractions. The women—Elsa, Fräulein Bürstner, the washerwoman, Leni, the debauched young girls who surround Titorelli—offer K. specious comfort. They confirm his egotism, his mundane and meddlesome instincts, even when they reject him. (No women are accused in the novel, nor are any executed, though they find condemned men attractive.) Only K.'s landlady, Frau Grubach, says shrewdly about his arrest: ". . . it gives me the feeling of something learned which I don't understand, but which there is no need to understand." [60] The officials of the Court engage in absurd or obscene proceedings, in slapstick and sinister rituals. K.'s colleagues at the bank mock or annoy him; his uncle, his lawyer, offer the counsel of confusion. K. continues to seek information about the Court, from a manufacturer, from a painter. The painter, Titorelli, caps the comedy of facts and myths about the Law by distinguishing three categories: definite acquittal, ostensible acquittal, and indefinite postponement. " 'Both methods [ostensible acquittal and indefinite postponement] have this in common, that they prevent the accused from coming up for sentence.' 'But they also prevent an actual acquittal,' said K. in a low voice, as if embarrassed by his own perspicacity. 'You have grasped the kernel of the matter,' said the painter quickly." [61]

K. grasps the kernel of the matter only abstractly. The humiliations of Block, the admonitions of the priest, fail to change his heart. K. may no longer cast about for aid or tolerate distractions; he may recognize his reduction. Yet he can not renounce the imperatives of his old self, the demands of his old mind. The priest concludes: ". . . it is not necessary to accept everything as true, one must only accept it as necessary"; and K. answers: "A melancholy conclusion. . . . It turns lying into a universal principle." [62]

The end of K. appears as a paradox that resolves itself into further questions. He hurries his executioners along the way but refuses to participate in their ritual. He and his executioners seem one: "It was a unity such as can hardly be formed except by lifeless matter." [63] When a mysterious human figure leans out of a window, arms outstretched, K. can only ask:

> Who was it? A friend? A good man? Someone who sympathized? Someone who wanted to help? Was it one person only? Or was it mankind? Was help at hand? Were there arguments in his favor that had been overlooked? . . . Where was the Judge whom he had never seen? Where was the High Court, to which he had never penetrated? He raised his hands and spread out all his fingers.[64]

The final questions of K. are heroic clichés of a consciousness that adheres desperately—and heroically!—to clichés as principles of its own existence.

The underlying force of *The Trial* may be holy or demonic, gnostic or agnostic. Kafka presses only for a change in our awareness of the categories of existence. This he attains clearly in certain images or details which submit to a curious metamorphosis before our eyes. Titorelli, for instance, rolls up his sleeves and goes to work on a picture of the figure of Justice:

> . . . and as K. watched the delicate crayon-strokes a reddish shadow began to grow round the head of the Judge, a shadow which tapered off in long rays as it approached the edge of the picture. This play of shadow bit by bit surrounded the head like a halo or a high mark of distinction. But the figure of Justice was left bright except for an almost imperceptible touch of shadow; that brightness brought the figure sweeping right into the foreground and it no longer suggested the goddess of Justice, or even the goddess of Victory, but looked exactly like a goddess of the Hunt in full cry.[65]

Kafka repeats the motif. The darkness of the lawyer's room suddenly yields the figure of the Chief Clerk of the Court; the gloom of the cathedral unfolds the enigmatic portrait of the knight; the lumber-room in a bank reveals a warder whipping another. Nothing is what it seems, and what seems changes into new semblances as we watch: this is the black comedy of *The Trial*. In nature's absence—trees, hills, rivers, clouds, the moist earth—all appearances flit in a sealed mental space. Symbols make their statement by defying their semantic functions. The statement cannot be made otherwise. "For language," as Politzer recognizes, "does not travel far enough to reach these limits. Only by raising questions can it point in their direction; only by ambiguities can it break the silence of the inexpressible." [66]

## VII

In *The Castle*, the question becomes a quest. All of Kafka's life, all his calm and melancholy dreams, become allegory. The King never appears to claim little Franz from his dark corner, as the *Diaries* say, and take him to the Castle.[67] The affair with Milena adds the loss of one love to another. (Brod gives evidence for associating Frieda with Milena, Klamm with her legal husband.[68]) European Jewry finds in this novel at last an expression worthy of its intolerable and holy history.

Interpretations of *The Castle* abound; it is in the nature of the work to create and to destroy interpretations. But the action compels us mainly to realize that we can neither choose the Self nor the Other, neither K. nor the Castle. Thus Kafka increases the tension between consciousness and reality. The nature of human effort, of will and desire, remains profoundly problematic, the relation between cause and effect inscrutable. Perhaps all that we understand by human may be finally irrelevant. We sense that Kafka parodies or simulates these concerns —even love!—that he may empty them of their profane content. We sense this precisely because *The Castle* is his most novelistic work. The intricacies of plot, character, and humor, the precarious plausibility of everything we hear and see, can not conceal the android quality of the narrator. Kafka removes himself from the human reality, while still rendering accurately its surface, for a purpose: he wants to create a unique state of mind. This symbolic state includes all the known aspects of awareness, yet puts each aspect in an enigmatic relation to the others. Like "The Burrow," *The Castle* may be read as an allegory of consciousness seeking itself, and seeking deliverance from itself.

"It was late in the evening when K. arrived. The village was deep in snow. The Castle hill was hidden, veiled in mist and darkness, nor was there even a glimmer of light to show that a castle was there." [69] This is the appropriate beginning of K.'s quest, K. the outsider, stranger to reality, who still comes to survey the land, to map and measure, whose profession implies in German (*vermesser, sich vermessen*) some presumption. K. begins with egotism, vanity, greed; he can threaten, argue, fuss, wheedle, and exploit. K. is man, our nasty, hypocritical brother. The sacred or demonic complexity of the novel has but one end: to alter K.'s consciousness before our eyes, and thus to alter our own consciousness even more. The rhythm of action and reaction, success and failure, knowledge and doubt, brings him over the seven days of his fictional life to a point of equivocal stillness. Kafka decides to avoid a happy ending to the story, and presents seven days of quest as a prelude to true patience or perhaps to new creation.

Everything is designed meticulously to defeat our certitude. The native town of K. seems "hardly inferior to this so-called Castle," with its flaked, ramshackle buildings resembling a small town; the Castle itself cannot be distinguished from the adjoining village; the main street leads nowhere. No clear difference can be discerned between the peasantry and the inmates of the Castle. The assistants of K. look alike; are they also his old assistants? To the query of K., eager to take up his duties as Land Surveyor, a voice from the Castle answers through the phone: "Neither tomorrow nor at any other time." [70] Yet Barnabas brings a letter to K., over the illegible signature of Klamm, praising work he has not yet performed. K. tries in vain to reach Klamm through Frieda. The Mayor attempts to explain everything to K.: the Castle makes no errors except in petty affairs; the importance of a case does not depend on the amount of work it entails; there are many Control Authorities in the Castle; Klamm's letter may be a private message; K. cannot prove a single contact with the authorities; the pronouncements of the Castle should not be taken literally. The Mayor concludes: "Nobody keeps you here, but that surely doesn't amount to throwing you out." [71]

This conclusion never changes; only our awareness of its meaning grows. Even K. begins to realize that "there was nothing more senseless, nothing more hopeless, than this freedom, this waiting, this inviolability." [72] K. is humbled to the position of a janitor in the school; he loses Frieda to one of his assistants, and subsequently to Klamm. "That you always longed for Klamm while you had me was bad enough," Frieda says to him in a crucial scene, "but that you seem to have stopped trying to reach Klamm now is much worse. . . . According to the landlady your happiness, a questionable and yet very real happiness, would end on the day when you finally recognized that the hopes you founded on Klamm were in vain. But now you don't wait any longer even for that day. . . ." [73] This is the point of tension or stillness at which K. may be truly transformed. Perhaps the closest he comes to it is at the Herrenhof. Waiting for his nocturnal interview with Erlanger, he blunders into the room of another "secretary," Bürgel, dozes and dreams while the other drones, and finally falls asleep clutching Bürgel's foot. This brief moment of oblivion makes its own case. At the same moment, a servant loses the file on K., and thus brings the matter to an indefinite end. The "last" chapter of *The Castle* joins that incorrigible pair, Pepi and K. The latter now knows enough to say: ". . . my own guilt is by no means clear to me; only when I compare myself with you [Pepi] something of this kind downs on me: it is as if we had both striven too intensely, too noisily, too childishly, with too little experience, to get something. . . ." [74]

But the repudiation of the Self does not commit us to an acceptance of the Other. Kafka holds both within the structure of his ambiguities. The Castle, for instance, seems in turn a void, a labyrinth, an echo chamber, and a ubiquitous authority. The facts in the novel contradict each other; they are open to interpretations; they are subject to the veracity of each reporter. The characters have different points of view, and the collision of their statements leaves the "truth" shattered. The characters themselves shift and exchange their identity; the eyes of Klamm flash through Frieda's and sparkle in the mischievous gaze of the assistants. Motives, not entirely clear, constantly deny or oppose each other. Parallels and parodic contrasts complicate the invisible relations between events: Gardena, Frieda, and K. are related through Klamm; the assistants mimic K. in their childish play; Amalie and Sortini, Frieda and Klamm, K. and the Count suggest suppliant pairs; the interview with Bürgel and the interview with Lasemann mirror one another.

Parables reflect upon parables, and stories upon other stories: the tale of Amalia and Sortini, told by Olga, compounds the allegory of K. with Amalia's silence. Authorities reveal themselves only in surrogates: Barnaby as messenger, Erlanger as secretary. Even the names Kafka chooses for his characters—Count Westwest, Sortini and Sordini, Bürgel, Klamm—exploit onomatopoeia, homonyms, and puns. Statements are seldom direct: when K. is compelled to accept the post of school janitor, Frieda answers for him. " 'Really,' she said, 'he accepts the post, don't you, K.?' So K. could confine his declaration to a simple 'Yes,' which was not even directed to the teacher, but to Frieda." [75] Omissions of history and geography, politics and economics, sociology and theology, give a sense of pure space in which all definitions depend on the authority of the negative.

This is not to say that *The Castle* has no meaning. It may be read as a pursuit of grace, a search for community, a quest for self-discovery, or a parable of man in the modern world. It may be read, even more specifically, as a hieratic statement on Gnostic religion, the Cabbala, totalitarianism, death, or incest. The epistemological comedy of Kafka and his absurd humor, his satiric sense that human existence can neither be accepted nor dismissed, his gay and gentle feeling about the contingency of consciousness, his style, in short, hold the novel together. Yet *The Castle* is also a statement that includes itself. It is a symbolic creation that explores the motives and means of its creation, the limits of awareness. Its art radically disturbs the categories of our thought and carries us to the threshold of despair. Daniel-Rops rightly says that Kafka is an artist "who creates his work out of that which essentially destroys both the artist and his work." [76] Yet the art of *The Castle* carries us also beyond despair. It evokes a new consciousness in the reader to replace the consciousness it has destroyed in K. so that the true quest may be seen at last: a quest for questlessness.

## VIII

Some good fortune places Kafka where he belongs, at the very center of this work; he is the key figure in our search for a postmodern literature. More than any major modern writer, he brings the future into our midst. He haunts all authors who follow him here, and gives to that ancient event, the dismemberment of Orpheus, the air of a prophecy secretly fulfilled.

The place of Kafka is not only in literary history. He seems to see sharply something we do not see and thus demands from us new patience, the full mystery of response. It is certain that he plays out the luminous drama of human consciousness on a level that few of us can attain. In doing so, he makes the clinging antinomies of man—hope and despair, union and solitude, health and disease, power and impotence, eternity and death—so complete as to become once again whole. For him, completion lies on the other side of art, the scrupulous and holy art of ambiguity, on the far side of silence where all is pure meaning.

Kafka either envisions the end of man or the emergence of a new being. Meanwhile, we learn enough from him to live without alternatives, within contradictions. We may even learn to enter, through his words, into an Orphic trance, looking onto the enormous calm of existence.

CHAPTER V

# *INTERLUDE:*

## *From Existentialism to Aliterature*

It seems that one cannot be an honest man of letters,
unless one is disgusted with literature.
Jean Paulhan, *Les Fleurs de Tarbes*

### I

THE POSTMODERN SPIRIT lies coiled within the great corpus of modernism—the work of Proust, Mann, and Joyce, Yeats, Rilke, and Eliot, Strindberg, O'Neill, and Pirandello—gnawing at the nerve of certain authors, diverting others into mad experiments. It is not really a matter of chronology: Sade, Jarry, Breton, Kafka acknowledge that spirit. It may be rather a question of "Terrorism," as Jean Paulhan says in *Les Fleurs de Tarbes:* a sense that literary language can no longer carry the burden of consciousness, an intuition that culture can neither mediate nor contain. Paulhan knows that a fanatic purity of soul makes inordinate demands on language, and thus leads to Terror and to Silence. The Terrorist, above all, is a "misologue." [1]

Paulhan makes his statements in the midst of another reign of terror: World War II. The crisis of the Western mind enters a new phase. Everywhere, then as now, men wonder at the enormity of things. After the Six Million, comes continuous genocide; and the world's body itself, earth, water, space, threatens us with fire the next time. Literature responds to the threat of apocalypse, responds diversely, encompassing the full range of human possibilities under impossible stress. In choosing the particular development of letters from Existentialism to Aliterature, then, I offer but a single example, once again from France. The development shows no single purpose, no pure outline. It eludes, even more than Dada and Surrealism, the dominance of a major figure. It seeks, nevertheless, to answer the challenge of earlier movements, restating the issues of language, culture, and consciousness in terms of its own.

Both existentialism and Aliterature reveal a certain rage for concreteness. If the writers of the period share any tendencies, they are these: a phenomenological awareness of existence, a sense of its contingency, a feeling of particularity, discreteness, and discontinuity in words and things. Thus the reification of experience begun in the nineteenth century ends by imposing the muteness of language against which Sartre, Camus, Sarraute, and Robbe-Grillet struggle. All recognize that death compounds the futility of human life in a universe without pre-established norms. All place on consciousness the burden of self-vindication, with clarity and good faith. Literary genres, inherited from another age, appear to them quaint or alien. They want to remake, to reconceive, that fundamental activity of mind we call literature. In retrospect, Michel Butor accurately describes their intentions in fiction when he says: ". . . all real transformations in the form of the novel, all fruitful investigations in that domain, can only take place within a transformation of the idea of the novel itself. . . ." [2]

## II

Jean-Paul Sartre stands at the crossroads of post-Hegelian thinkers: Kierkegaard, Nietzsche, Marx, Freud, and Husserl. I can do no more than establish him as a point of reference, a landmark of the times; the intricacy of his philosophy, the range of his literary and political work, the impact of his life may appear only in hints. My focus is on the early Sartre, his role in a tradition of silence.

He names his autobiography *The Words* and shows a guilty intimacy with language from the start: "The liar was finding his truth in the elaboration of his lies. I was born of writing. Before that, there was only a play of mirrors." [3] Jean-Paul is actually born on June 21, 1905, in Paris. His Catholic father, a marine engineer, dies when the child is two; his mother brings him up in the Calvinist, Alsatian household of her own parent, Charles Schweitzer, scholar and grand patriarch, sire of Albert Schweitzer of Lambaréné. Sartre has his mother all to himself. "Being nobody's son, I was my own cause and was filled with both pride and wretchedness," he writes; and again: "I always preferred to accuse myself rather than the universe, not out of simple good-heartedness, but in order to derive only from myself." [4] Fatherless, Sartre pretends to possess no supergo; doubtless, he derives his heroic asceticism and promethean drive from old Charles. The mother remarries, again a marine engineer, when the boy is eleven; he feels desolate. But at La Rochelle, where the family now takes residence, Jean-Paul trains himself in arduous freedom. He imagines himself a "faux bâtard," the orphan become foundling. Young Sartre shares something with Baudelaire and even with Genet, about whom he will write extraordinary books. Unlike them, however, he refuses to accept a role created by Others: Bastard, Thief, Dandy, Intellectual. Thus he refuses Abstraction, the Absolute; his alienation remains simply a condition of lucidity.[5]

In 1924, he begins his work in philosophy at the École Normale Supérieure. When he graduates, in 1929, he ranks first in the *agrégation*; Simone de Beauvoir ranks second. Their *liaison* endures. He studies for a year at the Institut Français in Berlin, where he comes under the influence of Husserl and Heidegger; he knows German from his Alsatian childhood. Sartre then teaches philosophy in the provinces, in Le Havre, in Laon, developing his thought, his aversion to bourgeois life and mendacity, finishing his first phenomenological work, *L'Imagination* (1936). A year later, he transfers to the Lycée Pasteur in

Neuilly and makes his presence known in Paris. Gaston Gallimard publishes *La Nausée* (1938), giving it its title; Jean Paulhan publishes "Le Mur," in the *NRF* (1938).

It is, of course in the shame of the Occupation and the dread of the Resistance that Sartre, Camus, or Malraux, learns how extreme the human situation suddenly becomes, how continuous the exertion of individual freedom. Death and torture dissolve our preconceived notions of man. Sartre spends the early part of the war in the Maginot Line, flying useless meteorological balloons; the absurd seems ingrained in experience. When the Germans capture him in 1940, he persuades them to release him as an ailing "civilian." Back in Paris, Sartre writes with new ferocity. He produces *Les Mouches* (1943), under the nose of the Germans though Orestes proudly declares: "I am my liberty"; finally, the Nazi censors close the play. He completes *L'Être et le Néant* the same year. Two volumes of his projected tetralogy, "Les Chemins de la liberté," *L'Âge de raison* and *Le Sursis,* appear by the end of the war, 1945. Sartre travels in the United States, Russia, Africa, Scandinavia, an ambassador of the embattled mind at large. His major works follow close upon one another: *Les Mouches* (1943), *Huis-clos* (1944), *Morts sans sépultures* and *La Putain respectueuse* (1946), *Baudelaire* (1947), *Les Mains sales* (1948), *La Mort dans l'âme* (third in the tetralogy, 1949), *Le Diable et le Bon Dieu* (1951), *Saint Genet* (1953), *Les Séquestrés d'Altona* (1956), *Critique de la raison dialectique* (1960), etc. In 1964, he declines the Nobel Prize for Literature lest his name, his *freedom,* become hostage to an institution. Philosopher, man of letters, political oracle of the Left, a conscience of nations, Sartre offers us this backward glance at himself: "One writes for one's neighbors or for God. I decided to write for God with the purpose of saving my neighbors. I wanted gratitude and not readers. Scorn corrupted my generosity." [6] Neither scorn nor generosity prevent him from progress, contradiction, or self-repudiation. He knows how to "flee forward." He knows also how to give dignity to disillusionment. "I've again become the traveler without a ticket that I was at the age of seven . . . ," he writes at sixty.[7]

There is no way yet to gauge the vast influence of Sartre. This need not prevent us from speculating on his contribution to the avant-garde. He adds both to the philosophy and the literature of vanishing forms, and gives to silence ambiguously.

Existentialism, we know, plumbs the solitude of man. It follows through the nihilism of Nietzsche, denies all essences, all *a prioris* in the human condition, and achieves a transvaluation of values despite itself. "I can neither seek within myself the true condition which will impel me to act, nor apply to a system of ethics for concepts which will permit me to act," Sartre says.[8] (The rubric "a philosophy of alienation" captures this failure of authority, man's separation from the universe, the ambiance of absence, but neglects the potential for transcendence that Existentialism often contains.) The early Sartre discovers in Nothing a crucial category; a totally free being "nihilates" himself. It is thus man who introduces Nothingness into the world. Taking from Husserl the concept of the "intentionality of consciousness"—its inevitable direction *toward* objects, like some bodiless wind—Sartre resists Husserl's idea of a Transcendent Ego that may re-invest consciousness with independent thought. As Knight puts it, "Existentialism came into being when it was seen that Husserl had tried to retain a *representative* consciousness after intentionality had rendered it obsolete." [9]

Up to *Being and Nothingness*, Sartre calls our attention to human subjectivity and gives to the void a new role in the mental drama. Consciousness shifts, changes, nihilates. The world itself seems gratuitous, absurd. "The individual," Iris Murdoch says, "is the center, but a solipsistic center. He [Sartre] has a dream of human companionship, but never the experience." [10] The image of "The Hole," that feminine and obscene "appeal to being" in Sartre's work, vividly reminds us of the terrifying contingencies of the self. Sartre's mood, his intellectual emphasis, will later change, heedless of contradictions. It is not entirely clear, for instance, how a kind of solipsism can translate itself into a new humanism—"In choosing myself, I choose man"—or how creatures who meet only in strife, as "competing transcendences," can ever love, politic, or testify. Still, Sartre aspires to answer the dumbness of creation, and his lapses, his inconsistencies, may make part of the answer.

Sartre also wants to answer the silence of language and turn literature into the sword of liberty. He understands his opposition; and writes penetratingly about the withdrawal from speech in two early essays, "L'homme ligoté," on Jules Reynard, and "Aller et retour," on Brice Parain. Sartre knows the heavy peasant stillness of Reynard's background, the silence of the fields toward the city. He recognizes Reynard's literary needs: discontinuity, pointillism, laconic darkness. The inner turmoils of man's nature defy all fictional forms and subvert the very statements he makes. Sartre knows Parain even better: "He is word-sick and wants to be cured." [11] Parain feels the oppression of language, the tacit way words come between man and himself, between one voice and another. Really to hear ourselves is to stop talking! "Having followed him," Sartre says, "we have arrived at the limit of the human condition, at that point of tension where man tries to see himself as if he were an inhuman witness of himself." [12] Behind Parain's quest for impossible silence lies the urge to test the self by the self, turning consciousness inside out like a glove. Sartre realizes the ontological limits of this endeavor. He counters: "I am 'situated' in language. I cannot be silent. In speaking, I cast myself into this unknown and foreign order, and I suddenly become responsible for it." [13] He concedes only "the emptiness and silence that I am, through which, nevertheless, there is a language and there is a world." [14] This concession unites two propositions: consciousness always reverts to emptiness, language defines existence in the presence of another. "Language is being-for-another," Sartre affirms, reclaiming words from the void into which they so easily tumble.

As a literary critic, Sartre also adheres to his ontological commitments. The Surrealist experiment, which seeks to replace words by a more immediate mode of action or expression, "and which abandons nothing of the disquietude from which it arises," seems to him no more viable after 1930.[15] *What is Literature?* refutes the Surrealists with Existentialist doctrine. Sartre remains largely in sympathy with their revolutionary temper, their loathing of the middle class, their flamboyant individualism. But he can not condone their anarchic zeal, their denial of objectivity, or their literary theory: ". . . they maintained that the secret goal of all literature lay in the destruction of language and that it was enough to speak without saying anything in order to attain that goal." [16] For Sartre, the writer is always "en situation"; to speak or write is to act; and literature only attains full self-consciousness in a classless society wherein author and public, form and content, become one. Every literary work is created and recreated by "the liberty" of its readers; one does not write for slaves. In an age of consumption, violence and gratuitousness help to preserve the freedom of words. In an exuberant passage, Sartre concludes:

> Thus, concrete literature will be a synthesis of Negativity, as a power of uprooting from the given, and a Project, as an outline of a future order; it will be the Festival, the flaming mirror which burns everything reflected in it, and generosity, that is, a free invention, a gift. . . . In short, literature is, in essence, the subjectivity of a society in permanent revolution. In such a society it would go beyond the antinomy of word and action.[17]

Sartre's view is no less utopian than the Surrealists'. He defends his more conventional literary practice by assimilating it to the historical process of revolution. The final goal is not the disappearance of art *from* culture but its disappearance *into* the culture, its coincidence with the "collective subjectivity" of a society. The two visions may not differ greatly. A quarter of a century later, Sartre will mock his youthful visions, and deny a special destiny to literature. Here is the withering statement of his autobiography: "For a long time, I took my pen for a sword; I know now we're powerless." [18]

An existential autobiography, however, remains something of a paradox, a noble absurdity. Sartre's admissions can not really cancel certain truths of his own imagination, the truths of *Nausea*, for instance. He confesses:

At the age of thirty, I executed the masterstroke of writing in *Nausea*—quite sincerely, believe me—about the bitter unjustified existence of my fellowmen and of exonerating my own. I *was* Roquentin; I used him to show, without complacency, the texture of my life. At the same time, I was *I*, the elect, chronicler of Hell, a glass and steel photomicroscope peering at my own protoplasmic juices. Later, I gaily demonstrated that is impossible; I was impossible myself. . . . I built with one hand what I destroyed with the other, and I regard anxiety as the gurantee of my security; I was happy.

I have changed.[19]

Sartre changes while Roquentin continues to exercise his peculiar authority as a hero of silence. He recoils from nature, reason, language, society. He strips, sheds, scours, driving ruthlessly toward authenticity, leaving no feeling or fact in the shadow of illusion; and comes to the terrible discovery that everything, including himself, is *de trop;* hence the total freedom of man and his measureless responsibility. Does he not glimpse the abyss that King Lear—"never, never, never . . ." —so tragically reveals?

But *Nausea* refuses tragedy. It is perhaps the first phenomenological fiction, exploring mental states that owe little to traditional modes of literature, gathering in its brilliant title metaphors of a new sensibility. For nausea is not merely a vague human malaise; it is a total response of the organism to the nature of existence. Consciousness contracts, curls in revulsion from its environment, seeking to empty itself out, to unmake words—hopeless task!—and to disgorge the limp, pasty, or viscous substance of things. But nausea also brings with it strange insights. Roquentin looks at the black, gnarled roots of a chestnut tree, and suddenly realizes that things are stark, alien, irreducible to language, that nothing seems congruent with the mind's reflexive order. Past nausea, within a new lucidity, lie premonitions of truth and freedom. There is a kind of madness in this new lucidity, as Claude-Edmonde Magny shrewdly notes, a dissolution of all our habits, all our old epistemologies: "Madness then appears, after magic and scientific technology, as the third stage in the evolution of thought." [20] The upholders of habit are "les salauds." Complacent, cowardly, hypocritical, these cheat reality, robbing themselves and others of life.

Sartre, however, offers us in *Nausea* more than a parable of his philosophy. Ironically, the author sets out to undermine the conventions of fiction, and to parody, as Henri Peyre shows, the literary devices of the masters.[21] He limits his powers to know all his characters, to encompass their world, to create, like Mann, Proust, or Joyce, a fictional universe, a complete imaginative space—in short, to confirm a prior idea of human destiny. Above all, he creates in this novel, as he does nowhere else, an original poetry through which the senses reject the evidence they so precisely render. An active form sets before us the thickness and fluidity of *one man's* experience without losing its noetic clarity.

Roquentin begins as an ordinary man, solitary, laconic and joyless; he shuns the sun. After much travel, he settles down in mud-colored Bouville to write his biography of the Marquis de Rollebon, an absurd and flamboyant figure of the past. Roquentin has left his mistress, Anny; the *patronne* of a café complies to his sexual needs. Before long, this ordinary man enters into a new relation with reality. Objects touch him back with a sweetish and sickening feeling. He looks out of a window, yawns, and begins to cry. The huge bronze statue in the square confirms the illusions of the citizens, their narrow ideals; but to him, the statue seems neither quick nor dead. "Things are bad! Things are very bad: I have it, the filth, the Nausea," he puts down in his diary.[22] The past yields only scraps, images, dubious tales. "This is what fools people: a man is always a teller of tales, he lives surrounded by his stories and the stories of others, he sees everything that happens to him through them. . . . But you have to choose: live or tell," Roquentin notes as Sartre writes and smiles behind him.[23] And what prompts the universal mendacity of men? Their fear of death. Take Doctor Rogé: "For this reason [mortality] he has carefully built up, furnished, and padded his nightmare compensation: he says he is making progress." [24] Death gives an invisible mandate to the novel.

Impressions pile on impressions without logic or necessity. Objects undergo a mysterious metamorphosis. Characters—Anny, M. Achille, the Autodidact, Doctor Rogé—merely pass through each other's field of vision. Nothing happens. For Roquentin, everything begins to happen. "I looked anxiously around me: the present, nothing but the present. . . . Now I knew: things are entirely what they appear to be—and behind them—there is nothing." [25] Thus the new *cogito:* "I am. I am, I exist, I think, therefore I am. . . ." [26] This cogito will uphold no humanist doctrine, no value on existence. "Absurdity: another word; I struggle against words; down there I touched the thing," Roquentin thinks. He thinks absurdity and lives it, perceptually.[27] In his three dreams, he reviews his futile life, as bourgeois, adventurer, and historian, all come to an end. The true resolution of that life is found not in Sartre's conclusion but in scattered passages of phenomenal poetry:

I exist. It's sweet, so sweet, so slow. And light: you'd think it floated all by itself. It stirs. It brushes by me, melts and vanishes. Gently, gently. There is bubbling water in my mouth. I swallow. It slides down my throat, it caresses me—and now it comes up again into my mouth. For ever I shall have a little pool of whitish water in my mouth—lying low—grazing my tongue. And this pool is still me. And the tongue. And the throat.[28]

Instead, Sartre chooses to conclude *Nausea* with Roquentin's response to a tune, "Railwaymen's Rendezvous," and his decision to create a similar melody in a novel of his own, a book that would cast "a little of its clarity" on his past. This is unwarranted, troublesome. Sartre, of course, prepares his readers by introducing the musical motif early in the story; Roquentin finds a "strange happiness" in the jazz record. Furthermore, Sartre tells us nothing about the outcome of Roquentin's artistic project; *Nausea* carries an "Editor's Note" explaining: "These notebooks were found among papers of Antoine Roquentin. They are published without alteration." [29] In short, Roquentin might have written nothing in his life other than the diary. Still, the tension between the ideas of contingent existence and harmonious art seems more than the devices of the novel can sustain. "To think that there are idiots who get consolation from the fine arts," Roquentin exclaims before turning to the pure realm of music, a realm beyond existence that Proust or Schopenhauer might have chosen.[30] We suspect that the ending of *Nausea* justifies the writing of Sartre's own novel more than Roquentin's.

The ambivalences of Sartre toward art conceal his uneasiness with silence. His will rejects passivity, acceptance, the dark fullness of nature. His consciousness insists upon itself, keeping Woman at a distance. (Sartre's heroines seldom attract us: they compromise Being and deflect the masculine drive toward freedom and lucidity with their opaque character.) [31] Yet his intelligence cries for engagement even as it retreats from the world's body to the edge of solipsism. He acts, he chooses continually, compelled by a radical intuition of the void, and so defines human existence. He wants to overcome his distrust of language by finding some way between the inherent duplicity of words and the muteness of life. He says: "The circularity of: to speak I must know my thoughts but how am I to fix my thought except in words? is the form of all human reality." [32] In the end, his nausea cannot drown the mind's discourse with itself.

## III

Albert Camus, who spends his later days disowning Existentialism, offers an even greater resistance to silence. His measure, as critics say, is Mediterranean, blue harmonies of sky and sea, bathed in sunlight. In 1957, at the height of his career, he accepts the Nobel Prize in Stockholm saying, "I have never been able to renounce light, well-being, the free life of my childhood." [33] This is also the man who makes death the keystone of his work and discovers in the Absurd a new reason for being; this is the man of poverty. Some ultimate spareness of of the spirit brings him within the purview of the avant-garde.

Camus is born on November 7, 1913, in the Algerian village of Mondovi. His father, of Alsatian origin, dies in the Battle of the Marne when the boy is less than a year old; his mother, of Spanish descent, brings up her two children, Lucien and Albert, on a charwoman's wages. The family, which includes a grandmother and a paralyzed uncle, lives in a two-room apartment in Belcourt, a working-class district of Algiers. The poverty of the family is acute though the beaches are free. Camus recalls a certain warmth spreading over his childhood, an enduring absence of resentment.[34] Later, he will both seek and dismiss luxury, give egotism subtler forms of self-rejection, and shun the glitter of "Tout-Paris."

The boy shows brilliance, and a sympathetic teacher prepares him for a scholarship at the Lycée. Camus reads widely—his mother remains illiterate—and his favorites include Nietzsche, Gide, and Malraux. He loves sports, particularly swimming and football. But in 1930, he suffers from an attack of tuberculosis, a recurring threat in his life. Like Kafka, about whom he will write resonantly, Camus experiences the knowledge of his mortality; unlike Kafka, he will never come close to reconciliation with the Absurd. Camus enters the University of Algiers in 1932 to study philosophy, coming under the influence of Professor Jean Grenier. He reads the Greeks, Augustine, Heidegger, Jaspers, and Shestov. He shows a political interest in the anti-fascist movement founded by Henri Barbusse and Romain Rolland. He joins the Communist Party in 1934, resigning the next year because, as he says, the Party exploits the issue of colonialism without true regard for the oppressed.[35]

During the thirties, Camus throws himself passionately into things. He develops a vigorous interest both in drama and in journalism. He establishes a worker's theatre, "Le Théâtre du Travail," in 1935, and writes his first work, *Révolte dans les Asturies* (1936), about a miners' uprising. He reports for the *Alger Républicain* on the callousness of colonial bureaucracy and the destitution of the Kabyle tribes. He publishes two volumes of limpid essays, *L'Envers et l'endroit* (1937) and *Noces* (1938), and finishes writing his most remarkable play, *Caligula,* which appears only in 1944. He begins to work on *L'Étranger* (1942) between two marriages, one in 1933 and the other in 1940. Throughout, his health seems frail, and when he volunteers for military service at the outbreak of the war, the army rejects him. He goes to Paris in 1940 to join the staff of *Paris Soir.* When the Germans invade the capital, Camus first flees to Lyons where he completes *Le Mythe de Sisyphe* (1943), and then returns to Oran where he starts working on *La Peste* before his twenty-eighth year.

The Resistance soon takes shape. Camus is back in Lyons, working secretly with Malraux and René Leynaud, sounding the underground call of *Combat.* The first open issue of the paper appears on August 24, 1944, with the name of Camus on the masthead. His celebrated editorial begins: "Paris fires all its bullets into the August night." [36] The man emerges from these years of risk and sacrifice a hero, an author of at least two works that sustain, amid the rubble of Europe, a new conscience for the times. Camus also works for the publishing firm of Gallimard. *Lettres à un ami allemand* appears in 1945, *La Peste* in 1947, *L'État de siège* in 1948, and *Les Justes* in 1950. By the end of the decade, the image of Camus "le Juste" inspires the young, in Europe, in America, to re-examine the possibilities of moral existence, without illusion or despair, in the clear-eyed certainty of death.

But Camus does not survive the next decade, full of richness, solitude, and confusion. *L'Homme révolté* (1951) precipitates the bitter quarrel with Sartre who accuses him of purism and conceit, and denounces him for willful neglect of History, of the ambiguities in every political act. Still, in the growing insanity of the cold war, Camus refuses to create victims or executioners, and to sanction violence in the name of historical necessity. He continues to speak up in his public voice through the three volumes of *Actuelles* (1950, 1953, 1958). The Algerian War tears his allegiances asunder and the terrorism of both sides violates his heart. He turns to theatrical adaptations from Calderón, Buzzati, Faulkner, Lope de Vega; and finally stages his great favorite, Dostoyevsky's *The Possessed* (1959). In 1956, he publishes his most troubling novel, *La Chute*. The Nobel Prize comes to him the next year; his first thought is: it should have gone to Malraux. More and more, like Jonas in "The Artist at Work," *L'Exil et le royaume* (1957), Camus fears that success may poison the source of his inspiration. Silence weighs down on his last years. On January 4, 1960, he dies in an automobile accident near Sens. They bury him in the Alpine village of Lourmarin. Sartre says: "I call the accident that killed Camus a scandal because it suddenly projects into the center of our human world the absurdity of our most fundamental needs." [37] A few years before, Camus himself confesses: "my work has not even begun." [38]

What would the work have been like? In the "desperate encounter between human inquiry and the silence of the universe," how full or hollow would the voice of Camus grow over the years? [39] The critics recognize powerful tensions and divisions in him, which he senses himself and hopes to overcome. The dialectic of affirmation and denial, paganism and Christianity, violence and justice, joy and cruelty, beauty and suffering—of Gidean plenitude and Baudelairian insatisfaction, as Sartre puts it—moves deep in his life.[40] Camus makes this explicit in the very first collection of his essays: "Between the right and inverse sides of this world, I do not want to choose. . . . The great courage is to hold the eyes open on light as on death." [41] That same volume derives from "the admirable silence of a mother," and the effort of a man to "counterbalance that silence" with justice or love.[42]

A mother's silence—his own, Spanish, enduring, unlettered—reveals to Camus the instant "Between Yes and No," containing the richness of negativity, cold indifference, and the immemorial warmth of the flesh. But the son also turns toward the sun, the active principle, reason and visible relation. Serge Doubrovsky is right: "The theme of the 'sun' . . . defines the fundamental category in Camus's ontology: participation." [43] Every time Camus speaks, he appeals to human solidarity. Even rebellion—"I rebel; therefore *we* exist"—proposes a metaphysical fraternity. Still, Camus never forgets a mother's silence and the darkness that lies behind it. His classic fidelity to limits, his gallic sense of measure, restrain a harrowing intuition of the depths. Indeed, he never accepts limits without some abandon or irony. "Here I understand what they call glory: the right to love without bounds," he says in "Noces à Tipasa"; and in "Le Désert," he asks: "The measure of man? Silence and dead stones. All the rest belongs to history." [44] Despite his birth under the sign of The Balance (Libra), there is a part of him—we see it best in *The Fall*—that reaches toward the shadows of Kierkegaard, Dostoyevsky, and Kafka.

A bright anguish lights his philosophical essays. *The Myth of Sisyphus* rebuffs Caligula—"Men die and they are not happy"—and his plea of a "superior suicide." [45] Condemned by Death, man discovers the Absurd; and he answers by refusing to assent to either. This is negative transcendence: "I leave Sisyphus at the foot of the mountain! One always finds one's burden again. . . . One must imagine Sisyphus happy." [46] *The Rebel* sets itself a larger task: to refute the terror of nihilism and totalitarianism, complete negation and demonic assertion, that shapes modern history. The book rejects murder even as it denounces existence: "One hundred and fifty years of metaphysical rebellion and of nihilism have witnessed the persistent reappearance, under different guises, of the same ravaged countenance: the face of human protest. All of them, decrying the human condition and its creator, have affirmed the solitude of man and the nonexistence of any kind of morality." [47]

But Camus knows the fate of the great rebels: "To be nothing—that is the cry of the mind exhausted by its own rebellion." [48] That is also the cry of the literature of absence since Sade. Camus takes his stand against it though his own heroes, from Caligula to Stavrogin, cry out for the void in the name of truth and terror. Even the nameless renegade priest, his tongue cut out by Sahara tribesmen, his mouth full of salt and desert, his mind reeling in the pitiless sun, acknowledges the sovereignty of Nothing: ". . . only evil is present, down with Europe, reason, honor, and the cross." [49] Genet will come next to fulfill the vision of emptiness that Camus, coming so near to it, defies till the end.

He embodies his difficult defiance in art. For Camus, the literary work does not detach itself from its creator; nor does it escape the absurdity of existence. "Creating or not creating changes nothing," he writes. "The absurd creator does not prize his work. He could repudiate it. . . . At the same time a rule of aesthetics can be seen in this. The true work of art is always on the human scale. It is essentially the one that says 'less.' " [50] Negating and magnifying at the same time, the absurd artist "must give the void its colors." [51] Like Caligula, who says to the poet Cherea: "I don't like literary men, and I can't bear lies," [52] Camus does not assign to art false powers of redemption. Like Jonas, who leaves a blank canvas with an ambiguous message—is it *solitaire* or *solidaire?*—Camus accepts the desperate faith of his mission. He knows that artists must share the trials of man in our time: "The hatred for art, of which our society provides such fine examples, is so effective today only because it is kept alive by the artists themselves. The doubt felt by the artists who preceded us concerned their own talent. The doubt felt by the artists of today concerns the necessity of their art, hence their very existence." [53] Camus can only give dignity to art by presenting it as an aspect of continuous rebellion. This is why he is cautious of Rimbaud whose silence "is also a preparation for the silence of authority, which hovers over minds resigned to everything save to the necessity of putting up a fight." [54] This is also why he is critical of Surrealism which "places itself at the mercy of impatience," existing "in a condition of wounded frenzy: at once inflexible and self-righteous," and "while simultaneously exalting human innocence," extols both murder and suicide.[55] Camus chooses another way. He dreams of transfiguring silence into plenitude:

> Ernst Dwinger in his *Siberian Diary* mentions a German lieutenant—for years a prisoner in a camp where cold and hunger were almost unbearable—who constructed himself a silent piano with wooden keys. In the most abject misery, perpetually surrounded by a ragged mob, he composed a strange music which was audible to him alone. And for us who have been thrown into hell, mysterious melodies and the torturing images of a vanished beauty will always bring us, in the midst of crime and folly, the echo of that harmonious insurrection which bears witness, throughout the centuries, to the greatness of humanity.[56]

The dream remains something of a dream. The novels of Camus tell a more ambiguous story. It is tempting to turn to his first fiction, *The Stranger*, and to Meursault, strange hero of quietness and the blinding sun, eternal outsider, whose sullen passion for truth qualifies him, in Camus's words, as "the only Christ we deserve." But Jean-Paul Sartre, reviewing this novel in 1942, already "places" it for us.[57] Sartre notes that a work about an absurd hero need not explain; it need only describe;

and thus appears "magnificently sterile." (Like *Nausea, The Stranger* predates the phenomenological novel.) He perceives the contradiction of the book: that it must use language and thought to render an absurd reality, that it must "translate from silence." Camus, therefore, resorts to analysis, discrete and discontinuous impressions, "islands of time," the technique of Nonsense that both Hemingway and Kafka adapt to their own uses. "The sentence is sharp, distinct, and self-contained. It is separated by a void from the following one. . . . The world is destroyed and reborn from sentence to sentence," Sartre says.[58] The nominalism of the style—it goes farther than Locke or Hume—denies any logic or relation in experience. The style reveals the action as if through a glass pane, mute and alien gestures, almost humorous. Sartre concludes: "This is what enables Camus to think that in writing *The Stranger* he remains silent. His sentence does not belong to the universe of discourse." [59]

But if Camus's first novel allows us to refer it with some ease to the tradition of silence, his last, *The Fall*, must trouble and complicate our sense of that tradition by its bitter intricacies. Its hero, Jean-Baptiste Clamence "at your service," will remind us of that other bilious, garrulous paradoxicalist, the speaker in Dostoyevsky's *Notes from the Underground.* Both are heroes of spite, ironists of a despair larger than night; and both represent, as Nathan Scott notes, the very antithesis of the Camusian rebellion or *mesure.*[60] Camus seems to turn completely about, making through Clamence the strongest case against himself, once again raising all fundamental questions—death, justice, human solidarity—as if he had never tried to answer them deliberately in his former books. I say "seems," for *The Fall* is a parable of ambiguities. These emerge, no doubt, from the author's inner development, as man and artist, toward the end of his life. But the ambiguities also become a moral and aesthetic principle of the novel, an element of its design. If the hero reminds us of Dostoyevsky, the method on a deeper level recalls Kafka.[61]

Jean-Baptiste Clamence, "judge-penitent," play actor," presents himself courteously to the reader as a monster. He is a monster of egotism, vanity, cowardice, mendacity, guilt, and despair—a monster, nonetheless, of culture and cunning. Let us admit it at once: he is the intractable, insufferable, irremediable Self. "I, I, I is the refrain of my whole life. . . ." [62] He thinks to dominate the universe from heights and holds court in a sailor's tavern, within the concentric canals of Amsterdam—circles of a bourgeois hell in the midst of Europe—adjoining a flat, dead sea, the Zuiderzee. And he tells his tale, no fuller than a novella in length, bottomless in selfhood, endless in spiritual lust.

It is a tale of success. A distinguished lawyer in Paris, Clamence has money, health, position; he enjoys the esteem of men; and women love him dearly. Eagerly, he confesses: "I lived with impunity. I was concerned in no judgment. . . . I freely held sway bathed in a light as of Eden." [63] He is himself the serpent in paradise. All his generosity reflects back upon him, and there is no one he can love. One night in November, a slim woman in black jumps to her death from the Pont Royal. The Seine is cold; Clamence walks on without looking back. The cry of the woman pursues him, he says, through the years, echoing sometimes as a laugh. Through knowledge of his guilt, Clamence achieves, he thinks, lucidity. He subverts his legal practice, spends himself in debauchery. But there is really no place to hide from the radical sin of existence. Clamence comes to Amsterdam. There he lives in a room bare and clean as a coffin—a stolen altarpiece stands in his cupboard, "The Just Judges"—and serves as "judge-penitent."

What demented profession is that? Clamence thinks we all live in our "little ease," a cell devised in the Middle Ages wherein the culprit can neither stand nor lie. The culprit, cramped to his dying day, comes to believe his guilt. "Everyman testifies to the crime of all others—that is my faith and my hope," Clamence says.[64] "Wherefore, since we are all judges, we are all guilty before one another," he repeats.[65] Thus Clamence becomes an advocate of universal slavery, perpetuating the judgment in every act of penitence. But his sophistry goes farther. "I am the end and the beginning; I announce the law. In short, I am a judge-penitent," he declares.[66] Clamence never refutes the clamoring self; I, he says, I. He consecrates himself to the task of revealing to his clients their guilt and ignominy, merely to extenuate his own, really to extend his powers. "And as for me," he concludes, "I pity without absolving, I understand without forgiving and, above all, I feel at last that I am being adored." [67] He permits himself everything; nothing has changed. A creature of spite and self-contradiction, dare we believe anything he says?

It is just possible to see Clamence as a fallen figure, expressing the Pauline doctrine of depravity, and his author as a man looking toward distant conversion. It is also possible to take the opposite view: "Far from seriously expressing a belief in universal human wickedness in *The Fall*, Camus is satirizing and attacking this belief. He sees it being used as a weapon for enslaving men," Philip Thody notes.[68] But the irony of Camus runs deep in this work, giving the reader few reassurances; and the autobigraphical references—unusual for him—conceal a special query or quest. I do not believe that he gives us an answer to his quest: how to live in a world without divine Grace or human Justice? Camus knows the true terror of his book: the difficulty, perhaps even the impossibility, of refuting Jean-Baptiste Clamence.

The book may be ambiguous anti-prophecy. Jean-Baptiste, as Carl Viggiani perceives, is a mock Baptist announcing no Messiah; Clamence offers no clemency.[69] The grey doves of Holland never descend from the air. This false lawyer of Paris with a false name plays false Pope in a concentration camp in Tripoli, acts as a false judge and prophet in Amsterdam, and slyly implies that his story may be a false tale. Yet his indictment of mankind—"A single sentence will suffice for modern man: he fornicated and read the papers"; "He has two faces: he can't love without self-love"; "Every man needs slaves as he needs fresh air"; "Spitefulness is the only possible ostentation"; ". . . woman is the reward, not of the warrior, but of the criminal," etc.—seems a compendium of truths struggling to deliver themselves from calumny.[70] And who among us can dismiss the vision of Clamence, that the future may only hold mass servitude?

As anti-prophecy, *The Fall* engages the tradition of silence in particular ways. It provides a total critique of Western man, casts a doubt on his destiny. More: it questions the sanity of consciousness. Clamence is the Self incapable of release except in manifestations of its own disease. Like Sade, he says: "In short, for me to live happily it was essential for the individual I chose not to live at all"; and at the end, he dreams of his decapitated head, held high above the crowd, dominating all.[71] The consciousness of Clamence is locked within its language, locked in "the negative landscape" of Holland, locked in its dubious being. "In order to cease being a doubtful case," he admits, "one has to cease being, that's all." [72]

But the negativity of the novel is still more complex. The hero addresses an interlocutor who never answers or speaks. Is he a character? Is he the reader? Or is he Clamence himself, a Parisian lawyer, an alter ego, cultured and cynical as the speaker? Certainly, the distance between speaker and listener shrinks as the novel comes to an end, the terms become more familiar, and the irony of style takes on the subtle hues of self-contempt. The opening pages of the narrative—divided in five days in parody of a neo-Classical tragedy—contain curious reflections on silence and language, the purpose of all speech. The entire life of the hero corroborates his statement: "Thus I progressed on the surface of life, in the realm of words as it were, never in reality." [73] Again, like our legendary Cretan, Clamence admits his lies. But he asks: "Don't lies eventually lead to the truth? . . . Don't they all have the same meaning?" [74] This compulsive deceiver, this hellion of modern history, this sciolist of degradation, ends by convincing the reader of one thing only: the horror of human speech!

It is no wonder that Camus, speaking in his own steadier voice, says earlier: "We live for something that goes farther than morality. If we could only name it, what silence!" [75]

## IV

With few exceptions—*Nausea, The Stranger*, and *The Fall*, perhaps—Existentialism tends to express radical thought in conventional literary form. Its ambitions are Promethean, didactic, or political; its judgments weigh on the language of art; and its personalities almost dominate the reader's awareness. By contrast, the literature that follows seems neutral, self-effasive. Pretending to eschew ideology, protest, and analysis, it cultivates a certain flatness—Roland Barthes calls it "*matisme complet*"—in order to avoid imposture. This literature goes by many names: anti-literature, objective novel, *écriture blanche, nouveau roman, chosisme, école du regard, école de minuit*. Germaine Brée may be right in asking for a new name to designate fictions of this type.[76] I simply choose the generic term of "Aliterature," intended by Claude Mauriac, one of its practitioners, to suggest the power of avoidance, of self-refusal, that this movement seeks.[77] The term will not greatly affect the authors themselves who include Nathalie Sarraute, Alain Robbe-Grillet, Michel Butor, Claude Simon, Robert Pinget, Marguerite Duras, and Jean Cayrol, among others. Obviously, so many authors are not likely to adhere strictly to a school. But their common rejection of tradition puts them in a certain relation to one another, and tempts them to explore certain possibilities of fiction.

Aliterature shares with the tradition of silence what Hegel calls the "patience and labor of the Negative," what Heidegger calls the "mystery of oblivion." [78] It moves toward a still center, and within that toward a point yet more still. Kafka anticipates its qualities; Beckett also, and in some measure Sartre and

Camus.[79] Even the interior monologue of Edouard J
*Les Lauriers sont coupés* (1887) may suggest a re
cedent. But Aliterature emerges mainly as the languag
consciousness at its reflexive task, the creative process giving phenomenological evidence of itself. It takes from Husserl the concept of "intentionality," and adapts it to a narrator who lacks an isolate self, an identity separate from what he may recall or perceive.[80] The nominalism of Aliterature, its concern with trivial *things*, sensations of the banal, is therefore epistemological. True knowledge resists abstraction; myth and metaphor yield to the feigned concreteness of fact; self and surface are one. But a sociological view is also thereby implied. As Lucien Goldmann shows, the active functions of capitalism in its last stages pass from men to things; the world of objects constitutes an autonomous order, a dominant structure, to which all human expression adheres.[81] The aesthetic of Aliterature responds to this bondage of postmodern man with a small measure of freedom. Out of the given data of experience—images, perceptions, memories—new patterns are created, new *fictions*. Fictions of this kind may exercise the only freedom of a mind threatened by nominalism on the one hand and solipsism on the other. Such fictions can refer only to the internal time of consciousness, not of history or the stars; they refer to the phenomenological present, where discontinuous reality escapes from each word even as it is read or uttered. Self-reflexive, Aliterature exploits its narcissism; it dramatizes on the page, Sturrock says, "the assembly of a novel;" and in doing so reveals "the opposition or tension that exists between language and silence." [82]

## V

Nathalie Sarraute begins writing in that mode before it receives a name. Born in 1902 in Russia, she divides her childhood between her divorced parents, living in Russia, France, or Switzerland. At the age of eight, she settles with her father in Paris. The ancestry of her stepmother is partly German; the young girl soon learns that language. Later, at the Sorbonne, she takes her *licence* in English, and afterward reads history at Oxford, 1921–1922. Later still she studies sociology at the University of Berlin, and law at the University of Paris. Decidedly, she knows her languages and shows no aversion to learning. She marries a fellow law student, practices at the Bar, gives birth to three daughters. But Mme. Sarraute begins to move toward another life. Her first book appears before the war, in 1939, an early version of *Tropismes. Portrait d'un inconnu* waits till 1948 for publication. The book, though it carries a famous preface by Sartre in which he speaks of the contemporary phenomenon, "lively and totally negative works that might be called anti-novels," scarcely makes a revolution.[83] Mme. Sarraute persists; she lectures and appears on radio interviews; she writes criticism for *Les Temps modernes.* Gallimard publishes *Marterau* (1953). As an editor of the Editions de Minuit, Robbe-Grillet brings out a new version of *Tropismes* (1957). *Le Planétarium* appears in 1959, *Les Fruits d'or,* which wins the Prix International de Littérature, in 1963. By that time, critics and plain readers know of the *nouveau roman,* though few may read the genre and fewer still appreciate what they read.

Two reasons, at least, account for the uncertain resistance to the new literature. Claiming for itself new assumptions, its fails to edify or entertain, indeed to render "reality," in any way that even a modernist reader expects. But claiming also for its theory more than its practice shows, the new novel leaves room for both adverse and sympathetic critics to question its achievement. The critical statement of Mme. Sarraute, *The Age of Suspicion,* reflects in some measure this uneasiness.

In her treatise, Mme. Sarraute pretends to reject psychological analysis, the idea of human depths: ". . . modern man, having become a soul-less body tossed about by hostile forces, was nothing, when all was said and done, but what he appeared to be on the surface. . . . The 'tumult like unto silence' that adherents of the 'psychological' had thought they saw in his soul was nothing, after all, but silence." [84] This is in keeping with the phenomenological doctrine of mind as a field of perceptual relations; it denies only one kind of psychology in favor of another. What Mme. Sarraute finds spurious is the convention of "character," that psychological prop on which the novel so often rests. The character of fiction, she says, has lost his ancestors, his well-filled house, his discernible manners; now he must lose his name. The novel must reckon with the suspicions of its author and reader: "For not only are they [author and reader] both wary of the character, but through him, they are wary of each other." [85] Moreover, both have become wary of fiction itself. The facts of outrage push reality to the very limits of our dreams: in a certain sense, Kafka can go no farther than Himmler. What more can the novelist say? Perhaps he can only present surfaces, render tenuous states of consciousness, as multiple, changeful, and ambiguous as the states of matter and energy, in modern physics. "Suddenly, the reader is on the inside, exactly where the author is. . . . He is immersed and held under the surface until the end, in a substance as anonymous as blood, a magma without name or contours." [86] In an age of mutual suspicions, Mme. Sarraute is grateful for the quality of doubt that compels the novelist to discover new modes of sensibility, and prevents him from repeating the efforts of his predecessors.

Yet her final view of literature is not altogether original: literature, she says, gives to its readers "a deeper, more complex, cleaner, truer knowledge of what they are, of their circumstances and their lives, than they can acquire alone." [87] Mme. Sarraute does not contemn words; on the contrary, she permits them to take the central place in fiction, in absence of character, plot, or setting. Her interest in "subterranean movements that are at once impatient and afraid" brings her closer to Marcel Proust, Henry James, or Virginia Woolf than her theory allows.[88] And her penchant for certain critical terms—"surface," "hard," "compact," "opacity"—seems at variance with her own fastidious style, refined secretly by poetic means. She sets fiction against itself, but ends with an art work as *made* in its way as a Mallarmé sonnet. Her true achievement may be a poetry of existence that evades the fond inauthenticities of older narratives. In an interview reported in *Tel quel* (Spring 1962), she says: "For me, the poetry in a work is what reveals the invisible. . . . Believing what I do about poetry, how should I not think my own works poetic? It would amount to believing that I do not reveal an atom of the invisible world." [89]

Poetry meets fragments of a new psychology, sentiments anterior to verbal expressions—*sarrauteries* they are sometimes called—in "tropisms." Dostoyevsky, here as elsewhere, is the acknowledged master of Nathalie Sarraute. She quotes a passage from one of his stories, "A Bad Anecdote": "We know that entire arguments pass sometimes through our heads instantaneously, in the form of sort of sensations which are not translated into human language and even less into literary language." [90] These "arguments," in the form of images or infra-discourse, suggest her own tropisms. Deriving from a Greek root, "to turn," tropisms "slip through us on the frontiers of consciousness" and present, in the collection of prose-poem-play-stories by that name, little, anonymous actions, sinister, quotidian, magical, "the secret source of our existence, in what may be called its nascent state." [91]

Mme. Sarraute retains tropisms as the "living substance" of her subsequent works, amplified into larger dramatic actions and more complex verbal interplays. *Portrait d'un inconnu,* for instance, is an account of domestic deceptions, desires, despairs, couched in the language, banal and insidiously poetic, of a hypersensitive observer. This voyeur looks inward to tell a phenomenological tale of an old miser and his sickly daughter. His tale could also be his own, for he too is the son of a father, the old friend, perhaps, of the miser. Speaking in the first person, his stream of modified consciousness becomes omniscient; his internal notations transform a mundane family affair into an archetype of existence, shuttling between self and other, appearance and reality, concreteness and generality. His cracked vision dwells on fragments of public experience, bits of quotidian life, moments of language and time, subverted continuously by his inwardness. For the speaker, nothing remains ordinary, without oddness, fear, lust, pain, or cruelty; nothing remains in its place. His phrases, even his images, bring all the small solaces of the daylight world; his dislocations of that world twist and snap underneath.

And what is the motive of that speaker? His erotic interest in the daughter, his fascination with her father, his guilt toward his own, his ambivalence toward all the others—they, they, they, their whispers, their rumors—blend into his compulsion to see "the other aspect," and to find discoveries in "old forgotten things." [92] "They" imagine a picture he paints, called "l'Hypersensible-nourrie-de-clichés." But his motive is deeper: he wants to rescue father and daughter from their fate as objects, heavy, opaque, created by the language of others; and deeper still: he wants to rescue himself from a worse fate as an object created by his *own* language. The Portrait of an Unknown may be that of a nameless old miser. But there is also a painting by that name, in a Dutch museum, to which the narrator returns. Its painter is as anonymous as the subject; so is the old miser; and so is the narrator. The painting itself, however, directs an "appeal" to the speaker, projects a "silent flame" that melts the chain binding him to "others." [93] "I ask only this, that they empty me, that they deliver me," he says to a medical "specialist." [94] We begin to see: Mme. Sarraute, a narrator, a painter, and several portraits of nameless people, within the context of a single artistic consciousness, search for mutual deliverance, separate authenticity.

The threat to authenticity comes from others, which is to say, from common parlance, words. But it also comes from death.

The old man speaks of "my awakenings of a condemned man." [95] The narrator goes farther; he senses that death weighs on language, smothers objects, and deceives men with the false euphoria of all clichés. In this novel, refrains, slogans, tropisms, serve to imply death continually, and to exorcise it in the silent prayer beneath the words. The novel ends:

> Everything will quiet down, little by little. The world will take a smooth and clear aspect, purified. . . .
>
> After death? . . . No, that too is nothing . . . Even that slightly strange air, as if petrified, that slightly inanimate look will disappear in turn. . . Everything will take care of itself. . . It will be nothing. . . Just one step more to take.[96]

*Portrait d'un inconnu* can be read as a novel about an egoistic miser near death, a family romance, a satire on bourgeois society, a philosophic reflection on language and consciousness. Its central impulse, however, comes from the need of the artist to define his form and function—indeed, his life—in the process of writing, without recourse to traditional definitions of art. The result, nonetheless, appears literary, richly allusive. Certain elements—ideas, objects, feelings of a viscous, opaque, and sweetish ("douceâtre") kind—remind us of *Nausea*. Mme. Sarraute also refers to other painters and writers, making complex use of their symbols, the mask of Prince Bolkonski, for instance, in *War and Peace*. Her incantations of foreign names and places, the meaningless patter of dialogue, recall the language of Nonsense, recall sometimes the secret rhythms of Ivy Compton-Burnett, sometimes of Ionesco: "Biarritz? huh? huh? Ustarritz? Do you know what it is? Do you know? Ustarritz? He rolls his *r*'s very strongly. Biarritz? La Bidassoa? huh? huh? Chocoa?" [97] Like Hemingway, she learns to omit, and makes her statement by exclusion; the silence on the other side of banality tells her tale. So does the sudden poetic image. In a crucial episode, the daughter steals a piece of a soap bar from her father; his mortal rage collapses in sleep; then: "The awakening is peaceful. The soap bar, on the board above the sink, shines gently in the morning sun, like rippling sand on a beach after a stormy night." [98] Still, Mme. Sarraute cannot maintain the tension between speech and silence throughout her novel; its final section has directness, rawness of emotion, almost the character of a climax or denouement. This shift betrays a larger issue, the inherent artistic problem of the *nouveau roman:* how to convert boredom and flatulence, the dumbness of things, into literary use? Diffused, diffracted, the attention of the reader may wander about; the purely imagistic resources of language cannot always hold it in place. In some real sense, the reader is released from conventions of the past as well as from significations of the future. Perhaps this is in the nature of Aliterature, which Mme. Sarraute brilliantly demonstrates in *The Golden Fruits,* a novel about a novel called *The Golden Fruits* which commits itself to oblivion in the act of reading.

## VI

The oblivion of Aliterature is largely symbolic; Alain Robbe-Grillet forcefully reminds us of it. His obsessive imagination, his technical mastery and versatility, his polemics, continue to energize literature. No doubt, he has something in common with Nathalie Sarraute as with other writers—Butor, Simon, Ollier—coerced for easy reference into a school. He has more to set him apart. Respectful, intransigent, he demurs on the tropisms of Mme. Sarraute: they imply depths and may unlock the trapdoors of psychology. Yet Robbe-Grillet himself is not the pure *chosiste* that some early critics, notably Roland Barthes, make him out to be; another aspect of him appears *humaniste.*[99] There are resonances in the man that a strictly visual interpretation of his work mutes.

Born on August 18, 1922, in Brest, the earliest memories of Alain Robbe-Grillet are the rocks, lichens, gulls, and seascapes of Brittany. His father is an engineer; both parents come from the Jura. The boy attends the Lycée de Brest and later the Lycée Saint-Louis in Paris. He studies engineering at the Institut National Agronomique and receives his *diplôme* in that subject. During the war, he works as a deported laborer in a tank factory near Nuremberg; his friendship with the writer, Claude Ollier, dates from these years. But Robbe-Grillet does not yet envisage a literary career. After the war, he returns to Paris, serving in the National Institute for Statistics from 1945 to 1948. As a colonial engineer, he travels to Morocco, French Guiana, Martinique, and Guadeloupe from 1949 to 1951. He decides finally that the imagination does not exhaust itself in number or geometry; he turns to language.

The earliest work of Robbe-Grillet appears later in the collection *Instantanés*, 1962. Editions de Minuit publishes his first novel, *Les Gommes* (1953). The association with the publisher, Jérôme Lindon, proves enduring; Robbe-Grillet becomes literary director of the Editions de Minuit in 1955 and remains in that influential position to date. *Le Voyeur*, which wins the Prix des Critiques, comes out the same year. Reviewers begin to take note of the new talent with unusual hostility: decidedly, this is not literature. Robbe-Grillet explains his work in a series of short articles, "Littérature aujourd'hui," in *L'Express* (1955-1956). Skilled in controversy, he enters the fray, participates in conferences and radio programs, carrying the literary debate, dormant since the early days of Existentialism, in open places. Beginning with Barthes, the younger critics of France, many of them novelists, support him: Maurice Blanchot, Claude Mauriac, Claude Ollier, Bernard Pingaud, Philippe Sollers. After *La Jalousie* (1957) and *Dans le labyrinthe* (1959), few reviewers call him a fad or hoax. The cause of Robbe-Grillet passes to America. Two famous film scripts, *L'Année dernière à Marienbad* (1961) and *L'Immortelle* (1963), bring him to the attention of the world; *nouveau roman* and *nouveau cinéma* at last meet in a luminous public dream. Robbe-Grillet collects his combative critical writings in *Pour un nouveau roman* (1963).

By 1965, when *La Maison de rendez-vous* appears, he seems already an avuncular figure on the literary scene, a benevolent influence on still younger authors writting for *Tel quel,* whom he also helps to publish at the Editions de Minuit.

Such an account may prove only that, in the language of academic citicism, men of letters pass from modishness to history without ever attaining to the danger, dignity, or doubt of experiment. Robbe-Grillet himself does not give us biographical clues to his sensibility. We sense his anti-romantic temper, his commitment to an Apollonian ideal of distance and precision, a visual measure of things. But we sense also his unavowed desire to participate—like the Surrealists—in the silent metamorphosis of things. Controlled, he pretends to surrender the initiative to objects. Detached, he still accedes to the frenzy of men. He pores over manuals of psycho-pathology, and notes: "I feel like the most normal of men, yet most of my main characters are mad." [100] In artists, madness cries for a style. We can believe Robbe-Grillet when he insists: "What is important for me in the novel is *structure,* or form." [101] The form creates a private, maniacal, sado-erotic world—*The Voyeur, Jealousy*—in which minute observation conceals derangement of the sense, in which sick solipsism reigns. Inevitably, we think back on the phenomenal disturbances of *Nausea.* But as Dennis Porter says, "Robbe-Grillet's technique is, in fact, the expression of a position that is significantly more radical than that of the Sartre of *La Nausée.* What it implies is that something close to a psychosis is a permanent condition of all our lives." [102] Mundane madness, close to number and surface and ratio, close to meticulous deduction, has its phenomenological correlatives too.

Critics will not agree on form or madness in Robbe-Grillet. He gives them a fictional labyrinth wherein they may lose themselves. He also gives them, in *For a New Novel,* tangled threads leading here and there. In this collection of reviews, essays, manifestoes, the author defends, attacks, defines, all the while pretending to explain himself, at most presuming to outline a new kind of art. Modestly, a little slyly, he writes: "The novelist's critical consciousness can be useful to him only on the level of choices, not on that of their justification. . . . And when we ask him why he has written his book, he has only one answer: 'To try to find out why I wanted to write it.' "[103] Even more than Nathalie Sarraute, he feels that the Balzacian novel has come to an end, that the bourgeois world which it assumed has become as obsolete as Newtonian physics. The ideal of Flaubert, "un livre sur rien," presages the beginning of the end. A "new realism," closer to what we crudely call Surrealism perhaps, extends from Flaubert to Kafka, thrusting into the future. Novelists only lie by repeating mindlessly the past. Hence the familiar plea: no more character, plot, or inwardness, no more archaic metaphysics.

Robbe-Grillet, however, does imply a certain view of the universe, an anti-metaphysic. He refuses the absurdity of the Existentialists and their nausea: "But the world is neither significant nor absurd." It *is*, quite simply. That, in any case, is the most remarkable thing about it. . . . Around us, defying the noisy pack of our animistic or protective adjectives, things *are there*. Their surfaces are distinct and smooth, *intact*, neither suspiciously brilliant nor transparent."[104] But neither are their surfaces always smooth or distinct. Robbe-Grillet creates his own metaphysic *within* language. We know why. He detests older forms of anthropomorphism. Things are things and men are men, he says to Sartre through Roquentin. He detests pathetic fallacies, analogical styles, metaphors, adjectives. He detests the arrogance of humanism and the self-pity of tragedy, the assumption that man is everywhere and that the cosmos conspires miraculously to thwart him. He detests viscous, dark, and soulful depths. Almost in the spirit of Zen, he gives back the world to itself: ". . . we no longer consider the world as our own, our private property, designed according to our needs and readily domesticated. . . ."[105] He avoids abysmal despair:

"Confronting such a void, he [man] henceforth feels no dizziness. His heart no longer needs an abyss in which to lodge. For if he rejects communion, he also rejects tragedy." [106] But he still lives in language, and writing about Joë Bousquet, the dreamer, says of himself as well: "Hence beyond language there is probably nothing else. The world 'creates itself in us' and 'ends in speech. . . .' " [107] This is why the nominalism of Robbe-Grillet accords with his idea of "total subjectivity," hallucinations with the "new realism," and formalism with inverted metaphysics. All meet in words.

Formalism, without pejorative connotations, subsumes his aesthetic. The artist puts nothing above his work: ". . . he soon comes to realize that he can create only *for nothing;* the least external directive paralyzes him. . . ." [108] Commitment is full awareness of language; only style, *écriture,* is responsible. He takes *Nausea* and *The Stranger,* twin masterpieces, to task for their self-betrayals, lapses into outrage. He admires the Surrealists for their achievement, in restoring, "by systematic investigation, to the 'apparent miracles which cast so lively a doubt on the common vision of reality' all their value and all their weight"; but chides them for their blurred interiority.[109] He prefers the language of Nonsense, Jarry, Carroll, Roussel, Beckett; and encourages new writers, like Robert Pinget, who "spoil" their own books.[110] He defines narrative time and space in the new novel: "A few paragraphs more and, when the description comes to an end, we realize that it has left nothing behind it: it has instituted a double movement of creation and destruction which, moreover, we also find in the book on all levels and in particular in its total structure—whence the *disappointment* inherent in many works today." [111] Disappointment, or autodestruction, then, becomes the latest mask of art for art's sake, an art, nonetheless, requiring of each reader wakeful participation, active assistance. To what end? So that human consciousness may play its role, Robbe-Grillet will simply say. "Today's life, today's science are dissolving many of the categorical antinomies established by the rationalism of past centuries. It is natural that the novel, which, like every art, claims to precede systems of thought and not to follow them, should already be in the process of melting down the terms of other pairs of contraries. . . ." [112] There is always something new under the sun.

*For a New Novel* simplifies certain literary and philosophical issues; in part, it serves as apolgetics, perhaps even as rationalization. Yet in doing so, it manages still to construct a vivid model of the new literature, and to construe its spirit with wit and charity. This spirit owes much to the power of the Negative; Robbe-Grillet proves it repeatedly in his own fictions. The spirit itself, however, is less one of absolute negation than of inquiry into the ordeals of meaning, of language, at a particular moment of Western society; or as Roland Barthes puts it, the "degree zero" of form is never attained, negativity turns always into its opposite." [113] We are not surprised that Robbe-Grillet withholds his final judgment on the "death of the novel"; the fits and starts of a genre, he thinks, may mark a renascence.

His own novels do not cease to appear with some regularity, varying in theme as in formal ingenuity.[114] Compact, controlled, sustained emotionally without cryptomania, *Jealousy* offers an example of the genre at its best. The novel creates unbroken tensions between description and suppression, reason and madness, objectivity and obsession. Its violence derives from a gap in language and structure, what the author calls "un creux." We see what an invisible character, the jealous husband, sees, a consciousness without pronoun, a "je-néant." [115] The husband sees; he feels only by implications of language, in the presence of a reader; if he acts to murder his wife or her lover, we only feel without seeing it. *Jealousy*—the word in French also means a window blind—renders reality sharply in certain slants of light, through slats, both hiding and revealing. Like a blind, like jealousy itself, the novel invents the landscape by selective omissions. The eye which *is* the screen is also tormented by what it inwardly sees. "We may compare in that sense the text of *La Jalousie* and the essays in the 'simulation' of psychological states, including paranoia, written by Breton and Éluard in *L'Immaculée conception* during the surrealist period," Morrissette notes.[116] Surrealism yields to the new realism of demented objectivity.

The techniques of disorder are precise. Robbe-Grillet provides a table of contents for the eight sections of the novel, four of which begin with the word "now," the first and last beginning with the phrase "Now the shadow of the column. . . ." He draws a plan of the house set in the midst of a banana plantation, with doors, windows, and furniture carefully sketched in. The eye leads, "the eye falls," "the eye reaches." We only begin to suspect whose eye it may be when we hear there are four chairs on the veranda: one for A, the wife; one for Franck, a neighboring planter; one empty, for Franck's wife, who never appears; and simply the fourth chair, at some distance, farthest from the chairs of A and Franck, placed sideways. Jealousy is the mystery of innuendo, the imagination creating its own chaos and fictions, the *artist at work*. The jealous husband: is he not an author, someone akin to Robbe-Grillet? "Memory succeeds, moreover, in reconstituting" each fact, both author and character seem to agree, as surmise engenders further surmise.[117] The smile of A, Franck's bent head, a letter, a song, all become parts of a verbal paroxysm, and parts of the squashed centipede on the wall. And what is that centipede, sometimes moderate in size and sometimes huge, that the husband sees Franck squash, over and over again, with all kinds of narrative, spatial, and chronological inconsistencies, against the dining-room wall? We are told that A goes to town with Franck to make vague purchases, and that their car, so they say, breaks down on the way home. We are also told of the rows of banana trees, their number and geometry, arranged in trapezoids. Are these answers not equally valid? Out there in the jungle, animals makes their noises:

Shrill and short, an animal's cry sounds quite close, seeming to come from the garden, just at the foot of the veranda. Then the same cry, after three seconds, indicates its presence on the other side of the house. And again there is silence, which is not silence but a succession of identical, shriller, more remote cries in the mass of the banana trees near the stream, perhaps on the opposite slope, reaching from one end of the valley to the other.[118]

And people look through blinds:

When the blinds are open to the maximum, the slats are almost horizontal and show their edges. Then the opposite side of the valley appears in successive, super-imposed strips, separated by slightly narrower strips. In the opening at eye level appears a clump of trees with motionless foliage at the edge of the plantation, where the yellowish brush begins.[119]

Both passages hint at the method of this story; both answer.

The time of the narrative is that of non-Euclidean perspectives in collision; or the time of icy compulsions, repetitions with small, pointless variations that acquire undue significance against the background of berserk monotony—back to Nick Adams in "Big Two-Hearted River." "The narrative," Robbe-Grillet says, "was on the contrary made in such a way that any attempt to reconstruct an external chronology would lead, sooner or later, to a series of contradictions, hence to an impasse." [120] Now, now, now, the author repeats, knowing that temporality gratifies our expectations and instantaneity destroys them; knowing also that consciousness makes its own time, which the novelist must equalize between narrator and reader so that both may share, as long as it may take to experience a work, the same consciousness. Thus the transitions from one paragraph to another seem entirely spatial, imagined to be simply there, without anecdotal sequence, in space. "Robbe-Grillet's objects never decay: they mystify or they disappear," Barthes says; "time is never a corruption or even a catastrophe, but merely a change of place, a hideout for data." [121] This makes for the ultimate ambiguity of *change*.

Even the sentence cannot absolve itself of ambiguity: "His sentence ends in 'take apart' or 'take a part' or 'break apart,' 'break a heart,' 'heart of darkness,' or something of the kind." [122] Descriptions of a novel that Franck and A are presumed to read lend themselves to blatant self-contradictions in parody of the novel we ourselves are reading.[123] Beckett's bitter comedy of exhaustive enumeration here becomes a travesty of surveillance, depiction, and ratiocination. Unmeaning details—a native crouching by the bridge, the hair of A, various shadows—coalesce only in some unspecified state of erotic anxiety; on a concrete level, they prevent the story from becoming whole. Hands and heads and feet move as if they obeyed no central intelligence, no organic unity. Everything remains separate, discrete, clear in itself only, and, like the white ship in A's calendar, totally fictive. Everything in the novel resists, as long as the reader can endure, conventional meaning.

A disturbed narrator, both absent and omniscient, leaves no alternatives to the reader but to become himself that narrator or else close the book. Once again we stand within the circle of subjectivity, on the thresholds of solipsism, believing only what we have no other means to disbelieve. We are still in the presence of man, of human consciousness oppressed by itself in the midst of things—a chestnut tree, the sun, centipedes. But Robbe-Grillet pushes language, farther than Sartre or Camus, toward a certain line of artistic "insignificance." We defeat him by forcing upon his structures familiar closure or extrinsic meanings—jealousy, paranoia, colonialism, etc.—and by denying him the patience he labors to earn from his readers. His art may not refute the possibility of art in the future. His perspective, nonetheless, is posthumanist, anticipating a change in the structure of consciousness, and helping to effectuate that change by means of new fictions. Thus, in the words of Bernard Dort, the novel pursues its vanishing form:

> First it had exercised itself against bourgeois values; then it took umbrage at value, however this was conceived; now it has turned

against reality, the world, and finally against literature, which is to say against itself. Hence the preeminence accorded in such novels to the *artist* who, more than mere hero, becomes the novel's theme. Hence today's culmination: Beckett or Genet. A literature of silence.[124]

Dismembered, Orpheus returns to the objects he once moved, the limbs of his own body, to retrieve his consciousness, a guilty song.

CHAPTER VI

# GENET:

## *The Rites of Death*

Je suis donc mort. Je suis un mort
qui voit son squelette dans un miroir.
Genet, *Miracle de la rose*

### I

LITERARY EXISTENTIALISM proposes a new definition of Man: it probes his consciousness; it becomes familiar with his terror. But man outdoes himself in breaking his definitions and outshining his terrors. Existentialism yields to a more subtle temper, antic in its dread, cold in its inversions. A non-Euclidean geometry envelops literature. After Sartre comes Genet.

Sartre publishes a brilliant and maddening work, *St. Genet: comédien et martyr*, in 1952. Once and for all, the work impresses the name of Genet on the history of letters. It also rushes to refute its own refutation—Genet's essentialism—and to extend the domain of Existentialism beyond itself. This dialectic hagiography carries an accusation. It also marks the transition from one era to another.

The deep ambivalences of Genet repel, and may thus elude, the virile mind. The intentions of Being and the intentions of Doing, as Sartre argues, clash in Genet's character, and subject him to a sophistical fate. Genet wants to be evil because he does Evil, and wants to do evil because he is Evil. The game derives its rules from mirrors. We shall see Genet's face in countless mirrors. For the moment, let us simply admit that he reflects the void. The glass looks back on Sade darkly, on the Surrealists who made the world transparent, on Hemingway's mortal knowledge, and on the outrageous metamorphoses of Kafka. The glass also projects a new image of human shame, transfigured in ritual death.

## II

The life of Jean Genet spreads underground; he invents his true biography within black prison walls. Gradually, the life emerges, from blighted soil, as a complete artifice, a synthetic flower of evil. The flower casts a shadow that we call art, visible to the sun.

Genet, who never forgives motherhood, is born of woman. She is a prostitute; sometimes, he imagines her a noblewoman of France. The father remains unknown. They find the infant in Paris, in 1910. At the age of seven, the National Foundling Society bestows him on peasants of the Morvan. The simple ways of the country, they think, will do him good. The region recalls the atrocities of Gilles de Rais. Little Genet, a solitary by birth, keeps to himself and excels in school. The child, weak, quiet, exemplary almost, begins to learn the mysteries of autism. But as Sartre says, a crack runs through the fullness of Genet's being. It will become an abyss. "Being nobody's son, he is nothing." [1] He owes his existence to the state, to foster-parents, to friends; he is obliged to everyone. One day, the boy, now ten, steals. We can call it revolt, experiment, desire. We can theorize that theft fills his space with an imagined essence of all things absent. The act must remain inexplicable.

The others, however, promptly call him a thief. Suddenly Genet has a name, an identity. He steals again; the name sounds continually in his ears. They have found a scapegoat; he has found a role. Very well, he will be a thief. The boy never repudiates completely the morality that condemns him. Like Sade, he merely inverts it. The judgment of others stands on him through eternity; the judgment reduces Genet to an object. Sartre rightly concludes: "Genet is a child who has been convinced that he is, in his very depths, *Another than Self*." [2]

The boy is incorrigible, and also cruel. He gouges the eye of another with a penknife. There are reform schools for his like, for instance the Colony of Mettray. The young criminal now confirms his fate. He must endure the degradations of the Colony; thus he makes them his own. His revolt takes on the hue of submission; his pride thrives on misery. He will come to love Mettray as in ancient times men adored the Terrible Mother, and will denounce her guilt by celebrating his own.

From Mettray, the boys gaze at the grim outlines of the Centrale de Fontevrault; thence, the most hardened criminals disappear into Devil's Island. The gaze awakens secret aspirations. For young Genet, Fontevrault shines with the splendor of myth, of destiny. Theft, treason, homosexuality, acts of a solitary imagination, give him access to all the prisons of Europe. The vagabond can only repeat his quest; the condemned man can only relive his death. Wherever Genet finds the desperate outcasts of the world, there he finds himself. He joins the Foreign Legion; he deserts it. The war does not transform him into a *maquisard*. He rejects the heroics of history from his cell. Finally, they sentence the recidivist to life imprisonment.

But the fate of Genet, almost perfect in its closure, betrays one flaw, a single freedom: his writing. This man chooses to sing. He begins to write poetry, at La Santé Prison, on a dare. Then he writes *Notre-Dame des fleurs* while serving a sentence at Fresnes in 1943. A turnkey destroys the manuscript and Genet writes it over again. The work appears in 1944. Genet becomes an author. *Miracle de la rose* follows in 1946, *Pompes funèbres* and *Querelle de Brest* in 1947, and *Journal du voleur* in 1949. Some of the early editions are clandestine, fragmentary, or anonymous: some contain drawings by Cocteau. Genet, child of silence, becomes an author, and opens his agony to language.

He opens it, that is, to his fellow men. In 1948, a group of eminent writers, including Claudel, Gide, Cocteau, and Sartre, submit a petition to the President of the French Republic. President Auriol grants Genet a pardon from the dread Relégue and invites him to dinner at the Palace of the Champs-Elysées.

The prisoner now enters literature. He moves, aloofly, among artists and writers; occasionally, he appears in the salons of the high bourgeoisie. Sartre produces his prodigious volume on Genet. Simone de Beauvoir chats about him in *The Forces of Circumstance.* The "virilization" of "Jeannot-du-Matin" takes place. The master of masks and mirrors creates a unique theatre: *Haute Surveillance* (earliest written, 1949), *Les Bonnes* (1947), *Le Balcon* (1956, 1960), *Les Noirs* (1958, 1960), and *Les Paravents* (1961). Only the theatre of Samuel Beckett rivals these plays in originality and in stillness. Genet ceases to write.

## III

The imagination of Jean Genet takes flight in solitude and returns to the void; his destiny barely escapes the circle. Foundling, pariah, deviant, he knows that isolation is the sign of his birth; he will make it the means of his salvation. Even his characters exclude him from communion. He lives an erotic liturgy of the self:

> The cafe disappeared, and Divine was metamorphosed into one of those monsters that are painted on walls—chimeras or griffins—for a customer, in spite of himself, murmured a magic word as he thought of her: "Homoseckshual." [3]

The outcast rebuffs not only society but also the very order of things. He works against nature, invents his sex and self, in order to sever all ties with creation. No memory of a mother or of woman's flesh connects him to the earth. Nothing truly sensual must mar his loves: "I am indicating to you, in this way, the form that my sensibility took. Nature made me uneasy. My love for Stilitano, the roar with which he burst upon my wretchedness . . . delivered me to the elements. But they are malicious." [4]

The outcast invents his guilt, and then inverts it. He must outdo others in the labor of his own humiliation. "The only way to avoid the horror of horror is to give in to it," Genet says.[5] The scapegoat, after all, assumes reciprocity in evil; the victim conspires with the victimizer. Genet imagines every prison to offer him the security of a palace, constructed for him alone. Necessity first, then pride and poetry, compel him to invert morality. Let evil be my good, and denial my everlasting yea! The agony of Judas, perhaps greater than the passion of Christ, makes the latter possible. Evil becomes an ascesis, a demanding and mysterious discipline. It haunts his sensibility: "Where Evil is concerned, we do not know whereof we speak. But I know that It, alone, can inspire my pen with the enthusiasm of language, a sign of the loyalty of my heart." [6]

Genet, of course, refuses to admit his Manichean fascination. For him, Evil explores the world and transforms consciousness. It is a form of *creation*. "If I cannot have the most brilliant destiny, I want the most wretched, not for the purpose of a sterile solitude, but in order to achieve something new with such rare matter," he boasts.[7] The boast is not entirely idle; Genet knows the form his courage takes. In his autobiography he writes:

> Refusing to accept a God of light in accordance with the explanations of the theologians, I felt God—or, rather than Him, a sickening impression of mystery—by means of a few evil and sordid details . . . of the Roman liturgy. "From this nausea," I said to myself, "has arisen the magnificent structure of the laws in which I am caught."
>
> My courage consisted of destroying all the usual reasons for living and discovering others.[8]

Evil defines the dignity of Genet, and may even whisper to him of a new world rising from the ashes of the old. But its quality is also compulsive. Like Sade, Genet yields to the erotics of Evil. Pilorge, Harcamone, Weidmann, Angel Sun, Snowball, all the glorious murderers of Genet, hold him in sexual thrall. The motive of magnificent crime is neither anger nor revolt but *lust:* "With fanatical care, 'jealous care,' I prepared for my adventure as one arranges a couch or a room for love; I was *hot* for crime." [9] And again: " 'They're treacherous' softened my heart. Still softens me at times. . . . Their sinuousness and the multiplicity of their moral lines form an interlacing which I call adventure. . . . This *pursuit* of traitors and treason was only one of the forms of eroticism. . . . Thus do I realize that I have sought only situations charged with erotic intentions. . . . I am aware that there exist adventures whose heroes and details are erotic. Those are the ones I have wanted to live." [10]

Proud, fearless spiritually, sometimes cruel, Genet still clings to a passive, a feminine, mystique of his destiny. Poetry plays its part in shaping the equivocal identity of this "woman." Thus Genet describes Divine: "For if, to define a state of mind that she felt, Divine dared use the feminine, she was unable to do so in defining an action which she performed. And all the 'woman' judgments she made were, in reality, poetic conclusions. Hence, only then was Divine true." [11] The "woman," the sinuous moralist, the masochist poet, thrill to masculine force.

Genet puts it simply: ". . . confronted with the universe I am lost, but the simple attribute of a potent virility reassures me." [12] Later, he will acquire some virility of his own. Still, the muscles of dominant toughs—*les marles, les durs*—the bulge in their crotch or swelling in their thighs, the lethal indifference of booted Storm Troopers, the sudden theophany of an assassin dragging his chains to the guillotine, flood his senses. Genet seeks force, in pimps, sailors, guards, or Naxi hoodlums, seeks it above all in Evil, because only thus can he replenish his emptiness. Philosophically, force—the camp at Belsen or at Auschwitz—annihilates the bourgeois order that has condemned and exiled him. This is part of Genet's dream. Erotically, force turns men into objects, and this is the other part of his dream.

In Genet's work, sexual force rules a world closer to fantasy than to nature, static, hierarchic, and repetitious. Every outlaw occupies his precise place, ranging from the lowly *lopes* and *cloches,* through the *vautours,* to the *durs* and *marles* and *casseurs,* to the sacred murderers at the top. The hierarchy rises in violence and virility, and culminates at a point where Being and Nothingness seem to meet in the great—yet curiously asexual!—killers. This irremediable world suddenly reveals itself to the lucid eye: ". . . instead of acting and knowing we are acting, we know we are acted upon . . . the order of this world—seen inside out—appears so perfect in its inevitability that this world has only to disappear." [13] But the world does not really vanish; it only repeats itself in order to perpetuate its laws. Divine walks down the street, sees another handsome young man. "It's the Again that has clutched me by the throat," she cries.[14] We begin to understand: force, status, destiny, and repetition, Genet's entire universe, depend upon a fantasy. "A man must dream a long time in order to act with grandeur, and dreaming is nursed in darkness," he writes.[15] All symbols —the Swastika as well—derive their power from unacknowledged desire. It is Dream that makes Force finally possible.

Thus, the imagination of Genet activates his life. Theft and treason become a form of art. Both transpose appearance and reality; both partake of beauty. Every seduction enacts a ritual of love. Myth, magic, and archetype transform Genet's existence into an artifice of eternity. He does not stand in historical time. His hierophanies emerge from the sacred and cyclical time of myth. He writes: "The Eternal passed by in the form of a pimp." [16] As Sartre recognizes, a stubborn Platonism, a mystic sense of participation in Eternal Qualities, determines Genet's ritual perceptions. The ritual leads inevitably to a drama of masks. Richard N. Coe puts it well: "Appearance *is* reality, argues Sartre. Appearance is more real than reality, counters Genet: the mask is more real that the face; to pretend to act, or to act a pretence, is more essential than sincerity. . . ." [17] Like the characters of his plays, Genet himself plays continually with masks, and refuses to distinguish between truth and falsehood. He plays with masks reflected in mirrors. This dazzling drama of mirrors befits Narcissus in the underworld.

Narcissus does not drown in his watery image, as the myth tells; he drowned earlier and seeks thereafter, hopelessly, to save himself by an image looking down at him from the bank. Only the dead know the speech of mirrors. This is why Genet speaks the language of silence. "In order to think with precision, Divine must never formulate her thoughts aloud, for herself," he writes.[18] Language turns back upon itself, as Narcissus beholds eternally his image, or Onan accepts his pleasure. Language becomes, in fact, Genet's prison mirror. Sartre sees the point:

> To Genet . . . there is no connection between the particular character that language has for him and the universal, socialized, content of words. It is not even possible for him to express unambiguously the most immediate manifestations of his consciousness.[19]

The language of Genet recalls the spirit of Mallarmé rather than of Rimbaud. His language is contractive, not explosive; discrete, not continuous; sometimes it approaches the vacant reference of number. Sartre sees the point again: "His aim is not to present externality as an expansive power, but to make of it a nothingness, a shadow, the pure perceptible appearance of secret unities." [20] The language of silence, of absence and exclusion, of flesh become number, is the language of the Negative. If consciousness proceeds by elimination, *néantisation* or negation, a process foreign to brute nature with its massive existence, then the language of the Negative must also be that of pure Consciousness. Thus Genet touches from afar the autism of Sade. The world loses its substance in the mist of the eye.

The imagination annihilates the world in quest of the Absolute Self and in this process figure and image, good and evil, male and female tend to naught. Everything vanishes into consciousness, and consciousness itself vanishes into the void. This is the sacred rite of death. Here is the first step:

Envisaging the external world, its indefiniteness, its confusion, which is even more perfect at night, I set it up as a divinity . . . . And little by little, through a kind of operation which I can not quite describe, without modifying the dimensions of my body . . . it was within me that I established this divinity—origin and disposition of myself.[21]

The second, the final, step is more stark:

This book, *The Thief's Journal,* pursuit of the Impossible Nothingness.[22]

Genet brings to his pursuit the excess of saints: "And this, in effect, is saintliness, which is to live according to Heaven, in spite of God." [23] He reinterprets the passion of Christ in the context of his own pain: "Let us ignore the theologians. 'Taking upon Himself the sins of the world' means exactly this: experiencing potentially and in their effects all sins; it means having subscribed to evil." [24] In the end, he conceives saintliness as union with the Absolute, the judge and judged atoned.

St. Genet seeks the Absolute, and its name is death or the void. Even murder, the apotheosis of all crime, symbolic assault on divinity, projects as its true end self-extinction. Ultimately, revolt must strike at the source of life itself. Here is Pilorge, the murderer: "He spatters the wall with a brilliance that can be expressed only by the confrontation of the two terms that cancel each other. Night emerges from his eyes and spreads over his face. . . ." [25] Here is Genet speaking in his own voice: "I long for the noise of cannon, for the trumpets of death, so that I may arrange an endlessly recreated bubble of silence." [26] Genet offers us this paradox: a dead man still longing for oblivion.

This paradox conceals the hidden freedom of Genet. His imagination takes flight in solitude and returns to the void, but the circle fails to close completely. For Genet becomes an author, an artist. He even develops an aesthetic. We should distinguish between his aesthetic theory and his literary practice. The former seems a pure invention, a poem imitating a poetics. The latter, an invention too, changes with time, with mood, and depends on the concrete mediations of language.

The aesthetic theory of Genet acquires body in a remarkable ballet, *'Adame miroir* (1946)—Adam, Madam, mirror, artist, etc.—that he writes for Roland Petit. But the theory lends itself better to discursive analysis in two aphoristic essays, or poems, "L'Atelier d'Alberto Giacometti" (1957) and "Le Funambuliste" (1958). Genet discerns in Giacommetti's sculpture the art of sacral solitude: "To the kingdom of the dead, the work of Giacometti conveys the knowledge of the solitude of every being and of every thing, a solitude, which is our most certain glory." [27] Art blossoms from the wound of loneliness, and offers itself to the innumerable nation of the dead. The parable of the funambulist starts at the same point. We see the equilibrist bring to life the steel wire upon which his life depends; each seems to give the other reassurance, for a brief moment, in space. When the funambulist dances in the air, he dances only for his image, he becomes Narcissus. "Death—the death of which I speak—is not the death that will follow your fall, but the one which precedes your appearance on the wire," Genet writes. "It is before mounting the wire that you die. The person who will dance will be dead—intent upon and capable of all beauties." [28] The dead man nevertheless courts high danger; he paints his face gaudily, maintains his cold iniquity. He despises the crowd and the money they bring to him. Each of his jumps transforms itself into a pack of wild and exact beasts. True art is a *politesse* of emptiness. Genet repeats himself in order to be perfectly understood:

In order to acquire the absolute silence he needs to materialize his work—which is drawn from a void that it will, at the same time, fill and make manifest—the poet can exhibit himself in whatever posture is most perilous to him. He clearly thrusts aside any curious observer, or friend or inducement that tries to orient his work toward the world. If he wishes, he can do this by emitting an odor so nauseating, so dark, that he himself is lost in it. He will be alone. His apparent malediction will enable him to be supremely audacious since he is undisturbed by any gaze. He now moves in an element akin to death: the desert.[29]

Thus can aesthetic theory embellish the attempts of a blighted life to justify, and indeed to renew, itself.

## IV

The literary practice of Genet extends his autobiography into art. Five prose works carry the tendencies of his existence till fiction and confession merge in rituals of self-redemption.

With *Our Lady of the Flowers,* Genet begins to create a consciousness that includes his will to unconsciousness. The book is a work of transubstantiation: an adolescent murderer turns into an image of the Virgin, an aging queen dies in sanctity, a solipsist outlaw becomes a writer. And always in the background, the child Culafroy, the legendary boy who becomes Genet, dreams his fate. Dedicated to Maurice Pilorge, who thumbed his nose at the executioner, and composed in honor of three other criminals who carry about them the holy sign of the monster—eyes blue and vacant, "sky-blue, like the razor's edge to which clings a star of transparent light"—the book begins with Divine's funeral among other Montmartre queens and ends with her death in a pool of vomited blood, alone in a garret.[30] Between the terms of death—death alone puts a nimbus on reality—Genet moves freely. Dream, dialogue, and reflection, incantation and invective, myth and obscenity, past, present, and future mingle; and such is the poetry that all movement freezes, all contradictions become translucent as crystal. The characters, Divine, Our Lady, Darling Daintyfoot, Seck Gorgui, even the *flics,* participate in ceremonies of fixity.

Genet admits the motives of his verbal fantasy. Writing can be autoerotic; about Darling he says: ". . . if I think about him, I can't stop praising him until my hand is smeared with liberated pleasure." [31] Writing also serves to furnish his cell; it enchants prison walls, fills and transforms the space he inhabits. Then, too, writing invokes the Archetype, touches from afar the Absolute. Thus Genet asks: ". . . will my books ever be anything but a pretext for showing a soldier dressed in sky blue, and a brotherly Negro and angel playing dice or knuckle bones in a dark or light prison?" [32] Above all, writing brings lucidity to a soul seeking to hurl itself through a subterranean sky.

Divine—"he" or "she" according to mood—maintains a vile discipline: humiliation, jealousy, theft, treason, the indirect murder of a child. Genet trades roles and pronouns with Divine, the Quite Soft, the Quite-Quite, votary of the Absolute, watching his own pain reflected in hers, watching her suffering refracted by others:

> If it were only up to me, I would make her the kind of fatal hero I like. Fatal, that is determining the fate of those who gaze at them, spellbound. I would make her with hips of stone, flat and polished cheeks, heavy eyelids, pagan knees so lovely that they reflected the desperate intelligence of the faces of mystics. . . . Let her consent to be the frozen statue.[33]

The frozen statue has a past, a childhood. Little Culafroy danced between the sheets hanging from his mother's washlines, and the mother, Ernestine, put on all her jewels before trying to kill him. The past still trickles into Divine's existence; like Genet himself, she cannot escape memory, pain, or desire, and thus put herself beyond humanity. Our Lady, by going farther, gives the book its title. He kills an old man, confesses his crime gratuitously, and remarks at the guillotine obscenely. "Thus, acts have esthetic and moral value only in so far as those who perform them are endowed with power." [34] The Negro murderer,

Clement Village—a model of Gorgui—possesses even greater powers. He maintains "his mind in a superhuman region, where he was a god, creating at one stroke a private universe where his acts escaped moral control." [35] Village evades banality, transcends himself. But Divine knows only nonentity. As a child, she desecrates a ciborium in church, and suddenly realizes that every true miracle derives from its absence. "God was hollow. Just a hole with any old thing around it," she says, to which Genet adds, speaking in his own voice: "Thus I lived in the midst of an infinity of holes in the form of men." [36]

The style of Genet escapes from the Fresnes Prison to seek the magical moment, the anagogical link, the alchemical secret of things. It permits the sudden metamorphosis of men and beasts, matter and essence. The style conrtacts into poetry, which opposes nature by its willfullness. Taut, elliptic, fragmentary, the sentences cunningly slip toward shocking self-revelation: "Girl-queens were carrying wreaths of glass beads, the very kind I make in my cell, to which they bring the odor of wet moss and the memory of the trail of slime left on the white stones of my village cemetery by snails and slugs." [37] Sometimes, a long sentence, almost purely Proustian in its structure, coils into a single sombre image:

> But the fact is that my longing for a splendid imaginary destiny has, as it were, condensed the tragic, purple elements of my actual life into a kind of extremely compact, solid, and scintillating reduction, and I sometimes have the complex face of Divine, who is herself, first and at times simultaneously, in her features and gestures, the imaginary and yet so real creatures of election with whom, in strict privacy, she has contentions, who torture and exalt her but who allow her no rest and give her, by subtle contractions of wrinkles and the quiverings of her fingers, that disquieting air of being multiple, for she remains silent, as shut as a tomb and, like a tomb, peopled by the unclean.[38]

For Genet has no interest in expansion or modulation. He must bring everything back to the cell where he sits; he must shut out. He must also repeat, using the future tense only to reveal the grip of Destiny. Genet's style, at its best, is like his existence: white bones and dark flowers, timeless.

We know that Divine performs a macabre dance, a pantomime of desolation, a thousand gestures, in order to elude God: "She had to stand her ground, whatever the cost. Had to hold her own against God, Who was summoning her in silence. Had to keep from answering. . . . She assumed poses as astounding as those of certain Japanese acrobats. . . . Finally, one day, when she wasn't expecting it, as she lay still in bed, God took her and made her a saint." [39] But for Genet himself, *Our Lady of the Flowers* records another struggle, the struggle between word and dream, time and eternity, society and self. With all the leisure at his disposal, he begins to suspect the insufficiency of autism:

> My mind continues to produce lovely chimeras, but so far none of them has taken on flesh. Never. Not once. If I now try to indulge in a daydream, my throat goes dry, despair burns my eyes, shame makes me bow my head, my reverie breaks up.

For the first time, Genet gives to fantasy the equivocal reality of *language!*

*Miracle of the Rose* transmutes, even more fully, fantasy into poetic symbol, the heart of Harcamone into a Mystic Rose, and Genet's own life into a threnody. The miracle takes place at Fontevrault. Appropriately, the Centrale stands on the ruins of a medieval abbey where Plantagenets lie buried. Appropriately, Genet arrives in a Black Maria on Christmas night, to become an "exact visionary," past all disillusionment. The sacred aura of death does not prevent him from seeing things as they are: "The inmates are merely sorry creatures with teeth rotted by scurvy; they are bent with illness and are always spitting and sputtering and coughing. . . . They are now only scurrilous caricatures of the handsome criminals I saw when I was twenty." [40] Genet now looks about him with male eyes; toughs and broad-shouldered pimps cease to awe him. Their glamor depended, in his youth, on a fairy's fancy.

Fontevrault contains Mettray within its circle as a man encloses his past. Genet returns to his childhood, however, only to celebrate the "Kingdom of Darkness or Transparency." Mettray, with its unique *argot*, emerges, like some sunken Atlantis, babbling in the language of forgotten gods. There is no time. Past lovers, Divers and Villeroy, fellow prisoners, Botchako the masher or the handsome fag Bulkaen, even the guards, arrange themselves around the still center: Harcamone. The implacable hierarchy of prisons becomes a mystic community, bathed in the radiance of a single cell on Death Row. There the King of Nemi awaits his sacrifice with empty eyes.

*Miracle of the Rose* transmutes reality and at the same time keeps its terror intact. The accounts of Mettray—the scene of the bishop's visit, for instance—render with unholy fidelity the crimes of society, the collective degeneracy of man. We shudder at this wasteland that only great spite or malevolence can redeem. We understand Genet when he cries: "I stole in order to be kind." [41] They offer him squalid servitude. He knows that his response must be either abjection or invention. He goes farther; he responds with both; and in doing so, defines the method of symbolism. His literary style, which assumes hell ubiquitous, grants the damned a secret grace: they convert hell while accepting hell as eternal. Thus Botchako's savage voice cracks into pure song.

In *Miracle*, the roses of Harcamone symbolize love, friendship, death, and silence. Quietly, Genet steals one of them, seeking to penetrate their fragrance, their bloom. But the same roses reek with the red blood of Rosewood, the murdered turnkey, and the blood of Harcamone himself, beaten in revenge by the guards. Genet knows this. Harcamone may swell into the sacred body of the world, and a thousand white doves may fly from his cell; still, his head must roll beneath the blade. The crime that the *Miracle of the Rose* confesses is that no miracle, save in Genet's consciousness, ever takes place. All the triangles of love—Genet, Bulkaen, Rocky; Genet, Harcamone, Bulkaen; Genet, Villeroy, Divers; Genet, Divers, Harcamone—have but a single apex in the author's mind.

Genet's work develops only within the iron cast of his needs. The next two novels evince greater objectivity, an expanding narrative structure. Fragments, flashbacks, daydreams, the little talismans of his desire coalesce into the semblance of design. The author, furthermore, begins to associate himself with aggressive heroes who complicate the patterns of homosexual love, the play of active and passive principles. For the first time, too, Genet presents in the Little Skivvy of *Funeral March* a touching image of bereaved womanhood and portrays a brothel Madame, in *Querelle de Brest,* with subtlety. But let us not deceive ourselves: these developments remain superficial, their artistic merit dubious. Genet's lyrical cry from the depths becomes muffled in conventions. The formal breakthrough will come late, in drama.

*Funeral March* fails. Jean Decarnin, a young Communist beloved by Jean Genet, dies in the street fighting of Paris, August 1944, shot by a French militiaman. Jean's double dies in a world cataclysm, so that Genet, "drunk with violence and despair," may compose an elegy. The elegy conceals a sexual theory of Hitlerian history; the theory conceals a familiar dream of sleep. Sensing this, Genet asks: "Why is my choice limited and why do I see myself depicting before long the third funeral in each of my three books?" [42]

The grief of the author, who rarely speaks of himself in the first person, takes a startling form. He invents Decarnin's killer, a young thug called Riton; he invents Riton's lover, a blond Panzer officer, Erik Seiler; and he invents Erik's former lover, the Berlin Headsman. The grief of the author, an extension of his autism, creates nevertheless a desperate paradox. The enemies of Decarnin—the chain of malevolence goes back, through the Headsman, to Hitler—emerge as aristocrats of evil whom

Genet admires. Riton executes young patriots with glee, and thinks of himself as the scourge of French motherhood. Erik, who makes Decarnin's mother his mistress, shoots a child to watch himself murder, and so consummates the lesson of the Headsman. And Paulo, Decarnin's traitorous brother, participates in the unspeakable orgies of Hitler. We thrash about in an airless room, among the cobwebs of pornography, even as we realize that Genet has chosen to entomb us, together with his love, in human evil. The effect misses tragedy.

For once, history overcomes Genet's symbols. Hitler refuses to melt into Jeanne d'Arc. Genet writes: "The Boches—the word clearly shows that grief invents a whole symbolism whereby one hopes to act mystically. . . ." [43] But facts and ashes deny his example. Moreover, the demoniac will of Erik or Riton, supremely single, loses its outline in universal chaos. In the same way, Genet's love for Decarnin, stated repeatedly and never shown, loses itself in a macabre and cannibalistic fantasy, in which the author ingests his friend, then spews him back again in words. "To eat a youngster shot on the barricades, to devour a young hero, is no easy thing. We all love the sun. My mouth is bloody. So are my fingers." [44]

The personal voice vanishes almost entirely from *Querelle de Brest*. "Finally, to be visible to you, to become a character in a novel, Querelle must be shown outside of ourselves," Genet dutifully records.[45] The characters disengage themselves from the harbor mist; the story moves in scenes crowded with action and rich slang; the setting looms like the glum, granitic ramparts of Brest, anchor of the ocean. *Querelle,* in short, pretends to be a traditional novel. But the novel, of course, exalts murder, and its hero stands in solitude like the Angel of the Apocalypse, feet skimming the black waters. The book's form, except its *argot,* except the snatches from Seblon's diary, explores no new underside of consciousness.

Genet simply decides to elaborate his argument in more ample and dramatic terms. He employs doubles; he constantly fuses the sexual identity of his characters even as he polarizes their will. He creates an erotic structure of moral analogues. Nono, the master of a bordello, and his police accomplice, Marco, project powerful complementary presences; Querelle and his twin brother Robert present a more profound ambiguity; Gil Turko buckles beneath his crime as Querelle never buckles, and Roger looks up to Gil as Gil looks up to Querelle; Dede informs on everyone and loves Mario; Lieutenant Seblon discloses his feminine nature to Querelle only; Mme. Lysiane, Nono's wife, tries to enclose both Querelle and Robert in her love, in terror of the abyss between their two images; and, finally, Querelle decides fiercely to submit, homosexually, first to Nono, then to Mario, thus creating a new nature, a new imperative issuing from himself alone. The mirrors of "La Feria," the port brothel, reflect the central drama of the novel: "The mirrors were empty, pure, surprisingly close to unreality, having no one and hardly an object to reflect." [46]

The discourse on murder confirms the conclusion of mirrors. After killing his first man, Querelle knows—he alone among Genet's killers escapes the guillotine—that he has died himself, or more precisely, that he has put himself, beyond death, in a region where divinity coexists dangerously with the void. Murder absorbs all other actions, establishing a magical connection between all objects within its realm. It absorbs everything because it demonstrates, irremediably, the force of negation, of absence, at the center of existence. Through Querelle, Genet tries to push this compulsive dialectic to a new synthesis. For Querelle appears both male and female, muscular and sensitive, murderer and traitor, self and other. He commands, as sailor and seer, a larger experience than prisoners or hoodlums usually understand. Genet wants him to stand before us as a symbol of the human condition, decked sharply in white and blue, with the knowledge of the empty seas in his eyes. Querelle, in fact, still hesitates to leave behind Genet's personal Legend in order to live freely, like Ahab or Svidrigailov, in the symbolic space of fiction. His equivocal being obeys the equivocations of his author toward language.

The autobiographical Legend of Genet ends with a journal. More than ever, the author becomes conscious of the curious intent of his words:

> This journal is not a mere literary diversion. The further I progress, reducing to order what my past life suggests . . . the more do I feel myself hardening in my will to utilize, for virtuous ends, my former hardships. I feel their power.
>
> To speak of my work as a writer would be a pleonasm. The boredom of my prison days made me take refuge in my past life, even though it was vagrant, austere or destitute. Later on, when I was free, I wrote again, in order to earn money. The idea of being a professional writer leaves me cold.
>
> When, in the Santé Prison, I began to write, it was never because I wanted to relive my emotions or to communicate them, but rather because I hoped, by expressing them in a form that they themselves imposed, to construct an order (a moral order) that was unknown (above all to me too).
>
> Unless there should occur an event of such gravity that my literary art, in the face of it, would be imbecilic and I should need a new language to master this new misfortune, this is my last book. I am waiting for heaven to fall across the corner of my face. . . . Through writing I have attained what I was seeking. What will guide me, as something learned, is not what I have lived, but the tone in which I tell of it. Not the anecdotes, but the work of art. Not my life, but the interpretation of it.[47]

Genet quibbles, sensing the duplicity of his Muse. He rarely feels comfortable with the motives of his art. Now he pretends that the Legend will obviate the need for words. *The Thief's Journal*, however, proves to be a partial exercise in silence.

The *Journal* retraces the vagrancy of a young man in the underworld of Europe. His guiding star is Uranus where animals, crushed by their weight, drag themselves heavily, and ferns creep on the ground: "I want to mingle with these humiliated creatures which are always on their bellies." [48] Pushed to the limit, passivity becomes a source of power, and the miraculous wound of childhood perpetuates itself like a stigmata. Even the ruthless and stupid pimps, Armand and Stilitano, who dominate Genet, dimly recognize this negative force, this rage for the Absolute, that sustains itself on endless fantasies of misfortune: "I wanted to be the young prostitute who accompanies her lover to Siberia or the one who survives him, not in order to avenge him, but to mourn him and magnify his memory." [49] Genet leaves Central Europe in order to accuse himself in his native tongue. He flees Nazi Germany because, among a nation of outlaws, crime offers no secret rewards. Only in France can he savor the sweet fruits of transgression; only there can he experience a shudder each time he sees a *flic*.

Genet wages his struggles in the imagination, and wins his victories over himself. But the victories are nevertheless real. When the Spanish police seize on his person a dirty tube of vaseline, they mean to shame him with a sordid sign of pederasty. But the tube transforms itself, first into an image of "the most cherished of mothers," then into an object of "perpetual adoration." Genet concludes: "Lying on the table, it was a banner telling the invisible legions of my triumph over the police." [50] The invisible legions come into being—they are Genet's readers—and the proof of the triumph is the *Journal* itself. The paradoxes suggested by this incident express the tensions of Genet's career as man and writer. The ascesis of evil, full of humiliation and beatitude, ends not in sainthood but in art. The artist, however, persists—and rightly so!—in his pursuit not of art but of authenticity. And the solitary rebel behind both saint and artist confesses at last: "The prison . . . toward which I go offers me more joys than your honors and festivals. Nevertheless, it is these which I shall seek. I aspire to your recognition, your consecration." [51]

*The Thief's Journal* tells of Genet's quest between 1932 and 1940, the birth of his lucidity, the beginning of his "success." It also tells of his love for Lucien Sénémaud, hero of the poem

"Le Pêcheur du Suquet," many years after. "I lacked a taste for earthly happiness," Genet writes. "Now, when I am rich but weary, I ask Lucien to take my place." [52] The *Journal* offers us a happy ending without happiness. The innate contradictions of Genet can never resolve themselves into joy; they can only sink to a new level of stillness. Happiness is for another.

V

Genet now chooses drama over autobiography. Curiously, he turns from the most personal of literary forms to the most public. The choice is profound. In drama, he satisfies his need for ritual while preserving the blankness behind every act. He practices the consummate art of illusion under pretense of objectivity. He counterfeits reality before the eyes of an audience without recourse to a first-person narrative. In short, Genet creates a dramatic form that forces universal truth on a solipsist's fantasy.

The plays appear as "reflections of a reflection," metaphors of a metaphor. "One can only dream of an art that would be a profound web of active symbols capable of speaking to the audience a language in which nothing is said but everything is portended," he notes.[53] He makes characters transparent, turning them into signs as remote as possible from what they are meant to signify. "My characters are all masks," he states. "How do you expect me to tell you whether they are true or false?" [54] He imitates the pomp and mystery of the Mass, and the barbaric cruelty of the Mau Mau, till ceremony and terror meet, revealed in the ineluctable Moment. By his own admission, Genet detests the Western theatre, detests its social, realistic, and psychological tradition. He wants a sacred drama, founded on the heroic rigors of despair. Against rhetoric, he pits a poetry from the abyss. He even subverts his own poetry, as Roger Blin remarks, destroys the audience's credibility, awakening them to his duplicity in order to sink the poetry deeper into their souls. At last, all appearances melt, all shadows, images, masks, leaving us with a pure Lie, an intuition, as Sartre would say, of Evil or Nothingness.

*Deathwatch* adheres closely to the old obsessions of its author. The prison setting, the invisible demiurge, Snowball, the eternal hierarchy of death, personified by Green Eyes, Lefranc, and Maurice, the insidious presence of treason and flowers, arrest the single action, Lefranc's murder of Maurice, into a *tableau vivant*. The point that Green Eyes makes, in the hard light of the stage, among violent colors, with a dead timber, is familiar: one is elected to misfortune as to grace. "It chose me. It fell on my shoulders and clung to me. I tried everything to shake it off. I struggled, I boxed, I danced, I even sang. . . ." [55] Suddenly we learn from this morality play one thing new: Genet, the dungeon dreamer, can write dialogue with the force of a chained demon.

But great theatre requires more than good dialogue; it demands a new shape of reality. In *The Maids,* Genet coolly shatters reality into countless flickering shards. Two boys play the roles of the two girls who play the two maids, Claire and Solange. The two maids alternately play the roles of Madame and of each other. Thus, only impersonation—lying—reveals the truth of any condition—being a servant, being a mistress. Images beget further images without benefit of an original. When, at the outset, Claire plays Madame, and Solange plays Claire, in a ceremony of murder never completed, they spark a reaction of true and false feelings, without an ending.

Playing Madame, Claire satisfies both her hatred and love for her mistress; playing Claire, Solange satisfies the same feelings about both Madame and Claire, her sister. Their *double entendres* quadruple in meaning. Their kicks, their blows, their gobs of spittle miss no target within themselves or without. Claire and Solange also dream as they playact, and so give their performance another dimension. Claire, playing Madame, pretends that she has betrayed Monsieur. She dreams:

Claire, Monsieur will be led from prison to prison, perhaps even to Devil's Island, where I his mistress, mad with grief, shall follow him. I shall be in the convoy. I shall share his glory.

Suddenly all the levels collapse into one when Solange, still playing Claire, says to Claire, still playing Madame:

I'll follow you everywhere. I love you.[56]

But Madame herself soon enters on the scene, and speaks about Monsieur in a manner that parodies the dream of a maid playing at Madame:

I'd follow him from place to place, from prison to prison, on foot if need be, as far as the penal colony.[57]

Once again, the levels of reality pull apart, showing the mad perspectives of a play that calls the reality of the audience into question by denying its own.

In *The Maids,* Genet contructs a model of the self-reflexive imagination. To do so, however, he must employ models of a provisional identity. The women, who have a "negative" being, appear on the stage; the two men, Monsieur and the Milkman, who have "positive" being, remain invisible. The genius of the play transforms negative beings into a frightening presence. This becomes possible because the women exchange active and passive roles within a field of erotic force; they play the Eternal Couple, male and female, criminal and saint.

Claire seems the sweet, the feminine partner, the dreamer, She imagines the devil carrying her away in fragrant arms. She submits to the slaps of the older Solange, and accepts the fall from grace. But she also refuses "the dreary exile" of her sister's imagination—the ceremony never means the same thing for the two maids. And in the end, it is Claire who dares to bring God and the Holy Virgin into the ceremony; it is Claire who completes the death ritual by drinking the poisoned tea. Madame dies symbolically. Claire commits suicide. Solange will go to prison as the murderess of Claire. In the final soliloquy, Solange cries:

Madame is dead. Her two maids are alive: they've just risen up, free, from Madame's icy form. All the maids were present at her side—not they themselves, but rather the hellish agony of their names. And all that remains of them to float about Madame's airy corpse is the delicate perfume of the holy maidens which they were in secret. We are beautiful, joyous, drunk, and free! [58]

The freedom of the maids, Genet does not conceal from us, derives from their inability to love Madame, or each other, or themselves. Without any love for this world, they are free. And freedom declares itself in a dream of murder. Shrewdly, Sartre observes: "Genet prefers imaginary murder to real murder because in the former the will to evil, though remaining entire, pushes the love of nothingness to a point where it reduces itself to impotence." [59] Beyond hatred, master and slave embrace, serene at last in the nullity of a mirrored existence. This is the politics of absence.

With *The Balcony*, Genet displays his "politics" in a more lavish theatre. Words mean less than costume, setting, or gesture; plot gives way to nine ritual scenes, mixing politics and desire, history and hierophany. We are perhaps closer to the genre of Brecht than of Pirandello, though neither author contributes to Genet's intent, which is to terminate the world with a negative apocalypse. Ineluctably, we move from the brothel, house of dreams, to a colossal mausoleum, where all dreams sleep. This is the central transformation of the play.

The action takes place in "Le Grand Balcon," a brothel. Genet, who likes to exploit the erotic force of symbols, gathers all the elements of his vision into one place. Thus Madame Irma describes her establishment: "Like a Chinese lantern left over from a carnival, and waiting for the next one, or, if you prefer, like an imperceptible light in the imperceptible window of an imperceptible castle they can enlarge instantly whenever they feel like going there to relax." [60] The brothel also contains civilization. There the Bishop, the Judge, the General, and later, the Chief of Police, disclose their true, emblematic quality, their mode of non-being, untarnished by any historical function. Their mysterious brilliance appears to the audience as they "precede themselves" into a universal consciousness. The brothel contains personal satisfactions. It repels vulgarity, remaining sterile and chaste. It sanctions the longing for transgression, and unites opposites, saints and sinners, victims and executioners, into loving couples. It consecrates itself to cruelty, "a skilful, vigorous heading towards Absence." [61] It counterfeits life, and thus touches the principle of disintegration in all things. As the Bishop says: "The Devil makes believe. That's how one recognizes him. He's the great Actor." [62] The Devil inhabits the brothel—Genet's largest symbol—turning life into an artifice, turning every action into a "scenario," repeated meticulously unto death.

Outside this citadel lies the real, the obscene world. There, revolutionaries struggle for freedom against the Chief of Police; there Chantal, the prostitute, fights and sings. But the revolution must fail because its actions melt into dreams, and all its actors surrender to the brothel Nomenclature, peepholes and mirrors creating eternal Names. The Chief of Police is anxious to know if anyone asks to impersonate him, and Irma sadly replies: "The time's not ripe. My dear, your function isn't noble enough to offer dreamers an image that would enshrine them." The Chief is stubborn: "Nobody yet! But I'll make my image detach itself from me. I'll make it penetrate your studios, force its way in, reflect and multiply itself. Irma, my function weighs me down. Here, it will appear to me in the blazing light of pleasure and death." [63] Genet's spite demands this irony: the rebel leader, Roger, will ask to impersonate the Chief. Roger stands in the real; he struggles against Chantal becoming a revolutionary myth; he opposes play and the eternal. His home is the freedom of time and decaying flesh. But Genet prevails. Chantal dies in myth. Irma becomes the new Queen. The Chief of Police repudiates Irma, his only love, in order to join the Great Figures. And Roger, self-castrated, enters the brothel in the guise of his former enemy. The only winner is Death. As Irma, Queen of the Night, exclaims: "Glory means descending into the grave with tons of victuals!" Her last words plunge the audience into fright: "You must now go home, where everything—you can be quite sure—will be even falser than here." [64] When the curtain drops, we hear a burst of machine-gun fire in the distance.

The politics of Genet close around us as tightly as his cosmogony. The Great Figures rise eternally to satisfy mankind's dream of order. The audience itself dwells in one of the brothel's "studios." Death writes our history in capitals; and reality spreads its limp forms, like the Queen's invisible lace handkerchief, or a pair of pants devoid of legs and thighs. The presiding spirit of *The Balcony* is the Envoy who speaks with the cool authority of the Void: "I know only too well how hard it is to assume the appearance of our abyss." [65] Yet, despite all its exotic intricacies, its poetry of semblances, and its scattered references to European history—the medieval Festival of the Boy Bishop, Joan of Arc and the Hundred Years' War, the French Revolution, Napoleon, Franco—the play thwarts our sense of dramatic justice. A pure shaft of hatred transfixes the audience. Later, the audience will suspect that its destiny was willed arbitrarily, and its experience denied.

This is not true of *The Blacks*. The play's hatred finds a correlative in the terror of our streets. Genet now reverses himself: the rebels, who are blacker than tar, win. They triumph precisely because they are children of darkness, spawn of evil. It is not justice that vindicates them but lucid cruelty. Genet does not really concern himself with the "plight" of the Negro. He asks, instead, ". . . what exactly is a black? First of all, what's his color?" [66] The question seems rather specious since Genet already knows his answer. Black is the opposite of White; Black is excluded being.

The play transforms this familiar intuition into a genuine dramatic experience. It claims the freedom of total theatre, including dance, poetry, mime, jazz, circus, church ritual, black minstrelsy. It assaults the white audience, forcing upon it the sense of witness and victim. From the start, it establishes the pitch of ceremony and madness, magic and fatality. From the start, the catafalque of the White Woman stands at the center to remind us that the drama has already been concluded, the murder has already taken place. The actors perform just "one more time" to confirm their triumph, to exorcise the demon of whiteness, to round out the grief of the audience and make clear, for all time, that communication in *this* theatre is impossible. As it turns out, the play itself is a sinister subterfuge; the whites have been hoodwinked once more; a "real" execution, of a black traitor, takes place off stage. The leader of the blacks in "real life" turns out to be the abject white Valet on stage.

Genet, we see, puts before us the lie within the lie, within yet another lie, etc. The actors are not professional actors; they are Negro citizens—a medical student, a prostitute, a bootshine —who pretend to act blacks. Some don white masks and stand on a platform, impersonating both the white audience and its representative authorities. All re-enact the murder of an imaginary White Woman, for whom a "fresh corpse" must be provided every evening, played by a renegade black man, Diouf. All divert the attention of the real audience in the theatre from an execution which does not really take place. The voice of the group, Archibald, states with pompous insolence that their "clown show" communicates nothing.

Despite the vindictive confusion of images, *The Blacks* makes two dialectic assertions quite clear: black love must be invented and universal death must prevail. The scenes between Village, the ritual killer, and Virtue possess a passionate tenderness unique in Genet's work. Virtue suspects the sexual motive in Village's murder of the White Woman, and Village struggles against the white idea of love perpetuated in the world. Archibald says: "You think you love her. You're a Negro and a performer. Neither of whom will know love." [67] And when

Village declares, too simply, "I love you," Virtue responds: "That's an easy thing to say. An easy sentiment to feign, especially if it's limited to desire. You speak of love, but do you think we're alone?" pointing to the white Court.[68] The point is crucial. For the first time, Genet seriously explores the possibilities of love, heterosexual love! And he concludes: the world as we know it—in terms of the play, it is a *white* world—must be annihilated before man can recreate love!

To annihilate the world means, in Genet's cosmogony, to summon blackness and bear witness to death. Village intones: "Oh darkness, stately mother of my race, shadow, sheath that swathes me from top to toe, long sleep in which the frailest of your children would love to be shrouded, I know not whether you are beautiful, but you are Africa, oh monumental night, and I hate you." [69] The whites embody livid emptiness, the blacks transcendent darkness. Against the eternal, sculpted ruins of the white Queen, Felicity proclaims the tenebrous life of Dahomey: ". . . and that lovely tree, that crime of mine, is all Africa! Birds have nested in it, and night dwells in its branches." [70] Good will be reversed into evil, white into black, and absence into rich death. When the Queen abdicates, it is the human race—not merely Colonialism, not Western man only—that gives us its breath. The blacks rise in poetry to petrify our corrupt blood. Cunningly, Genet diverts this horrendous fate into a dramatic feint as Archibald, addressing his fellow actors, concludes:

> The time has not yet come for presenting dramas about noble matters. But perhaps they suspect what lies behind this architecture of emptiness and words. We are what they want us to be. We shall therefore be it to the very end, absurdly. Put your masks on again before leaving. Have them escorted to Hell.[71]

But the actors themselves stand under the same sentence of death as the white audience. Archibald declares: "Every actor knows that at a given time the curtain will fall. And that he almost always embodies a dead man or woman. . . ." [72] Thus the imagination finally reflects upon itself the nullity of the human condition.

We look only from one angle at the plays of Genet; a narrow beam flickers here and there on their surface, leaving the rest to the night. Our words, like pebbles, barely sound their still depths. But the plays rely, less and less, on verbal language; increasingly, they approach the purity of the absurd. Our criticism, which seemed partial, now becomes officious. This is particularly true of *The Screens.*

Genet writes his longest drama, with ninety-eight characters, in seventeen major scenes. The action, evoking the Algerian war of independence, melts into parody of Surrealism. The world breaks into split levels on a stage, into countless painted, shifting screens. Genet writes his longest drama, performed precisely, by masked figures lost among artificial objects, in a theatre open to the sky, and his purpose is this: to affirm the Negative Hero against Genet's own temptation through the years. We know the temptation by many names, Virility, Happiness, Freedom; they are all names of the Positive that Genet abhors. Twenty years after *Our Lady of the Flowers,* an artist of international repute, summoning the forms of his mature genius, still keeps faith with the sombre oath of his childhood.

It is Saïd, of course, who contains the demonic pathos of his author. Outcast, man of many sorrows—he marries Leila, the ugliest woman in the province—Saïd evolves into thief, jailbird, and traitor to his own people. He refuses every role and circumstance; he seeks only the ultimate stringency of his solitude. The Cadi says to him: "You steal often. I spend my time sending you to jail. You sense something. . . . You know that by going to jail you escape the obligations that are now going. . . ." [73] Saïd transforms the world, *his* world, with treason and poetry, sees steamboats crossing the rye fields, and sailors in the alfalfa. Unlike the Colonists and the Rebels, he discards reason and purpose; like his Mother, he knows the flies of death each by its name. Saïd seeks the irrevocable. He joins the dead who are the last pariahs on earth; or rather, does not quite join them, not even the dead, but merely exists as a song between two states. The others, one by one, Arabs and Europeans alike, travel obscenely to the region of shadows, drain themselves and empty their bowels, and await for Saïd to appear. Ommu says to him: "We're embalming your sordidness, your shittiness;" and he answers: "Does that mean I'm going to keep rotting until the end of the world in order to rot the world, is that what it means?" [74]

The principle of dissolution must triumph until the universe reconstitutes itself. The Arab Rebels have the edge on the Colonists; hatred is on their side. But the Rebels enjoy a community of purpose. The true outcasts—they are, besides Saïd, mostly women: Leila, the Mother, Kadidja, Ommu—wither into lonely truth. In *The Screens,* Genet offers a radical critique not of colonialism or capitalism, but of existence. He defends consciousness against all limits. He defends it with the negativity of Saïd and with the poetic expression of that negativity. As Marc Pierret puts it, "For Genet poetry is an act of stripping away. He creates death. When the human landscape surrounding Saïd is touched by the falseness of his acts, it crumbles and collapses." [75] Evil, poetry, and death redeem the squalid life of man. This is why Ommu can say to the Arab Combatant:

> Soldier! . . . Soldier of ours, young prickhead, there are truths that must never be applied, those that must be made to live through the song they've become. Go die facing the enemy. Your death is no truer than my raving. You and your pals are proof that we need a Saïd. . . .[76]

Before the truth can live through a song, however, language itself must shrivel. The colonist, Mr. Blankensee, grows roses; he boasts: "We're the lords of language. To tamper with roses is to tamper with language." [77] The rose gardens of Blankensee burn; his flowers fall on arid ground. The Logos disappears among thorns and nettles. *The Screens* stands both as proof and refutation of parched silence while the moon serenely betrays its white mission.

## VI

A scholar asks: "Can we afford not to dismiss Genet?" This is like dismissing evil, and worse, dismissing a chance to redeem it. We know where Genet fails. His great hate condemns him to repetition; thus he avoids liberty. He longs to transcend his fate but remains a slave to transgression. He cannot finally create a new ethic because the hold of the old on him is irrevocable. He denies woman her flesh, and her fecund womb, seeking a new zone in Nature where nothing is of use. Sperm turns to excrement; Being spends itself. His glacial consciousness—Georges Bataille saw there the coward's spite—gives to the world nothing.[78] Yet somewhere within the black tundras of his vision, Genet sees a light. He follows the inhuman to the edge, and sees new shapes of love among the shadows. Secretly, he hopes that Evil may cleanse the universe and recreate God in another image. This is the theme of his miraculous song.

Few Modern songs ring clear or simply true. Genet says: ". . . poetry is the break (or rather the meeting at the breaking point) between the visible and the invisible." [79] It is also the language of beauty recognizing its own falseness, the speech of treason, the verbal action of the negative, the voice of the anarchic and inviolate self. Genet writes to create anti-forms: autobiography degenerates into onanism, and drama disintegrates into the infinite emptiness of appearances. The sentence defines itself by rejections, moving against itself: "Within me, the destruction of the [penal] colony corresponds to a kind of punishment of punishment: I am castrated, I am shorn of my infamy." [80] The argot of crime, we think, implies a mystic, a secret, a terrorist society. It conveys even more: Genet's resistance to all communication, his refusal. He knows what words can do: "One puts an honest hand on one's heart and talks. Speech kills, poisons, mutilates, distorts, dirties." [81] When Genet speaks at all, it is as if he speaks to watch himself speak. He makes few direct statements; instead, he quotes from himself, standing back to see what would happen if indeed he had said what he merely pretended to say. He cannot bear to commit language to any discrete—i.e. profane—reality. Everything changes, metamorphoses into another, within the same circle of autism. Yet the prose itself, though elliptic, seems so very clear! Sartre is not deceived: "Genet's prose is the *medium* of his poetry. It is Being, it is Good: it is therefore created only for Evil. . . . One never sees . . . the poetry; it appears only at the *expense* of a prose sentence: it is a leprosy of prose." [82]

Genet sings to destroy reason, history, and society. So do the Surrealists. Genet, however, rejects love, humor, and surprise, rejects any collective or unconscious truth. He sings to undermine all the assumptions of Being. He probes anti-consciousness. "Long before Robbe-Grillet and Robert Pinget," Coe writes, "before Butor and even before Nathalie Sarraute, Genet was puzzling away at the fundamental question of the *nouveau roman*, in so far as this form of the novel is directly related to phenomenology." [83] Coe adds: "There is nothing superficial about Genet's *chosisme*; it is inherent in his vision of the world and of society. For if the meaning of an object is the voice which is given it in terms of its social function, and if Genet rejects lock, stock and barrel the key concept of the society which gave it that voice, then the meaning of every object becomes utterly arbitrary, dictated only by itself and the bare fact of its existence." [84] We can go farther: Genet sings finally to dissolve language into a silence deeper than Aliterature.

He does not, of course, succeed. Singing of the rites of death, he reclaims part of his existence from nothingness, and reclaims part of ours from our small versions of oblivion. He shows us, in language, the very end of solitude, of revolt, of endurance. Drawing palm trees on a screen, we can still sit in the shade; we summon the breeze. Meanwhile, Orpheus and Narcissus embrace in a black pool.

CHAPTER VII

# *BECKETT:*

## *Imagination Ending*

No trace anywhere of life, you say, pah,
no difficulty there, imagination not dead
yet, yes, dead, good, imagination dead imagine.
Samuel Beckett, "Imagination Dead Imagine"

### I

SAMUEL BECKETT pursues the vanishing form till it nearly vanishes. He is an apocalyptic by reduction, possessed by the idea that the universe must evacuate itself; a visionary comedian who knows that human consciousness cracks into a bitter joke; and a supreme example of the postmodern artist, turning the malice of language against itself. "My work," he says, "is a matter of fundamental sounds made as fully as possible, and I accept responsibility for nothing else!" [1] The sounds and the silences dramatize, in Cartesian parody, the very laws of thought; in bits and pieces, they summon universal man, *quidam*, "somebody; one unknown."

Beckett inherits the verbal deviltry of Ireland and shares the black humor of Swift. He learns from Joyce, learns enough to trust his own voice. He begins by parodying the inventories of *Ulysses* and the puns of *Finnegans Wake* and ends by devising a system of combinations and permutations more pure than Joyce ever invents. It is as Kenner observes: art becomes a "closed field" and the total verbal competence of Joyce yields to the thorough "incompetence" of Beckett.[2] The Dadaists by comparison seem lax. More than Hemingway, Kafka, or Genet, Beckett gives himself to Pythagorean stringency and truth. He reaches beyond Existentialism, beyond Aliterature, into a silence that sings.

## II

Beckett's reticence about his life recalls the anonymity of his creations. Peggy Guggenheim sketches this rare portrait:

> Ever since his birth, he had retained a terrible memory of life in his mother's womb. He was constantly suffering from this and had awful crises, when he felt he was suffocating. He always said our life would be all right one day, but if I ever pressed him to make any decision it was fatal, and he took back everything he had previously said. . . .
>
> Though I adored talking to him and being with him, conversing with him was very difficult. He was never very animated and it took hours and lots of drink to warm him up before he finally unravelled himself. He was a very fascinating lanky Irishman with green eyes and a thin face and a nose lke an eagle and his clothes were very French and tight-fitting. He was extremely intellectual and abstract as a person and had an enormous passion for James Joyce, and had once been engaged to his daughter.
>
> Beckett was not Joyce's secretary, as everyone has since claimed, though he was perpetually doing errands for him.[3]

This is rather pert. But does the portrait not remind us of Beckett's fictions, his heroes waiting interminably for the end?

The facts, however, are more sober. Samuel Beckett is born in 1906 at Foxrock, near Dublin. His family is Protestant, middle class. He attends the Earlsfort House School in Dublin, then Portora Royal School, Ulster. Beckett is a brilliant scholar and a popular athlete, playing cricket and rugger. In 1923, he enters Trinity College, Dublin, to read French and Italian. He travels for the first time abroad, to France, in the summer of 1926. The following year, he receives his B.A. with honors, and the university nominates him for a lectureship at the École Normale Supérieure, Paris. Beckett takes another trip to Florence in the summer of 1927, teaches briefly in Belfast, and begins his duties at the École Normale as *lecteur d'anglais,* in the fall of 1928.

The literary life of Beckett begins. Beckett meets a young *agrégé* in English, Alfred Péron, and persuades him to cooperate in the translation of "Anna Livia Plurabelle," from *Work in Progress.* He also participates with Dujardin, Valéry, Soupault, Fargue, Romains, Sylvia Beach, and of course Joyce—there are others, the whole company requiring the service of a chartered bus—in the famous *Déjeuner Ulysse* arranged by Adrienne Monnier at the Hôtel Léopold, Les Vaux-de-Cerney, on June 27, 1929. He wins his first literary prize, in a competition inspired by Nancy Cunard and judged by Richard Aldington, with his poem *Whoroscope* (1930), about Descartes.

Beckett returns to Trinity College to obtain an M.A. in 1931, continuing his research on that French philosopher. Time haunted, he also studies Proust, and the same year publishes a probing book on him. Until 1932, he lectures on French at Trinity College. But four terms in Ireland are all Beckett can endure; he leaves again for the Continent. His wanderings bring him always to Paris, and in Paris Beckett always visits Joyce. Often, they sit in silence or interchange enigmas. Joyce's daughter, Lucia, whose mental state is already precarious, develops a passion for the visitor, and Beckett must tell her flatly that he comes to see her father .(Some years later, he tells Peggy Guggenheim "that he was dead and had no feelings that were human; hence he had not been able to fall in love with Lucia." [4]) He publishes a collection of stories, *More Pricks than Kicks* (1934), and a collection of poems, *Echo's Bones* (1936). The following year, he settles finally in Montparnasse.

His association with Eugène Jola's periodical, *Transition,* makes him known in small literary circles. Echoing from a distance the sentiments of Dadaism and Surrealism, the periodical attracts gifted writers who have no program in common but share certain attitudes toward history and art. Here is a typical editorial: "We are still living in an epoch of transition . . . in the face of a materialistic despotism which places 'concept' before the living imagination, and the force of the will before that of life. . . . The new TRANSITION, having little faith in Reason or Science as ultimate methods . . . in a spirit of integral pessimism, proposes to combat all rationalist dogmas that stand in the way of a metaphysical universe." [5] Beckett's distinctive work takes shape among the bustling, bristling movements of France *entre deux guerres*; and Dada touches it from one end as does Existentialism from another.

In 1938, Beckett's first major work, *Murphy*, appears in England with the encouragement of Herbert Read. The war breaks out; the Germans occupy France; Beckett goes underground though he is a citizen of neutral Eire. He is active with Péron in the Resistance. The Gestapo takes interest in their activities and arrests Péron in 1942. Beckett absconds to the unoccupied zone, earning his living as an agricultural laborer in the Vaucluse, near Avignon. He writes his second novel in English, *Watt*, which appears only in 1953. After the war, Beckett makes a sullen trip to Ireland, returning shortly to France. "I just made it in time," he writes.[6] All exiles, Henry Miller reminds us in his book about Rimbaud, exile themselves from the world's body, the mother's flesh.

Holed up in his Paris flat, like the Unnamable in his bin, Beckett writes. He translates *Murphy* into French, and in that language composes *Molloy* (1950), *Malone meurt* (1951), *En attendant Godot* (1952), *L'Innommable* (1952), *Nouvelles et textes pour rien* (1954), *Fin de partie* (1957), *Comment c'est* (1961). The true exile must also refuse his mother tongue. To Herbert Blau, who rightly sees in Beckett's attraction to a foreign language a form of self-repudiation, he says: "Yes, there were some things about himself he didn't like . . . French had the right 'weakening' effect. It was a weakness he had chosen, as Melville's Bartleby 'preferred not to' live. . . ." [7] Still, Beckett translates most of his published work back into English, and writes some pieces, *All That Fall* (1957), *Krapp's Last Tape* (1958), *Embers* (1960), *Play* (1964), originally in that language. In 1969, he shyly accepts the Nobel Prize. His fame barely touches him. Quiet and still unassuming, he lives with his wife, avoiding literary coteries, dividing his time between a small country house and a Paris flat.

## III

Certain motifs emerge from Beckett's earliest efforts and return to give his major work shape. In his essay on *Finnegans Wake*, "Dante . . . Bruno. Vico . . . Joyce," he admonishes the readers of Joyce: "This writing that you find so obscure is a quintessential extraction of language and painting and gesture, with all the inevitable clarity of the old inarticulation. Here is the savage economy of hieroglyphics." [8] It is as if Beckett speaks of himself. Even in the matter of hieroglyphs, both Joyce and Beckett believe that things with common numerical characteristics—the four Gospels, the four seasons, etc.—tend toward significant relations.

Joyce may be Beckett's transubstantial father and Kafka closer to his secret self, but it is Proust who helps to define his artistic conscience. Like Proust, Beckett confronts in every work that "double-headed monster of damnation and salvation," Time, with its twin attributes of Habit and Memory.[9] "The individual is the seat of a constant process of decantation," Beckett notes in his *Proust*, "decantation from the vessel containing the fluid of future time, sluggish, pale, and monochrome, to the vessel containing fluid of past time, agitated and multicolored by the phenomena of its hours." [10] The art of time, of entropy, is really a comic routine. If music is the formal analogy to Proust's art, vaudeville is the analogy to Beckett's. With uncanny foresight, Beckett defines vaudeville as "the comedy of an exhaustive enumeration."[11] We are prepared for the bitter hilarity of numbers.

Beckett continues his dour reflections on Time in *Whoroscope* which puns obscenely on celestial knowledge and degrades the movement of the spheres. If life is abortive—"How rich she smells, / this abortion of a fledgling!"—the history of the Western mind that Descartes began and Beckett must continue is no less so.[12] Decartes's voice prays: "grant me my second / starless inscrutable hour."[13] This is also Beckett's prayer. Crowded with scientific details and sexual allusions, the poem presents an embryology of Time. But it is also, in its puns and biographical references, an ironic tribute to Descartes, Seigneur du Perron, the one figure in intellectual history whom Beckett can neither accept nor ignore.

In the poems of *Echo's Bones* and the stories of *More Pricks than Kicks,* Beckett tests out his comic devices: garbled quotation, twisted cliché, jargon, pun, incongruity, etc. Belacqua appears as the hero of a vanishing consciousness, and his inactions evoke the mysterious banality of Beckett's world. Bicycles and clocks, madness and suicide, objects and abstractions, mingle in satiric or macaronic patterns of verbal dexterity. On the surface, Beckett seems to question the social and moral reality of middle-class Dublin. Beneath, he struggles toward a metaphysical question: man's sordid awareness, alienation, in the universe.

This leads us to the background of his thought. The patterns wherein his learning and imagination mesh, his metaphors of the human condition, derive from poets and philosophers of the past. Beckett adapts these patterns and metaphors to the postmodern world with consummate irony; his work seems a parodic reflection on Western history.

Once again, we return to Descartes. For Beckett, the universe of reason has withered, and the great philosopher who predicted the unity of all sciences in a rational method has become a glorious scarecrow in the fields of thought. Cartesian certainties, which depend on the uniformity of the mental process and of mathematical analysis, now yield to universal doubts. And as metaphysics once yielded to the scientific method, so the latter must give way, Beckett believes, to epistemological mysteries. The starting point of meditation is no longer the Cartesian "Je pense, donc je suis," but rather, "Je me doute"; and the point is quickly reached where the facts of inquiry dissolve into the reality of the inquirer, casting further doubt on both. Moreover, by making the reflexive act of consciousness the seat of reality, Descartes ushered dualism into Western thought while admitting solipsim by the back door. For the French thinker saw clearly the essence of the material world as extension and motion in space; the problem remained for him to explain how, in a dualistic universe, mind and matter could ever touch. His ruse was to assume that the pineal gland, the *conarium* on which Beckett puns obscenely, brought together the invisible world of the mind and the divisible world of matter. But Descartes's hapless disciple, Geulincx—Beckett refers to him in *Murphy* and again in *The Unnamable*—denied his master's ruse. Like the later Occasionalist Malebranche, Geulincx did not agree that mind and matter need be united; both were separate and real, though only mind could be known directly to man. Beckett adopts this absurd dualism with a vengeance. In his recurrent figures of men riding on bicycles, "Cartesian Centaurs," he gives us an image of bodies whirring in space like machines and of an intelligence superimposed on it grotesquely; the mind discards the body as a man discards his bicycle.[14]

Matter, then, in Beckett's world is alien, obdurate, and even threatening; nothing functions well; some metaphysical rust clogs all mechanism. His characters seek peace in entropy, in silence. Beckett writes: "To restore silence is the role of objects." [15] Meantime, however, mind is set free from decaying matter; it turns endlessly upon itself, droning words, dribbling numbers.

The fate of consciousness in a closed system may be glimpsed in the works of Ludwig Wittgenstein whose *Tractatus Logico-Philosophicus* and *Philsosphical Investigations* also envisage the possibilities of solipsism in word and number. Wittgenstein finally prefers to conceive of language as a game, a concept that Beckett's work puts to constant practice. Wittgenstein says:

Systems of communication . . . we shall call "language games." They are more or less akin to what in ordinary language we call games. Children are taught their native language by means of such games. . . . We are not, however, regarding the language games which we describe as incomplete parts of language, but as languages complete in themselves, as complete systems of human communication. To keep this point of view in mind, it very often is useful to imagine such a simple language to be the entire system of communication of a tribe in a primitive state of society. Think of primitive arithmetics of such tribes.[16]

Much of Beckett's prose seems like the arithmetic of a primitive tribe, struggling to convey in numbers its dim sense of reality. His anonymous heroes solemnly perform combinations and permutations; they repeat their words and vary their gestures *ad nauseam;* they add and tabulate all the trivia of existence. They are what happens to the mind when the mind has nothing to contemplate but its own symmetry, when language, caught in the paradox of its own self-denial, aspires to ratio. What began as Cartesian science ends as fiction, and fiction, Geulincx once argued, is intelligence demonstrating its sole freedom. Thus the tabulators of Beckett are also narrators. Their story, like a surd, tends toward silent infinity.

The heroes of Beckett, we see, are metaphysical clowns, *jongleurs* of solipsism. They are also morbid quietists, cripples, impotents. They suffer from radical acedia. Thus Dante's Belacqua, reclining in Purgatory, becomes the archetype of all Beckett's heroes who delay their salvation through spiritual indifference. Beckett, of course, knows his Dante exhaustively, identifying him with the coherence of faith, as he identifies Descartes with the coherence of reason. The shadow of Belacqua, tinged by more self-parody than we suspect, falls on all the heroes of Beckett—from Belacqua Shua to Murphy strapped in his rocking chair to Pim crawling through the mud—in testimony to the vanity of all human effort.

Yet human effort, in Beckett's view, appears not only vain; it is also blighted from the start. His pessimism frequently sends him to Calvin, Augustine, and Paul, to the Gospels and the Eucharist, in search of images of man's ambiguous fate. He echoes the famous statement of Augustine, "Do not despair: one of the thieves was saved; do not presume: one of the thieves was damned," in various works. The image of the Crucifixion, agony in geometric form, the two thieves proposing the final alternatives of salvation and damnation, fascinates Beckett. At times, he seems to accept Descartes's postulate of a malevolent deity; at all times, he identifies man's sin as the sin of birth. "Beckett's characters," Hoffman says, "suspecting or knowing themselves as defective creatures, are deeply suspicious of their creator." [17] Beckett's own suspicion is deeper. If God is dead, then nothing is permitted, and man is superfluous.

The intellectual tradition that Beckett finds most congenial appears melancholy indeed, though there are other writers, like Bruno or Vico, who seem to have aroused his interest. John Fletcher also traces the ideas of the Pre-Socratics in Beckett's early fiction: Pythagoras and Empedocles, Heraclitus, "the lachrymose philosopher," and Democritus, "the laughing philosopher," who appear in *More Pricks than Kicks* and *Murphy*.[18] To Democritus, called the Abderite, Beckett makes a number of allusions of which the most Beckettian occurs in *Malone Dies*: "Nothing is more real than nothing," quotes Malone.[19] This intuition, a source of cheerfulness to Democritus, becomes a source of epistemological despair to Beckett who feels closer, no doubt, to the ideal of the Nonent propounded by a Sicilian sophist, Gorgias of Lentini. The Nonent, in the terse paraphrase of A. J. Leventhal, assumes:

1. Nothing is.
2. If anything is, it cannot be known.
3. If anything is, and can be known, it cannot be expressed in speech.[20]

In Beckett's world, then, epistemology reveals only ambiguity. It is as if persons, objects, and events were observed hazily from a distance, and the act of observation itself, as in his *Film* (1967), invalidated both subject and object. The senses are seldom offered data sufficient for judgment, and when they are, the time lag between perception and expression condemns the latter to eternal obsolescence. The senses thus end by refusing to distinguish between illusion and reality, and consciousness, far from directing action or controlling matter, ends by displaying its infinite mutations. The principle of causality seldom operates. As a result, no logical relation obtains between particulars (objects) and universals (concepts). When definitions are attempted, they are usually made in the negative, by a process of elimination, a protocol of reduction, as if to define the world were to empty it. In the game that the mind plays with itself, language, of course, is the original flaw. As Molloy says:

> There could be no things but nameless things, no names but thingless names . . . the world dies too, foully named. All I know is what the words know, and the dead things, and that makes a handsome little sum, with a beginning, a middle, and an end as in the well built phrase and the long sonata of the dead.[21]

If habits, of which language is the deadliest, deaden, only the "suffering of being" awakens all the faculties of man. Against the silence of the dead, there is the silence of the agonized living. The latter may be the highest value in Beckett's world, this side of apocalypse. Thus from *The Unnamable*, who is Molloy eons later:

. . . it's to go silent that you need courage, for you'll be punished, for having gone silent, and yet you can't do otherwise than go silent, than be punished for having gone silent.[22]

On this foundation, the impossible art of Beckett rests.

Comedy restores that art to the realm of possibility. The comedy is clownish, cruel, absurd. It recalls some ideas of Henri Bergson on laughter. Bergson identifies the cause for laughter as everything rigid, mechanical, or eccentric, everything that threatens the elasticity that social life requires. His main insight which applies closely to Beckett's work, is that automatism and repetition are of the essence of comedy. "We laugh," Bergson says, "every time a person gives us the impression of being a thing." [23] Thus the fundamental processes of comedy are "Repetition," "Inversion," and "Reciprocal Interference of Series." Comedy is after all akin to number; its variations are a product of lucidity become automatic. Absurd comedy, however, introduces another element: it combines number and dream, drawing on images and obsessions that only dreams contain. This is the comedy of Beckett par excellence, and its laughter is never benevolent. Though laughter may finally serve to redress social evils, its immediate impulse is darker. In the laugher, Bergson discerns "a degree of egoism and, behind this latter, something less spontaneous and more bitter, the beginnings of a curious pessimism which becomes the more pronounced as the laugher more closely analyses his laughter." [24]

Vaudevillian and grotesque, Beckett's humor is essentially metaphysical; it assumes the absurdity of the universe and eludes conventional tragedy or comedy by confronting the automatism of number with the cruelty of nightmare. His satire is neither social nor even moral. It is the satire of a man who tries to bear his own company. Swift, Kafka, and Alfred Jarry, more than Rabelais or Joyce, define the tradition of the sadistic jest that Beckett exploits. The jest, as comedy often requires, calls attention to the carnal nature of man; and it transposes moral into physical concerns. Because the humor is reductive and sadistic, it tends to focus on scatological rather than erotic functions. Waste is the sole process of nature in a wasting universe from which Eros must be banished. Copulation, therefore, thrives but feebly, usually among cripples or octogenarians, as further proof of the mind's disgust with life. Beckett's three "modes of ululation," described in *Watt*, are the bitter laugh in the face of evil, the hollow laugh in the face of falsehood, and the mirthless laugh in the face of human wretchedness. All three laughs do not restore man to nature or society; they howl his alienation.

Beckett's concept of contractive comedy is implicit in his general view of art. In his essay on the Dutch painter, Bram Van Velde, Beckett is explicit. To him, art is a fidelity to failure, and also "a kind of Pythagorean terror, as though the irrationality of pi were an offense against the deity, not to mention his creature." [25] Art, then, is failure and frozen outrage. "I know," he says, "that all that is required now . . . is to make . . . this fidelity to failure, a new occasion, a new term of relation, and of the act which, unable to act, obliged to act, he [the artist] makes an expressive act, even if only of itself, of its impossibility, of its obligation." [26] Obligation, we see, wrestles with impossibility, and the result is always pyrrhic. The artist, like so many heroes of Beckett, can neither continue nor desist.

Since Beckett believes that the world "is expressed metaphorically by the artisan because it is apprehended metaphorically by the artist. . . ," it is not surprising to discover that his contractive tendency affects all aspects of his technique.[27] But contraction and even negation sustain a fierce life in Beckett's art, and silence implies an apocalyptic project for the transformation of consciousness. Though he comes closer than any other writer to piercing the heart of the Muses, there is far less love in him for "easeful death" than there is in Keats, Kafka, Genet, or Céline. "There are many ways in which the thing I am trying in vain to say may be tried in vain to be said," he confesses.[28] Beckett does not put aside the obligations of his vanishing forms.

## IV

The fictions of Samuel Beckett are products of the solitary game that the human voice plays by itself. A subtle dislocation of language appears in his earliest stories; later, we know, his words seek to meet their death in silence at some point projected outside of the word. Increasingly, the fictions map out the interior of the skull, which is Beckettland.

*Murphy* presents two of the most sympathetic characters of Beckett, Celia and Murphy, while parodying the love and quest motifs of traditional fiction. More than any other work, its events seem precisely placed and dated; its comic devices and rich allusions function as a principle of structure; and its intellectual virtuosity entertains, without dispelling the warmth of Celia's love. Her love fails, nevertheless, to redeem Murphy, "seedy solipsist." The need of Murphy's mind is to abolish itself; the need of all his friends is to make of his absence, his disappearance, a presence. Both needs are ironic equivalents, and it is irony that keeps the novel on the stretch.

The opening sentence of the book expresses the eternal aversions of Beckettian man: "The sun shone, having no alternative, on the nothing new. Murphy sat out of it, as though he were free, in a mew in West Brompton." [29] Working his rocking chair to a maximum rock, Murphy relaxes, hoping that the world will soon die down, "the big world where *Quid pro quo* was cried as wares and the light never waned the same way twice. . . . The rock got faster and faster, shorter and shorter, the iridescence was gone, the cry in the mew was gone, soon his body would be quiet." [30] His body sometimes finds peace; his mind never finds release, not even among the mental patients of the Magdalen Mercyseat which he joins as a male nurse. Like these patients, Murphy opts for the "small world" as against the "big," speculating on Belacqua's bliss, and on the three zones, "light, half light, dark," in which the mental and the physical fact, the kick *in intellectu* and the kick *in re,* finally correspond.[31] A defective gas stove explodes, killing Murphy in his rocking chair, before his speculations come to an end. Cooper drunkenly scatters Murphy's ashes on the spit and vomit of a public-house floor, and Celia returns to the streets. All the friends who seek Murphy seek really that deep calm, appreciated by the "higher schizoids" in their padded cells. The novel engages us with its wit and learning, its gay puns, its elegant constructions; and still we sense that silence, the "fourth highest astrological attribute" of Murphy, pervades its fictive silence.

*Watt* carries us further toward ataraxy and the mind's disgust with itself. As the first of Beckett's "epistemological novels," the work makes its case, through a deranged hero, that little can be known and less can be understood: "For there we have to do with events," Sam, the mad narrator reports, "that resisted all Watt's efforts to saddle them with meaning, and a formula, so that he could neither think of them, nor speak of them, but only suffer them. . . ." [32] Without any "vulgarity of plausible concatenation," in its plot, the novel also suggests the techniques of the anti-novel before Sartre coins the term.

The simple plot is almost devoid of novelistic content. Watt takes a tram, then a train, to the house of the enigmatic Mr. Knott. Replacing Arsène, Watt serves Knott for an indeterminate period, first on the ground floor, later on the first floor. Then, just as Watt has appeared mysteriously to replace Arsène, a new man, Micks, appears mysteriously to replace Watt. (Another man, Arthur, now replaces Micks on the ground floor.) Our hero makes his way to the train station and disappears. We learn that he is later institutionalized. Sam notes: "As Watt told the beginning of his story, not first, but second, so not fourth, but third, now he told its end. Two, one, four, three, that was the order in which Watt told his story. Heroic quatrains are not otherwise elaborated." [33]

The novel grimly rejoices both in order and absurdity. Watt walks with a "funambulistic stagger," flinging arms and legs like the perfect mechanical man. The composite age of the Lynches, who provide the dogs that eat Knott's garbage, always amounts to a thousand years. Arsène describes in detail the line of Knott's retainers, one serially ousting the other from each floor, reaching back to time immemorial. Watt plays games with language: "Then he took it in his head to invert, no longer the order of the words in the sentence, nor that of the letters in the word, nor that of the sentences in the period, nor simultaneously that of the words in the sentence and that of the letters in the word . . . oh no, but, in the brief course of the same period" all these inversions combined.[34] Watt's entire experience of the Knott (not?) household can be understood as an obligation to nothingness, an exercise in comic futility, a dim recognition of a reality that "might never cease, but ever almost cease." [35] The orderly plot, patterned according to a mathematical series, breaks up in absurd tables, catalogues, footnotes, verses, stories, musical notations, and verbal permutations, in ironic contempt of fictional forms. More significant, perhaps, is the impression Watt finally gives, that its author is pushing through "sempiternal penumbra" toward a starker goal.

The trilogy that includes *Molloy, Malone Dies,* and *The Unnamable* marks the highest achievement of Beckett in fiction. The heroes are no longer simply recumbent like Dante's Belacqua—the prototype of Watt and Murphy—who spends eternity holding his head between his knees; nor are they gradually alienated from the world of men and clouds and trees. The possibilities of motion for them are severely restricted, and their exile from reality is from the start complete. Sealed up in their mental space, they move about, fading, changing voices in the dark; constrained in all else, they lack the constraints of a particular identity. The fundamental categories of time, extension, and being are called into doubt as the fluid ego of one speaker flows into another, threatening the dissolution of all selves. The heroes of the three novels are virtually the same hero; he is the hero of all closed systems, subject to imperceptible decay.

*Molloy*, translated by Patrick Bowles in collaboration with Beckett himself, tends to be more faithful to the original than the translations made by Beckett alone. This novel, both stylistically and thematically, constitutes the broad foundation on which the trilogy rests. There are two sections in *Molloy*; each, narrated in the first person, depicts an absurd journey, the first by Molloy and the second by Moran. The stories, vaguely parallel, may be construed as anti-epics related to each other as Homer's epic, *The Odyssey*, is related to Virgil's *The Aeneid*. Taken together, the two stories form a statement on human impotence, on the questing consciousness and the creative imagination reduced to an obscene noise.

The first section begins with a series of ambiguities suggesting that one-eyed, toothless Molloy lies crippled in a room that once belonged to his mother; presumably, a man attends to him once a week. Molloy is a stranger to everyone, a stranger even to the hand affixed to his own body. His avowed purpose is "to speak of the things that are left, say my good-byes, finish dying." "They don't want that," he adds.[36] Molloy begins his tale by recalling that he once crouched on a hilltop, "like Belacqua, or Sordello," watching two men, A and C, approach one another on a country road. The two men are perhaps unimportant, like the two thieves on each side of the Cross, but one of them, with a cocked hat, is observed later in the novel by Moran. Molloy himself does not tell us much about these symmetrical creatures; he is more interested in finding his mother "who brought me into the world, through the hole in her arse if my memory is correct. First taste of the shit."[37]

(Both Molloy and his mother are ageless, sexless, sharing the same faulty memories and rancors; she calls him Dan and he calls her Mag; and they communicate by knocking on each other's skull.) Molloy's quest involves riding with crutches on a chainless bicycle, wandering through town and country, confronting the police who force him to recall his name. These trivial events seem part of the mythological present to Molloy who parodies the doctrine of eternal recurrence by his own solipsistic doctrine of eternal non-occurrence. As he lies in the real ditch in which he has really fallen, Molloy begins to think that all the world has died but for himself.

The antithesis of solipsism is love; but love for Molloy is an absence. On his quest for his mother, Molloy runs over the dog of a woman named Lousse and ends as her captive. His testicles droop; he is crippled, sterile, and impotent; yet Lousse "makes propositions" to him in the manner of Circe or Calypso, offering him love potions. (The only sexual experience Molloy recalls is with a woman, or perhaps a man, called Edith or Ruth, whom he meets in a garbage dump. "Perhaps after all she put me in her rectum," Molloy wonders. "A matter of complete indifference to me. . . . But is it true love, in the rectum?" [38]) Molloy does not even know why he stays with Lousse. Is it because he wants to free himself internally by accepting external bondage, as a man may feel free by walking eastward on the deck of a ship moving west? "I who had loved the image of old Geulincx, dead young, who left me free on the black boat of Ulysses, to crawl towards the East, along the deck." [39] When Molloy finally leaves Lousse, he discovers similar freedom at the beach where he collects pebbles and sucks them in every possible order to stay his hunger. "I always had a mania for symmetry," he admits.[40] The deadpan repetition of meaningless rituals, with hat or crutch or stone, is of course a parody of all rhythm and order; the conception of the body as a machine is a denial of organic life; and the confusion of erotic and excremental functions is a repudiation of the vital, binding instinct. Toward the end, Molloy meets a charcoal burner who offers him undesired attentions. Molloy kicks and clobbers him almost to death, and then crawls back, via a ditch whence he is rescued, to his mother's room. Cruelty in word or deed is a Beckettian correlative of impotence.

The second part of the novel focuses on Moran, a cold, precise, punitive man, who masturbates in front of a cheval-glass, carries a bunch of keys weighing over a pound, and likes to bully his thirteen-year-old son, called, like his father, Jacques. On a Sunday morning in the town of Turdy, a certain Gaber, sent by the mysterious Youdi, comes to Moran with orders to find Molloy. The fastidious life of Moran is gradually disrupted; he begins the day by missing Mass and ends it by experiencing a sharp pain in the knee, while giving his son an enema. He nevertheless makes elaborate preparations for his journey, delivering himself constantly of somber reflections on human destiny. It becomes obvious that he knows something of Molloy and that his relation to him is as obscure as the relation of Youdi is to everyone else. In his utter self-ignorance —he thinks of himself as gentle and generous—Moran gives the lie to what he says; Molloy, on the other hand, in his utter uncertainty, gives the lie to the very possibility of knowledge. Obviously, Moran lags far behind his quarry, Molloy, in grasping the wizened truth.

With his son, Moran takes the northern road toward the "Molloy country," traversing a market town called Bally or Ballyba, after warning his readers: "And it would not surprise me if I deviated, in the pages to follow, from the true and exact succession of event. But I do not think even Sisyphus is required to scratch himself, or to groan, or to rejoice . . . at the same appointed places." [41] One of his digressions refers to the "rabble in his head," a "gallery of moribunds": Murphy, Watt, Yerk, Mercier and all the others, avatars of the Beckettian hero, who also assayed the same futile quest. As might be expected, the adventures of Moran are arbitrary: his knee is stricken by anchylosis; he dispatches his son to procure a bicycle; he meets C, or someone like him, carrying a club; he meets a short man, who vaguely resembles Moran himself, and beats him to a pulp with a heavy stick like C's; his son returns three days later with a bicycle. After a violent quarrel with Moran, the son vanishes, and Gaber suddenly appears with orders for Moran—who is now wasting away—to return home. The journey home is as painful as Molloy's. The whole realm of matter conspires to balk and resist him. When Moran, now utterly decrepit, reaches his house in the spring, he finds everything empty, locked. He lives on, hobbling about on crutches, renouncing all things of this world. "I have been a man long enough, I shall not put up with it any more, I shall not try any more. I shall never light this lamp again," he states.[42] Outside, it is midnight and raining; or is it neither raining nor midnight? A voice persuades him to write a report.

In *Molloy*, Beckett is obviously employing two closed, interlocking structures that reflect one another. Molloy begins his story in his mother's room and ends it there with some ironic pastoral meditations. Moran records his search for Molloy, beginning his report in his room at midnight and ending it there. Molloy does not change much; he is what Moran will become. Moran, therefore, follows Molloy and turns into an absurd creator in his report. In this, Moran follows Beckett himself who writes the story of both Molloy and Moran, putting the reader in the same overseeing relation to Moran that Moran is placed to Molloy. Thus the futility of endless reflection may be recognized as infinite.

*Molloy* is a serious and original work. In it, Beckett introduces us to the hero as absurd narrator, a voice droning in the wilderness of its solipsism. In doing so, Beckett casts doubt not only on the evidence of the senses or the value of logical analysis; he further subverts the powers of the imagination. For Beckett's creatures are as suspicious of their creator as they are themselves contemptuous of whatever they can create; their creative acts are debased games that merely mirror another game, *ad infinitum.* The originality of the work also derives from its vision of shifting, merging beings, called by various proper names, who strain toward one another, seeking desperately a whole "*I*." This is apparent in the correspondences between the careers of Molloy and Moran, in their dim yet persistent awareness of each other, and in their occasional self-forgetfulness, as if their identities could suddenly dissolve into that of a mysterious self like Youdi's. Finally, *Molloy* presents us not only with a reflexive image of itself, but also with an inverted image of the world. Its cosmology is "inside out," its rituals are, like those of the Black Mass, parodies of church rituals. The excremental takes the place of the sacramental as Molloy speculates about his anal birth and constantly evokes the fecal associations of love. We move in a cone-like Inferno, the inverse below of what lies in the heavens above, which comes to a point in Satan's crotch. In keeping with this black cosmology, Beckett suggests Youdi as a parody of God and permits Moran to parody the Lord's Prayer: "Our Father who art no more in heaven than on earth or in hell, I neither want nor desire that thy name be hallowed, thou knowest best what suits thee." [43] In short, *Molloy* embodies the parodic impulses of Beckett in a complete form, a form that still scoffs at all possibilities of human order.

Malone, the speaker in *Malone Dies*, is still a more "advanced" case than Molloy or Moran. Thus he begins: "I SHALL SOON BE QUITE DEAD AT LAST IN SPITE OF ALL . . . Yes, I shall be natural at last. I shall suffer more, then less, without drawing any conclusions, I shall pay less heed to myself, I shall be neither hot nor cold anymore, I shall be tepid, I shall die tepid, without enthusiasm. I shall not watch myself die. . . ." [44] We begin to suspect that Beckett may be drawing a portrait of the artist as malicious player. For Malone forgives no one: "I wish them all an atrocious life and then the fires and ice of hell and in the execrable generations to come an honoured name"; and Malone wants only to play to death: "Now it is a game, I am going to play. I never knew how to play, till now. . . . Perhaps as hitherto I shall find myself, abandoned in the dark, without anything to play with. Then I shall play with myself."[45] Toothless, nearing a century of decay, Malone is fed soup by an old woman in his room—"Dish and pot, dish and pot, these are the poles"—unbeknown to his stupid flesh. With the help of a long stick, hooked at the end, he controls the world of matter in the skull-like space around him. His finicky mind takes endless inventories of his goods and reels out stories; the stories concern a number of fictional characters who become fused and confused with their creator who hopes to gain reality through them. What he writes is what we read.

In *Malone Dies,* then, Beckett does not employ two narratives, each reflecting the other; he forces the same narrative to reflect itself in the course of its own progress. (This reflexive quality is sometimes demonstrated in the same sentence, wherein the second part may comment on the writing of the first part.) Moreover, Malone, more than Malloy or Moran, depends for his existence on the act of narration; the absurd creator has no reality whatsoever outside the act that he condemns as absurd. When Malone ceases to scrawl, Lemuel is petrified; when Lemuel ceases to move, hatchet raised in the hand, Malone dies. And Beckett, who is behind Malone as Malone is behind Lemuel, by implication cancels himself out. Such are the prestidigitations of anti-form.

The contractive art of Beckett contracts more in *The Unnamable.* In *Malone Dies,* the interludes of self-examination become gradually indistinguishable from the episodes of narrative invention; reality and illusion are blurred in a state of consciousness that also subsumes death and life. Malone's cosmic indifference is really the obverse of cosmic acceptance. In *The Unnamable,* we are closer to the point where all these qualities fuse. The book thus begins: "Where now? Who now?

When now? Unquestioning. I, say I. Unbelieving. Questions, hypotheses, call them that. Keep going, going on, call that going, call that on." [46] The process of questioning puts itself to question. The narrator relies on statements, like the trilogy itself, that spiral toward zero and erase themselves semantically:

> The fact would seem to be, if in my situation one may speak of facts, not only that I shall have to speak of things of which I cannot speak, but also, which is even more interesting, but also that I, which is if possible even more interesting, that I shall have to, I forget, no matter.[47]

Yet we do manage to learn a few things about the speaker. He is alone. He is obstinate, determined to "go on," determined at all costs never to cease talking. Never! He is familiar with the other characters of Beckett, whom he calls puppets, surrogates, and "vice-existers." He sits in the self-same spot, hands on knees, gazing before him, his unblinking eyes streaming with tears. His origin coincides with the Beginning. "I am Matthew and I am the angel, I who came before the cross, before the sinning, came into the world, came here," he testifies.[48] Like the hero of an anti-creation myth, the Unnamable becomes the world he creates, becomes the creatures he invents, and takes life from the words they utter. He ends his preamble with the Berkeleyan resolution to speak of nothing but himself, about whom he knows nothing. What he says from that point on refuses paragraphing.

The ensuing soliloquy invokes all the surrogates of the Unnamable. Naturally, these evolve downward, from detested Basil, who somehow becomes Mahood, to Mahood, who becomes irreducible Worm. Again, Beckett constructs a deeply ironic form. The Unnamable, understood as the subject of the novel, wants his independence from the "master," the author, in order to cease existing; and the Unnamable, conceived as a creator of such fictions as Mahood and Worm, therefore an author himself, depends on them for his own existence. It is as if Beckett were saying that art and artist long to be free of one another; yet it is only in their mutual bondage that both exist to will their reciprocal destruction. At the end, a messenger as mysterious as the "master" comes in with an imperious order: Continue. Born obscenely "of a wet dream and dead before morning," the injunction imposes life on a hero who brags, "the testis has yet to descend that would want any truck with me, it's mutual, another gleam down the drain." [49] But the Unnamable does continue even if his words run obscenely in waste and excrement. Once again, Beckett cannot resist the most revolting transpositions of birth and death in the "creations" of his storyteller who lets down his trousers to "shit stories" on the whole world.

*The Unnamable* may be a novel of anal babble. Its hero may continue to summon surrogates even more lowly than Worm—at one point, Worm is almost displaced by a being with doll's eyes and a head splitting with "vile certainties." In the end, however, the book is a metaphysical leg-pull intended, like some Zen *koans*, to cripple the mind. Everything in this anti-novel seems to contradict itself as well as everything else. "This woman," he says, "has never spoken to me, to the best of my knowledge. If I have said anything to the contrary, I was mistaken. If I say anything to the contrary again I shall be mistaken again. Unless I am mistaken now." [50] Though he pretends to be condemned to speech by the masters who control his existence as well as the creatures whose existence he controls, he ends by yearning for his inexistence in "their language." We should not be surprised that the last words of the Unnamable concern the voice of silence:

. . . you must go on, I can't go on, you must go on, I'll go on, you must say words, as long as there are any, until they find me, until they say me, strange pain, strange sin, you must go on, perhaps it's done already, perhaps they have said me already, perhaps they have carried me to the threshold of my story, before the door that opens on my story, that would surprise me, if it opens, it will be I, it will be the silence, where I am, I don't know, I'll never know, in the silence you don't know, you must go on, I can't go on, I'll go on.[51]

Viewing the trilogy as a whole, we can discern something more than a pattern of contractions. The speakers, speaking always in the first person, are all exiled beings, shadows representing the universal drama of the Self. They enact, in the spirit of consummate parody, the ancient struggles between Mind and Matter, Fiction and Fact, Self and Other, Eternity and Time, Light and Dark, Word and Silence. Their struggle turns upon itself like a vortex and threatens to vanish though a central point, leaving us with an absolute blank. Like Cartesian clowns, they play out the farce of human identity in a cosmos turned inside out. They also serve as total satirists of our condition, leaving nothing holy or intact. Above all, they are the heroes of a new kind of consciousness, pure voices of subjectivity, recalling those "transcendental reductions" of Husserl that escape all phenomenological definitions. As Husserl puts it: ". . . the experiencing ego is nothing that might be taken *for itself* and made into an object of inquiry on its *own* account . . . it has no content that can be unravelled, it is in and for itself indescribable: pure ego and nothing further." [52] To reflect this new kind of heroic consciousness, Beckett is forced to abandon all the assumptions of the bourgeois novel and to create a fiction as reductive and as transcendental as its hero. Finally, he is forced to reject the possibility that art may ever realize this goal. If, as Ruby Cohn suggests, *Molloy* reveals the making of the artist, *Malone* the artist making, and *The Unnamable* the artist making comments on art while making it, all three share unequivocally a common destiny: heroic absurdity.[53]

After completing his trilogy, Beckett says in 1956:

The French work brought me to the point where I felt I was saying the same thing over and over again. For some authors writing gets easier the more they write. For me it gets more and more difficult. For me the area of possibilities gets smaller and smaller. . . . At the end of my work there's nothing but dust. . . . In the last book, *Innommable,* there's complete disintegration. No "I," no "have," no "being." No nominative, no accusative, no verb. There is no way to go on.[54]

He continues. *How It Is* is written not in one long continuous sentence as might be expected, but in short versets or paragraphs, each subdivided by natural breath pauses. No other form of punctuation halts the voice of its narrator who crawls in primeval slime through vast tracts of time, speaking only when he stops panting. His story is divided into three equal parts, each referring to the other, each dealing with his life before, during, and after Pim, each beginning and ending with the title phrase. The three cycles lock an infinite series. As for the speaker, he is obviously the latest incarnation of the Beckettian hero, "an ancient voice in me not mine." We can call him Bom, as indeed he calls himself sometimes, so long as we do not conceive of him as a distinct identity.

In the first part, before Pim, we learn that Bom progresses through the mud with a laborious movement at the pace of ten or fifteen yards . . . every eon? A sack of tinned food is strapped around his neck, and a can opener is in his hand. Sometimes, "images" of his life "up above" come back to him, memories of his mother's face. These images, he promises, will soon vanish; soon, even words, "quaqua," will also cease to come. Meantime, Bom wonders at the blue sky above, discusses Belacqua, Heraclitus, and Malebranche, and caresses the image of a girl who holds an ash-gray dog on a leash. Mainly, however, pain, laughter, and excrement occupy his thoughts. Waiting for Pim, Bom also tells us a good deal about the life with Pim to come. This "lover of arithmetic," we see, contrives somehow to incorporate in each section of the work parts of the others. The reflexive quality of the narrative becomes evident in the attention each part gives to its relation to the whole, as if the work had no aim but to comment on its own pattern, its geometry:

". . . there then behind us already at last the first phase of our life in common leaving only the second and last end of part two leaving only part three and last," Bom announces at the precise point of the narrative where this statement becomes true.[55] The first part, "the golden age," ends when Bom's claw feels the buttocks of Pim who is dragging *his* sack in the mud.

Bom tortures Pim outright; in his actions sexual sadism is explicit. Because Pim is something of a singer, the system of tortures that Bom devises for him is a parody of musical notations:

training continued no point skip
table of basic stimuli one sing nails in armpit two speak blade in arse three stop thump on skull four louder pestle on kidney
five softer index in anus six bravo clap athwart arse seven lousy same as three eight encore same as one or two as may be [56]

But this ghastly relation, insinuated to us as an archetype of marriage or friendship, indeed of all human covenants and contracts, fails to give life in the mud any meaning: ". . . orgy of false being life in common brief shames I am not dead to inexistence not irretrievably time will tell. . . ." [57] Both contrast the "LIFE ABOVE . . . IN THE LIGHT" with "YOUR LIFE HERE," and the contrast remains unredeemable. Absurd, revolting, and ludicrous as they may be, Pim and Bom still manage to convey in this section a deep intuition of pain and endurance: ". . . what age my God fifty sixty eighty shrunken kneeling arse on heels and hands on ground splayed like feet . . . we want to go on home at last." [58]

In the third part, Bom is sinking deeper in the mud, Pim has vanished, and the time is approaching when all "quaqua" speech will be lost in aboriginal silence. Yet Beckett, as usual, refuses to create a work with an ending. His central dramatic situation in *How It Is* seems a term in an infinite series. And so a creature called Bem is predicted to appear and to act toward Bom as Bom acted toward Pim. Thus from zero to eternity not three but an endless number of people will be caught in a procession, crawling between victims and tormentors. With berserk mathematics, Beckett actually works out some permutations on any given million creatures, as he does on any 777777 beings in search of a sack. The madness of number, the futility of repetition, and the solitude of consciousness in time are all implied in this seemingly frivolous device. But there are also times when Beckett makes his statement openly: ". . . but in reality we are one and all from the unthinkable first to the no less unthinkable last glued together in a vast imbrication of flesh without breach or fissure . . . and that linked thus bodily together each one of us is at the same time Bom and Pim tormentor and tormented pedant and dunce wooer and wooed speechless and reafflicted with speech in the dark and the mud nothing emend there." [59] It seems curious that the stunted discourse of the first two parts should suddenly yield, in the final part, to long stretches of connected speech and even eloquence. Beckett, however, is about to flash his trump card: he will repudiate clearly all that he has said equivocally. The anonymous voice, "self-style quaqua," that has been speaking to us throughout the novel says through Bom:

> . . . all these calculations yes explanations yes the whole story from beginning to end yes completely false yes
> that wasn't how it was no not at all no how then no answer how was it then no answer HOW WAS IT screams good [60]

Flat in the mud like a cross, Bom knows no answer; he merely guesses that he and his voice may be someone's dream in another world, the dream of an absent storyteller. Bom knows NO ANSWER, except the scream: "THAT'S MY LIFE HERE screams good . . . I SHALL DIE screams good." [61]

*How It Is* makes difficult demands on the reader; it can be hypnotic as well as soporific. Its broken rhythms and childish syntax—verbs and conjunctions are often dropped as in illiterate speech—suggest a type of consciousness that may be post rather than sub-human. The novel also explores a new kind of primitive, surreal, or dissociated poetry: short bursts of song between the futile efforts of the narrator to pull himself through the mud. Above all, its confirms the fierce austerity of its author. Moving still toward the East, with amphibious strokes in galactic mud, the narrator ends by losing even his voice, last vestige of solipsism. Does Beckett's savage irony leave us nothing then? It leaves this:

> . . . that for the likes of us and no matter how we are recounted there is more nourishment in a cry nay a sigh torn from one whose only good is silence or in speech extorted from one at last delivered from its use than sardines can ever offer [62]

Beckett's irony, which reduces the Fish, Christian symbol of redemption, to sardines, draws back in awe or reverence from human pain; for it is pain that presses silence into speech and speech back into silence.

## V

The pure and terrible art of Samuel Beckett finds its consummation in his plays. His novels are known earlier, especially in France; they appeal mainly to the *cognoscenti.* In the plays, however, the sound of a universal silence echoes in every act, and the rigorous game of living and dying takes ineluctable form. Since *Waiting for Godot,* Beckett comes to be known as the glum apostle of a new theatre. We call it generically, the Theatre of the Absurd. Martin Esslin notes: ". . . it is in this striving to communicate a basic and as yet undissolved totality of perception . . . that we can find a key to the devaluation and distintegration of language in the theater of the absurd." [63] No one carries the devaluation of language in drama further than Beckett; and no one maintains the tension between silence and speech, death and desire, at a higher degree.

*Waiting for Godot* is like the enigma a sphinx might dream. When Alan Schneider, the first American director of the play, asks the author about the meaning of Godot, Beckett answers, "If I knew, I would have said so in the play." [64] Yet critics continue to speculate about the identity of Godot. There are those who associate him with God; with a character in Balzac's *Mercadet*, named Godeau, who never appears on stage; with the bumptious and overbearing Pozzo; and even with Beckett's former patron, James Joyce. Anouilh wittily calls the play "a music-hall sketch of Pascal's *Pensées* performed by the Fratellini clowns." [65] And yet the most sensible statement about it may be that of an inmate of San Quentin, where the play is produced before a rapt audience:

> It was an expression, symbolic in order to avoid all personal error, by an author who expected each member of his audience to draw his own conclusions, make his own errors. It asked nothing in point, it forced no dramatized moral on the viewer, it held out no specific hope. . . . We're still waiting for Godot, and shall continue to wait.[66]

This is to the point. *Waiting for Godot* lends itself to social, political, psychological, and theological interpretations of the human condition; but in the end, it eludes all such views and focuses on Being mirrored in the inaction of waiting. What, then, can we say of the play? Certain general observations come to mind. The inaction of the play is cyclical, and its events are endlessly repetitious; its two acts are symmetric, both equal images of an absence. Two acts, as Beckett knows, are enough to represent a sequence stretching to infinity. And yet the force of entropy may be felt even in a cyclical system; the world of the play tends to run down. The stench of dissolution—the stinking breath of one tramp, the stinking feet of the other—hangs everywhere. Vladimir and Estragon are a little worse for wear toward the end; Lucky has become mute and Pozzo blind. Only the bare tree at center stage puts forth a few, ambiguous leaves in the second act, an ambiguity that is poetic as well as epistemological. Because matter repels mind, all objects—hats or boots, whips or leashes—retain their nasty and obdurate character. The same objects also serve as counters in a game, changing hands or changing heads in a parody of order. Anonymous and interchangeable, these objects, like the people who carry them, end by becoming quantities in an algebraic equation. Thus the four people on the stage are, in a sense, the same person as well as all of mankind. They all wear bowler hats.

Beckett contrives, however, to relieve this bleak scene. There are bits of business from the circus, music hall, and *commedia dell'arte*, the patter of feet and chatter of tongues. And there are subtle shades of discrimination between characters, characters who seem to complement one another in their common pursuit of futility. Pozzo, for instance, appears as the master and Lucky as the slave, and realistic Estragon is more active than his idealistic friend, Vladimir; but none can finally subsist without the other. Their ascetic dependence, more akin to bondage than love, can occasionally flower into tenderness. Hence the smothered note of affirmation in *Godot*. Its characters, after all, persist; they cleave desperately to one another when they fail to hang from a tree. Victim and victimizer are mutually dependent, and mediation between them is as perilous as mediation between lovers. Thus when Gogo tries to wipe Lucky's tears, the latter kicks him viciously in the shins. And Pozzo pontificates:

> The tears of the world are a constant quantity. For each one who begins to weep somewhere else another stops. The same is true of the laugh. (He laughs.) Let us not then speak ill of our generation, it is not any unhappier than its predecessors. (Pause.) Let us not speak well of it either. (Pause.) Let us not speak of it at all.[67]

Pozzo's system of thermodynamics, in which tears and laughter take the place of heat or energy, is a travesty of closed systems, a cruel joke on man. No wonder Didi keeps asking, "Will night never come?"

For their entertainment, while the luminous sky grows pale, Lucky dances. What is the dance called? Gogo guesses "The Scapegoat's Agony," and Didi, "The Hard Stool." But Pozzo informs them: "The Net." Lucky acts as if he is entangled in a net, then delivers his famous tirade, a mad jumble of puns, alliteration, and nonsense. It is as if Beckett were parodying Joyce and Joyce were parodying himself, and both were burlesquing all language and learning while restating the theme of the play:

> Given the existence as uttered forth in the public works of Puncher and Wattmann of a personal God quaquaquaqua with white beard quaquaquaqua outside time without extension who from the heights of divine apathia divine athambia divine aphasia loves us dearly with some exceptions for reasons unknown. . . .[68]

Lucky must be assaulted before he stops. After this speech, longest in the play, Lucky is literally struck dumb. The only effective death in the play is the murder of language. Time passes. The inscrutable message from Godot, delivered by the boy, lingers in the air.

The second act opens at the same hour, at the same place, the next day. The act of waiting is itself an expression of the futility of human desires; for even if the object of desire remains constant, the subjcet never does. "We always find something, eh Didi, to give us the impression we exist?" Estragon says.[69] The cruelty of their situation finds symbolic form in the German ballad that Vladimir sings about a dog that strayed in the kitchen and was killed with a cook's ladle. The cruelty of the song lies in its eternal cycle; the dogs that bury the stray dog write on its tombstone a story that ends where it began. And still the waiting continues. Didi tells Gogo to close his eyes if he wants to be seen by God. Enter Pozzo blind and Lucky on a shorter rope, carrying all the bags as usual. Is it Godot, they ask once again? Another boy enters, calling Vladimir Mr. Albert; he is a sheepherder with a message from Godot of the white beard. Tomorrow, without fail, he says! The two men promise to hang themselves if Godot does not appear. But in this play, all motion ends in stillness:

VLADIMIR: Well? Shall we go?
ESTRAGON: Yes, let's go.
(They do not move.)
Curtain.[70]

In silence and in stillness the pain of being may be felt. But the art of Beckett convinces us that parody is indeed the form our pain must now take. The play is conscious of itself as a game. The tramps are bent not on perdition but on self-entertainment, and Godot himself, their comic illusion, may be the game they best like to play. This gamesmanship prevents them from being ever committed, or, as Sartre would say, *en situation*. Their fate is existential only because it is stripped of most comforts; they are on their own. There is a formal sanctity in such a fate.

Besides circus, vaudeville, and *commedia dell'arte*, Beckett's plays owe something also to the Noh plays of Japan and perhaps to modern theories of games. *Endgame*, first performed at the Royal Court Theatre, London, on April 3, 1957, shows more affinity with these latter forms than does *Godot*. Beckett himself describes it as more elliptic and inhuman than his earlier play.[71] What is it about? All things final, the End of the World, an Ark that has survived one Flood and may not survive another cataclysm. We are in the presence of something taking its course, as Clov repeats, something about to finish. One critic identifies Hamm with the wounded Fisher King, Clov with Parsifal, and the jar of dry cookies with the Holy Grail; and another sees in the megalomaniac Hamm allusions to Joyce and in Clov allusions to Beckett, noting that Hamm is a mixture of Pozzo and Vladimir, as Clov is a mixture of Estragon and Lucky. Others attempt to discover the puns and allusions in the names: Hamm as Hamlet, as Ham who is Noah's son, cursed for seeing his father's nakedness, and also as hammer; Clov as the French word for nail, *clou,* and as the past tense of cleave; Nagg as the German *Nagel,* or nail; and Nell as knell, or as female nagger.[72] Almost all critics recognize that the action is laid out like a game of chess; the actors are pawns; and Hamm is the king near checkmate. But Stanley Cavell, in a marvellous essay, adds this: "The greatest endgame is Eschatology. . . . Now we are to know that salvation lies in reversing the story, in ending the story of the end, dismantling Eschatology, ending this world of order in order to reverse the curse of the world laid on it in its Judeo-Christian end." [73]

In the game of interpreting Beckett one should always refrain from simple- as well as single-mindedness. *Endgame,* I believe, may be seen as two symbolic dramas in one: an internal and an external action. The internal drama is simply that of human consciousness. The mind, the human personality, can be a closed system like chess; it can be ruled by habit and immutable laws; it may contain only one mobile impulse, Clov, ruled by a fixed authority, Hamm. And it may, therefore, be condemned to endless repetitions. (The question now is: Will Clov ever leave Hamm? The question earlier was: When will Godot arrive?) But Clov also looks outward, and the womb or skull-shaped room, designed originally for the play by Roger Blin, has two small windows that may be reached by a ladder—Clov has shrunk with time—and from which the emptiness of earth and sea and sky may be glimpsed. The play is not entirely solipsistic. Its action may be viewed, externally, as a phase in human history, time and events preceding that phase, a slow-motion apocalypse to come after, as indeed the numerous references to the Revelation of St. John the Divine suggest. These two symbolic facets of *Endgame* meet: the exhaustion of history and the exhaustion of consciousness are in the end both symptoms of a hidden wish: exhaustion of being. This is the central intuition of the play, crudely stated.

The curtain rises on a bare interior bathed in gray light. There, in two ash bins to one side, are Nagg and Nell. In the middle—or nearly in the middle—sits the imposing figure of Hamm, a blood-stained handkerchief on his face, a whistle hanging from his neck, the first a symbol of his passion and the second of his authority. Hamm can't stand or see, Clov can't sit; such is Beckett's fiendish symmetry. The first words are those of Clov: "Finished, it's finished, nearly finished, it must be nearly finished." [74] These words recall the last words of Jesus from the Cross; and their terror is augmented by the doubt modulating the syntax of Clov's sentence. Not even the end is certain. As for Hamm, he modulates his lofty misery with a yawn, and says: "And yet I hesitate, I hesitate . . . to end. Yes, there it is, it's time it ended and yet I hesitate to—(He yawns)—to end." [75] All of Beckett's art and Beckett's rage are in that sentence: his monstrous inventiveness in the techniques of desolation never yield finally to desolation. Clov looks at the wall without seeing *Mene, Mene, Tekel, Upharsin*, the words of Daniel which mean: "God hath numbered thy kingdom, and finished it. . . . Thou art weighed in the balances, and art found wanting. . . ." (Daniel 5:26) What he sees is his light dying—but never dead!

In their ash bins, Nagg and Nell represent the sedulous and obsolete past. They chatter in baby talk, try to embrace from their bins, recollect their youth at Lake Como, and eat dry biscuits. As usual with Beckett's characters, appetite, remembrance, and illusion survive all capacities to fulfill them. This is another source of comedy: not only decrepitude but also wretchedness is funny. As Nell says to Nagg: "Nothing is funnier than unhappiness, I grant you that." [76] To entertain her —for what is left to man in his dotage but to "tell old tales, and laugh / at gilded butterflies" like demented Lear?—Nagg offers to tell Nell, for the hundredth time, the story of the lazy tailor and the trousers. Hamm, too, amuses himself by telling tales and keeping an enormous chronicle that has run out of characters. And Clov pretends that he will be soon leaving, periodically scans the horizon with his telescope, and reports: Zero, Zero, and Zero. (But when he trains his glasses on the audience, Clov says, "I see . . . a multitude . . . in transports . . . of joy," using irony to deny the reality of the audience.) [77] For underlying all forms of the game is that terror of meaning which is the other side of faith. Nothing is ever allowed to mean or be. Even the life of a flea can disturb the balance of creation. The vicar of death on Beckett's earth is silence:

NAGG: (clasping his hands, closing his eyes, in a gabble) Our Father which art—

HAMM: Silence! In silence! Where are your manners? [78]

Hamm is the Chess King; and the Fisher King reigning over a land more waste than any we have seen; and Prospero declaring the end of revels that have never been, disavowing even the revels of parenthood; and Noah between the Flood and the Fire Next Time; and modern Man waiting in the enormous shadow of the Mushroom Bomb. Nagg nags: "I hope the day will come when you'll really need to have me listen to you, and need to hear my voice, any voice." [79] He nags in vain. Even Clov, who threatens with his departure the eschatological order of things, yearns for a final peace. All the characters, nevertheless, still grieve and rage. Sobs and laughter merely represent the subjective and objective responses to reality; the structure of the mind and the structure of history are really the same. Clov hangs up an alarm clock (Time) where a picture (Space) has been. But there is always an intruder into every system. He comes as a boy whom Clov espies as a potential procreator. The boy, however, seems to contemplate his own navel, fixing his attention upon himself, upon Nirvana perhaps, as if he were illustrating one of Beckett's favorite quotations from Democritus the Abderite: "Nothing is more real than nothing." Or is he rather the Buddha, raising us to another level of reality? The older French version is more explicit; it gives us a fuller sense of the religious possibilities of the episode. There may be, after all, a real life out there, a life by which the autistic characters may be redeemed. The suggestion is fleeting. Clov comes closer to leaving Hamm than ever before. At Hamm's behest, he articulates a few last words. These are the twisted words he utters "from the heart":

How easy it is. They said to me, That's friendship, yes, yes, no question, you've found it. They said to me, Here's the place, stop, raise your head and look at all that beauty. That order! They said to me, Come now, you're not a brute beast, think upon these things and you'll see how all becomes clear. And simple! They said to me, What skilled attention they get, all these dying of their wounds.[80]

"Enough," cries Hamm. He and Clov are still irrevocably obliged to one another. Yet the play and the playing go on. Hamm says:

me to play
(*Pause. Wearily.*)
Old endgame lost of old, play and lose and have done with losing.[81]

Both cry in darkness, in mutual witness. There is no guarantee that if Clov leaves, someone else (the boy outside?) might not take his place, thus repeating the cycle endlessly. For we can never know whether death's slow invasion works its way inward from the stillness outside or whether it moves outward from the dead center of the play. In any case, the horror and the poetry become real through intermittences in the game. With a vocabulary both limited and austere, *Endgame* manages to give us an authentic experience of waiting for the end of things, which may be also waiting for their beginning. It is Beckett's purest apocalyptic play.

## VI

In his later work, Beckett brings his "fidelity to failure" to ever shorter and newer forms: the radio plays, *All That Fall* (1957), *Embers* (1960), *Words and Music* (1962), *Cascando* (1963);

a play with tape, *Krapp's Last Tape* (1958); a television play, *Eh Joe* (1967); a pantomime, *Act Without Words I & II* (1960); a "dramaticule," *Come and Go* (1968); and an epistemological film script, *Film* (1967). The fictional pieces carry indicative titles: "Imagination Dead Imagine" and "Enough," both collected in *No's Knife* (1967). The point is clear. Opening and closing miming without words, waiting for the end, the "best yet to come," throttling the dead in the head, "that penny farthing hell you call your mind," coming and going, clasping in silence three pair of hands, filming an Eye and Object that shrinks from "perceivedness": Enough! [82]

There is the sufficiency of truth in the best work of Beckett; and also the sufficiency of poetry. Without faith in art or human consciousness, without benefit or ideology or dogma, Beckett still manages to regulate his "fundamental sounds" in the way poetry regulates itself from within. The poetry is like dry ice: it burns or freezes what ever it touches, leaves nothing superfluous in sight. It leaves us only with a fundamental intuition of what it feels to be human, feels to exist, try to exist, try not to exist. The poetry deeply acknowledges silence, eternal solitude, the last term in man's journey since the Sea gave up its life to Earth, since Thalassa broke in Number. Such silence—Orpheus of the severed head—speaks not only of vanishing things: it must also sing, on pain of universal stillness, of a new kind of love.

# *POSTLUDE:*

## *The Vanishing Form*

### I

THE DISMEMBERMENT OF ORPHEUS may be a continuous process, and literature may make and unmake itself forever. This view accords with the cyclical nature of myth. But we know that new beginnings do not always coincide with old ends. There is also schism, discontinuity, and perhaps apocalypse. The mythical world of recurrence, the historical world of continuity, prove inadequate temporal models of the world we are creating. There are those who believe that the future of the future can now be anything we want to make it.[1]

Do speculations about the destiny of man have a place in a study of literature? Literature speculates about little else. Moreover, the avant-garde helps to invent the future under the antic guise of experiment. For nearly two centuries now, these experiments have tended toward vanishing forms. They carry intimations of silence, a consciousness spinning loose of history, trying to twist free of words and things. Drawn to a strange vision of itself, the imagination invades the void. But as Antonio Porchia, who knows little about the avant-garde and cares less, says: "The void terrifies you, and you open your eyes wide." [2] Wide-eyed, the postmodern spirit sees everything—or nothing. It sees, anyway, that violated being gives rise to the tragedy of literary forms, and dares to wish an end to outrage.[3] This, too, is an Orphic mystery: man become god, the silent atonement of consciousness.

## II

The line that I trace from Sade to Beckett is hypothetical. Other lines can be traced, other authors named. And the moral that someone else draws from my tale may prove clearer than my own. Criticism is very seldom inevitable. Still, we may agree that the tradition of silence engages the varieties of contemporary experience in fullest measure. Culture and consciousness, turning against themselves, yield everywhere metaphors of inversion in anti-art. It is no longer the disintegration of the hero, or yet the death of a literary genre, that intrudes upon our criticism. It is rather the radical shift in the forms of our apprehension, in the possibilities of our life. We face, I think, new rigors of mortality. And our artists, mastering anew their "negative capabilities," seem to us, as Nathan Scott says, "hunger artists," waiters on indeterminacy.[4] In their peculiar patience we find active meaning. "Today at a later stage of individual despair," Stephen Spender writes, "there is a meeting ground in drugs, violence, sexual relations, hallucination, madness, between poets and non-poets who live the life of poetry regarded as experienced sensation." [5] Art undercuts itself in anti-art or loses itself in life.

Doubtless, the evidence of postmodern literature is quarrelsome, abundant, various. The trends change rapidly and change again from place to place. Yet the two accents of silence, heard throughout this study, persist in postmodern literature: (a) the negative echo of language, autodestructive, demonic, nihilist; (b) its positive stillness, self-transcendent, sacramental, plenary. Sometimes, these accents appear rhythmically, contrapuntally, in an author's work. More often, they sound a distinct keynote of his sensibility. It is impossible to survey the postmodern scene—from Artaud, Brecht, and Ionesco, to Harold Pinter, Peter Weiss, Edward Albee, and Fernando Arrabal (or Jerzy Grotowski and Julian Beck, for that matter); from the last

Joyce, Broch, and Céline to Iris Murdoch and Rayner Heppenstall, Günter Grass and Uwe Johnson, Philippe Sollers and Claude Ollier—without assaying a new work full of elaborations and qualifications. There are also some rare spirits of the age, most notably Elie Wiesel, who seem to converse immemorially in silence, carrying its dialectic beyond terror or even grace, beyond our reach.

Perhaps a few hasty instances of current American literature, least represented in this study, will suffice in this postlude. Nathanael West, writing at the edge of our contemporaneity, first comes to mind. He burlesques the mystery of feeling at the source, and burlesques, therefore, the very mystery of art. *The Dream Life of Balso Snell,* mock artist, proves to be a wet dream. More precisely, Snell imagines that he ascends into the bowels of the Trojan horse. This accords with his view of art as "sublime excrement." West seems to endorse this bilious irony: his own repugnance to life touches even his craft. His nausea, which no social despondency of the thirties can entirely explain, conceals itself in black comedy. A world of ugly doorknobs, dead dreams, and distressed loves, burns into the ash of parodic apocalypse. Thus West, turning violence into dubious merriment, is the new satirist laughing at the wound within his laugh.

Thirty years after, William Burroughs carries the excremental vision even farther. A devilish mimic, he transposes a world ruled by entropy, waste, and disease into a film of metallic laughter. His cosmic drama, a science fiction, the nightmare of some infernal machine, requires apocalypse for a denouement. Burroughs is haunted by metaphors of "total control": police, junk, language. His resistance to language especially—"to speak is to lie"—leads him to the "cut up method" of Brion Gysin and the "fold out method" of his own devising: neo-Dada compositions of random verbal collages. In the opening pages of *Nova Express,* he nastily asks: "What scared you all into time? Into Body? Into shit? I will tell you: 'the word.' Alien Word 'the.' 'The word' of Alien Enemy imprisons 'thee'. . . . Prisoner, come out." [6] Obscene idealist, satiric and visionary, lacing scientific jargon with poetic hallucinations, William Burroughs finally denies not only the Word but also the Flesh. His true aim is to free man by making him bodiless and silencing his language.

More versatile, John Barth may disguise his affinities with this tradition of silence by means of his verbal virtuosity. Yet he, too, is a radical skeptic who finds the phenomenal world gratuitous, and reality merely a "nice place to visit." Beginning with *The Floating Opera,* his heroes assert themselves as ironists of history and their own flesh, without connection to the earth, yet free, funny, and lucid in the region of "ultimacy," which lies, in Barth country, beyond fancy. In *The Sot-Weed Factor* and *Giles Goat Boy* he gives us imitations of the Novel by an author imitating the role of Author: he parodies himself in the act of parody. *Lost in the Fun House* goes farther in appropriating techniques other than the novel's. Living voice, printed word, and magnetic tape constitute a kind of aural montage, a generic conceit. The narrative can swallow itself by the tail, as in "Anonymiad," or vanish entirely in a Chinese box, as in "Menelaiad." The piece called "Title" considers the plight of the tale, the teller, and the told thus: "What is there to say at this late date? Let me think, I'm trying to think. Some old story. Or. Or? Silence." [7]

Beckett, of course, speaks mutely here, and perhaps Borges or Nabokov. Yet for the first time, so it seems, an American writer makes the dangers of silence explicit. Barth even elaborates the theme in an essay aptly called "The Literature of Exhaustion." The "death of the novel" becomes the inspiration of a new kind of fiction. With Borges in mind, Barth observes "how an artist may paradoxically turn the felt ultimacies of our time into material and means for his work—*paradoxically* because by doing so he transcends what had appeared to be his refutation, in the same way that the mystic who transcends finitude is said to be enabled to live, spiritually and physically, in the finite world." [8] The mystical analogy reminds us, once again, how easy it is to cross from one side of silence to the other. When West, Burroughs, and Barth give themselves to the deepest parodies, negations, they almost declare themselves, thereby, waiters upon transcendence. We can imagine Blake stepping into the white emptiness that Sade leaves in the mind.

The sacramental language of silence also has its representatives in contemporary American literature. We now tend to ignore J. D. Salinger, though there was a time when each new story bearing his name was regarded as a public event. Beginning with "Raise High the Roof Beam, Carpenters," the later works puzzle the critics; they are relieved, therefore, that Salinger writes no more. Ungainly, prolix, allusive, convoluted, tolerant of chance, whimsy, and disorder, these narratives define a kind of anti-form.[9] Their impertinent exhortations of reader and writer undercut the authority of the artistic act. Yet the impulse behind them is less parodic than religious. It is appropriate that Seymour Glass, the central character of this unfinished sequence, should be an absent *mukta*, a dead seer. It is also right that his author should explore, in the spirit of Zen, alternatives to speech. Like Burroughs, Salinger comes to distrust words. The Gettysburg Address should be the gesture of one man shaking his fist at an audience on the occasion of fifty thousand deaths; "the human voice conspires to desecrate everything on earth." [10] But the quality of distrust in the two writers is antithetical. Thus Franny can listen to the dial tone of a phone, after a disrupted connection, with something like rapture; and the heedless, aimless chatter of Buddy, her writer brother, expresses whimsical celebration. "Oh, you out there—with your enviable golden silence," Buddy teases himself and his readers.[11] The writer behind Buddy, Salinger himself, gradually becomes as silent as an ideal reader. At first, the silence is metaphoric: twisted and loving locutions, digressions, language shattered in its effort to free itself of *kitsch* and sentimentality. In the end, Salinger ceases to publish. Is this some form of holy refusal?

Not all contemporary authors push their reverence for silence so far. The Beats, we know, claim nature and ecstasy their own, the barbaric yawp, the mystic's trance. "Who knows, my God," Kerouac cries, "but that the universe is not one vast sea of compassion actually, the veritable holy honey, beneath all this show of personality and cruelty. . . . Live your lives out? Naw, *love* your lives out." [12] Following this beatific vision, the "prosody" of Kerouac—too evident from the titles of his essays, "Essentials of Spontaneous Prose," "Belief & Technique for Modern Prose," "The Origins of Joy in Poetry"—bobs on the bottomless flow of mind: "Blow as deep as you want to blow." [13] We are back with Surrealism, or at least some aspects of it: dream, spontaneity, syntactic derangement, etc. The hush that the Beats may approach is not the self-ironic silence of a depleted will, an entropic universe; it is, both at its worst and best, an indiscriminate effusiveness, a kind of abundance. Words rolls on, loosened from formal structures, as if seeking to become part of nature again, "swimming in language sea," as Kerouac says, or wailing and howling with Allen Ginsberg:

Holy! Holy! Holy! Holy! Holy! Holy! Holy! Holy! Holy! Holy!
Holy! Holy! Holy! Holy! Holy! [14]

Like his great master, Walt Whitman, Ginsberg is a poet of Orphic hopes: he wants to wed language to the flesh. But in his "angelic ravings," Jeremiah jostles Orpheus and Buddha: biblical anger, pantheistic joy, and mystic calm mingle. The sense of some irremediable outrage breaks through his sacred chants and litanies. The dual sense of apocalypse as revelation, completeness within the present, and as final, vengeful destruction, sustains his rhythms. Still, Ginsberg dreams of conjuring from "the national subconscious" of America a new language of the body:

Nobody publishes a word that is not the cowardly robot
ravings of a depraved mentality

the day of the publication of the true literature of the
    American body will be day of Revolution
the revolution of the sexy lamb
the only bloodless revolution that gives away corn.

His dream, prophecy, hallucination, high on Peyote or drunk on Ayahuasca, acid Surrealism of old loss or new consciousness, ends:

come Poet shut up eat my word, and taste my mouth in your ear.[15]

It would be misleading, of course, to tout all the Beats as sacramental authors of silence. For one thing, unlike the Surrealists, their experiments do not go far enough toward discovering alternatives to art. For another, their imagination, or their spiritual energy, seldom compels our assent in the realm of the ineffable. Still, they recover for postwar American literature the mystery of Orpheus's dismemberment: the Dionysian, creative-destructive, threat to language. Young poets, neither Beat nor yet Academic, must heed this threat. Thus, for instance, Robert Bly says: "In short, nothing we can do today with *form* will suggest to the instincts a way to better society, or take away our own sense of infinite expansion." [16] When language and form lose their authority, how can art not lose face?

Even Norman Mailer, prolific author, major and representative figure of our time, finds that he must turn from fiction to fact, from novel to pop, from art to legendary existence. "We've passed the point in civilization where we can ever look at anything as an art work," he says. "There is always our knowledge of it and of the making of it." [17] Mailer would probably resist an identification with either tradition of silence. In his essay on the American novel, "The Argument Reinvigorated," he still harbors heroical ambitions for the form, a destiny as large as the land. Yet in that same essay, he gives evidence only of artistic duress or diminishment, of fracture or failure in modern fiction. Hemingway can only take hold of the paw of the American beast and Faulkner of its dream. Younger writers shrink into moral earnestness or Camp. Mailer concludes: "And the important art in America became the art of the absurd." [18]

The art of the absurd is the penultimate conclusion of the line of silence extending from Sade to Beckett. In recent American fiction, its votaries include Joseph Heller, Thomas Pynchon, James Purdy, J. P. Donleavy, Terry Southern, Thomas Berger, Donald Barthelme, Ishmael Reed, Earl Rauch, Richard Brautigan, Ronald Sukenick, among many others. But literature lags, as usual, behind other expressions. The arts of silence show greater exuberance in random music, concrete poetry, computer verse, electronic dance, guerrilla theatre, deliquescent sculpture, autodestructive media, packaged nature, psychedelic spectacles, blank canvases, and plain happenings. Pop, Op, Funk, Concept, Topographic, and Environmental art proliferate, interpenetrate, even as new kinds of anti-art generate newer styles. As Harold Rosenberg says: "Today's styles are, increasingly, global in both conception and transmission. They are picked up everywhere at the same instant and shot back and forth from continent to continent as items of the total communications package." [19]

In this "total communications package," the history of artistic genres and forms becomes irrelevant. Even museum curators bend their gaze toward the future and help to *make* literary history by their choices. More significantly, "the total communications package" dispenses with the art object itself as well as its history. The raw material for art becomes in itself the fact, the event. Thus when Duchamp signs a spade, the act alone introduces it into the category of artistic awareness. "To understand the signed spade is to grasp an intrinsic development in human culture. . . ," Rosenberg continues. "Vital art works of this century are symbols of activities of mind that extend beyond the skill involved in their production." [20] As in Duchamp's supreme examples of artistic renunciation, the work becomes a complex transparency, a structure almost purely mental, a vanishing form.

Though my concern is mainly literary, I can not refrain, in a study of vanishing forms, from touching on the extraordinary example of Marcel Duchamp. Duchamp antecedes Cubism; he surpasses Surrealism; and he expresses, until the end, the most subtle impulses of the contemporary imagination. Apollinaire hails him. Breton recognizes that Duchamp spearheads the modern movements, noting: ". . . never has a more profound originality appeared more clearly to derive from a being charged with a more determined intention of negation." [21] In our own day, John Cage honors his memory with a marvelous series of plexigrams entitled *Not Wanting to Say Anything About Marcel*, and says: "Had Marcel Duchamp not lived, it would have been necessary for someone exactly like him to live, to bring about . . . the world as we begin to know and experience it." [22] The *Nude Descending a Staircase* rocks the Armory Show in 1913. For nearly a quarter century, Duchamp pretends to turn his back on art, playing chess with Man Ray, indulging his puns and spoonerisms, deivising pure activities of the mind. Then his masterwork, *The Bride Stripped Bare by Her Bachelors, Even* (*The Large Glass*), unfinished since 1923, finally appears still unfinished and necessarily so, to grace the Philadelphia Museum of Art in 1954. Duchamp watches his own posterity rediscover him, watches his own work, posthumously, so to speak, with cool and benevolent irony. Fittingly, his last work *Given: 1) the Waterfall, 2) the Illuminating Gas* is made public in the Philadelphia Museum only after his death.

The great refusal of Duchamp has many levels. Some may see in it contempt or self-punishment.[23] Others recognize there a rare, enigmatic charity. Duchamp, we sense, wants to imply a fourth dimension in his work: love. This emerges from Breton's brilliant interpretation of the *Large Glass*.[24] Duchamp himself prefers to say about that piece of lucid mystery: "There is no solution because there is no problem." [25] A master of self-devaluation, he declines to interpret his own work. Art is a "drug" without veracity; the artist is merely a "medium;" and language in any case betrays: "As soon as we start putting our thoughts into words and sentences everything gets distorted. . . . Language is no damn good—I use it because I have to, but I don't put any trust in it." [26] It is perhaps our entire aesthetic vocabulary that Duchamp derides. His ready-mades counterfeit reality; his self-inventories fake art history; his cryptic masks, jokes, and disguises impersonate human character. Duchamp loves to appear simply as a *respirateur*, a breather. Yet his paradoxes take us to the heart of postmodern life. A supreme intelligence of anti-art, he dedicates his existence to the artistic avant-garde. A total skeptic, Cartesian without a method, he emanates a sacramental irony toward creation, and says always to his friends: "yes." [27] He seems to combine the two languages of silence in a single vision. Here lies a prophetic consciousness, behind the Mona Lisa smile and mustache. Cage puts it better: "The rest of them were artists. Duchamp collects dust." [28]

## III

My comments offer but a foreshortened view of recent American literature, which is in itself but a partial reflection of the postmodern spirit. Everywhere, Western art—like science, politics, morality—participates in the renewal of shapes, straining the structures of human life. Thus the reign of terror, wonder, and burlesque in our age.

Admittedly the tradition of silence is selective, a choice of fathers for our fantasies. Sade forces upon us the extreme character of human consciousness. His successors, aristocrats of excess, push their hope or outrage beyond the limit of art. We are asked to discard culture and remake consciousness—Dada, Surrealism; to withstand the exclusive rage of death—Hemingway; to sustain all the ambiguities of the void—Kafka; to struggle with matter, history, and sensation in the name of mortal freedom—Existentialism, Aliterature; to embrace perversely images in a mirror within a mirror—Genet; and to silence language without bringing time or solipsism to a stop—Beckett. Seldom, it seems, has desire been so blighted. Seldom has joy given so freely to pain, authority to doubt, and communion to solitude. Indeed, never has literature asked so much of its readers, of man, for so little in return. Is this all that the avant-garde, alchemists of the spirit, can suicidally offer? I too may learn to dislike such authors.

But we know better. In loving or spiteful unattachment, these children of the void dream as no others can. Renouncing the stated world, foregoing even their own flesh, they reveal to us worlds within our common world. Eros, twisted or denied, unlocks all the caverns beneath the sea. In their case, life seems to enhance itself by deathly knowledge. Above all, art or anti-art, modern or postmodern, we recognize in their work a quality of consciousness validated by our own secret lives, by our own public existence. This is why the myth of Orpheus's dismemberment invades literary history, and why the story of vanishing forms refuses to remain merely a theory. We are compelled at last to discover in the tradition of silence, in some imaginary realm where Sade, Jarry, Tzara, Breton, Hemingway, Kafka, Sartre, Camus, Sarraute, Robbe-Grillet, Genet, and Beckett meet in common awe of human destiny, a meaning larger than criticism can yield. A part of us—at least a part—wants to join them in anticipating a reality which may become all together ours.

The game of prophecy is, as a game, both dreary and portentous. We still possess a divided mind wherein prophecy rebounds in forms of parody or irony. Then, too, the urgencies of the times and our own distractions grant few men the authority of shared vision: each of us gambles only on what *he* can see. I am aware of these difficulties in bringing this work to its necessary incompletion. Yet neither can the imagination abandon its teleological sense: change is also dream come true. To begin, then, where the vanishing forms of literature end, we may need primary vision more than second sight. But this is not the place for visions. I can only hope that after self-parody, self-subversion, and self-transcendence, after the pride and revulsion of anti-art will have gone their way, art may move toward a redeemed imagination, commensurate with the full mystery of human consciousness. Neither more nor less. Our revels then will have ended. Everyone then his own magician, and no man a magician alone. Prospero and the sea will change together, without need of drowning any book "deeper than did ever plummet sound."

# NOTES

(In the text, I have paraphrased in English all quotations, except poetry. The original is provided in the following notes.)

## PRELUDE: *Lyre Without Strings*

1 Edmund Wilson, *Axel's Castle* (New York: Charles Scribner's Sons, 1953), p. 25.
2 *Ibid.*, pp. 262f.
3 *Ibid.*, p. 298.
4 José Ortega y Gasset, *The Modern Themes* (London: C. W. Daniel, 1931), p. 86.
5 J. Hillis Miller, *Poets of Reality* (Cambridge, Mass.: Harvard University Press, 1965), p. 3.
6 Sigmund Freud, *Totem and Taboo* (New York: Vintage Books, 1946), p. 198.
7 Elizabeth Sewell, *The Orphic Voice* (New Haven: Yale University Press, 1960), pp. 5, 19.
8 Rainer Maria Rilke, *Sonnets to Orpheus*, trans. C. F. MacIntyre (Berkeley and Los Angeles: University of California Press, 1960), p. 11.
9 Geoffrey Hartman, *The Unmediated Vision* (New Haven: Yale University Press, 1954), p. 155.
10 I have given a plausible outline of this subject in *The Literature of Silence* (New York: Alfred A. Knopf, 1967), pp. 17–24. See also the fuller outline of Erich Heller, *The Artist's Journey into the Interior* (New York: Vintage Books, 1968), pp. 99–170. Professor Heller's gifted study, which I unfortunately saw too late, takes as one of its central motifs the statement by Hegel: "Art is and will remain a thing of the past."
11 See Elizabeth Sewell, *The Structure of Poetry* (London: Routledge and Kegan Paul Ltd., 1951).
12 See, for instance, Marcel Raymond, *From Baudelaire to Surrealism* (New York: Wittenborn, Schultz, Inc., 1950); Anna Balakian, *The*

*Literary Origins of Surrealism* (New York: New York University Press, 1965); Albert Béguin, *L'Ame romantique et le rêve* (Marseille: Cahiers du Sud, 1937); Mario Praz, *The Romantic Agony* (New York: Meridian Books, 1956).

13 Robert Martin Adams, *Nil* (New York: Oxford University Press, 1966), p. 246.

14 George Steiner, *Language and Silence* (New York: Atheneum, 1967), p. 89.

15 ". . . chaque livre était fait pour reprendre tous les autres, les consumer, les réduire au silence et finalement venir s'installer à côté d'eux, hors d'eux, et au milieu d'eux (Sade et Mallarmé avec leurs livres, avec Le Livre, sont par définition l'Enfer des Bibliothèques.)" Michel Foucault, "Distance, aspect, origine," in *Théorie d'ensemble, tel quel* (Paris: Éditions du Seuil, 1968), pp. 17f.

16 Roger Shattuck, *The Banquet Years* (New York: Vintage Books, 1968), p. 358.

17 George Steiner, "The Language Animal," *Encounter* (August 1969), pp. 13f.

18 Jacques Rivière, "Questioning the Concept of Literature," in *From the N.R.F.*, ed. Justin O'Brien (New York: Farrar, Straus and Cudahy, 1958), pp. 40, 46.

19 Frank Kermode, "Modernisms," in *Continuities* (New York: Random House, 1968).

20 Martin Esslin, "New Form in the Theatre," *The Nation*, April 22, 1961, p. 344.

21 *Continuities*, p. 23.

22 Renato Poggioli, *The Theory of the Avant-Garde* (Cambridge, Mass.: Harvard University Press, 1968), p. 61.

23 *Ibid.*, p. 226.

24 *Ibid.*, p. 110.

25 Quoted in *The Modern Tradition*, ed. Richard Ellmann and Charles Feidelson (New York: Oxford University Press, 1965), p. 120.

26 John Cage, *Silence* (Middletown, Conn.: Wesleyan University Press, 1967), pp. 109, 53, xii.

27 John Cage, *A Year from Monday* (Middletown, Conn.: Wesleyan University Press, 1967), p. 10.

28 *Ibid.*, p. ix.

29 *Ibid.*, p. 29.

30 Norman O. Brown, *Life Against Death* (Middletown, Conn.: Wesleyan University Press, 1959), pp. 68, 172.

31 *Ibid.*, p. 71.

32 Norman O. Brown, *Love's Body* (New York: Random House, 1966), p. 110.

33 *Ibid.*, p. 160.

34 *Ibid.*, p. 190.

35 *Ibid.*, p. 258.

36 *Language and Silence*, p. 24.

37 *Ibid.*, p. x.

38 Susan Sontag, *Styles of Radical Will* (New York: Farrar, Straus and Giroux, 1969), pp. 4f.

39 *Ibid.*, p. 23.

40 *The Orphic Voice*, p. 403.

41 Elizabeth Sewell, *The Field of Nonsense* (London: Chatto and Windus, 1952), p. 3.

42 *Ibid.*, p. 38.

43 Quoted and translated by Sarah N. Lawall, *Critics of Consciousness* (Cambridge, Mass.: Harvard University Press, 1968), p. 244.

44 *Ibid.*, pp. 230f.

45 Maurice Blanchot, *Le Livre à venir* (Paris: Gallimard, 1959), pp. 237, 265.

46 *Ibid.*, pp. 269, 304.

47 Roland Barthes, *Writing Degree Zero*, trans. Annette Lavers and Colin Smith (New York: Hill and Wang, 1968), p. 3.

48 *Ibid.*, p. 39.

49 *Ibid.*, p. 75.

50 *Ibid.*, p. 88.

51 Roland Barthes, *Critique et vérité* (Paris: Éditions du Seuil, 1966), p. 38.

52 *Ibid.*, p. 72.

53 Quoted by J. Hillis Miller, "The Geneva School," *Critical Quarterly*, VIII, no. 4 (Winter 1966), pp. 315f. Note that Miller himself also says: "Though writing is the only action which escapes the imposture of the merely human, at the same time all literature is necessarily a sham. It captures in its subtle pages not the reality of the darkness but its verbal image." *Poets of Reality*, p. 38. Murray Krieger further attempts to relate my own sense of "silence" to that of the Geneva School, in "Mediation, Language, and Vision in the Reading of Literature," *Interpretation: Theory and Practice*, ed. Charles S. Singleton (Baltimore: Johns Hopkins University Press, 1969).

54 Thomas Carlyle, *Sartor Resartus* (London: J. M. Dent & Sons, 1948), p. 164.

55 Walter J. Ong, *The Presence of the Word* (New Haven and London: Yale University Press, 1967), pp. 44, 91f.

56 Jerzy Peterkiewicz, *The Other Side of Silence* (London: Oxford University Press, 1970), p. 2.

CHAPTER I

## SADE: *The Prison of Consciousness*

1 *The Marquis de Sade,* ed. Richard Seaver and Austryn Wainhouse (New York: Grove Press, 1965), p. xvi.

2 *Ibid.*, pp. 138f.

3 *Ibid.*, p. 125.

4 Simone de Beauvoir, "Must We Burn Sade?" in *The Marquis de Sade,* ed. Paul Dinnage (New York: Grove Press, 1953), pp. 25, 26.

5 Seaver and Wainhouse, *The Marquis de Sade,* p. 113.

6 *Ibid.*, p. 157.

7 D. A. F. de Sade, *Les Crimes de l'amour,* 3 vols. (Paris: Jean-Jacques Pauvert, 1961), vol. 1, p. 15.

8 *Ibid.*, p. 28.

9 Dinnage, *The Marquis de Sade,* pp. 93f.

10 Seaver and Wainhouse, *The Marquis de Sade,* p. 170.

11 *Ibid.*, p. 173.

12 *Ibid.*, p. 185.

13 *Ibid.*, p. 220.

14 *Ibid.*, p. 231.

15 *Ibid.*, p. 252.

16 *Ibid.*, p. 254.

17 *Ibid.*, p. 359.

18 *Ibid.*, p. 338.

19 *Ibid.*, p. 272.

20 *Ibid.*, p. 344.

21 *Ibid.*, pp. 455f.

22 *Ibid.*, p. 460.

23 *Ibid.*, p. 478.

24 *Ibid.*, p. 520.

25 *Ibid.*, pp. 597–599.

26 *Ibid.*, p. 589.

27 Steven Marcus, *The Other Victorians* (New York: Basic Books, 1966), p. 22.

28 An earlier, garbled version was published by a Dr. Iwan Bloch, under the name of "Eugen Dühren," in Berlin in 1904. The edition of Maurice Heine, however, published in three volumes between 1931 and 1935, is generally considered the original edition of this work.

29 D. A. F. de Sade, *The 120 Days of Sodom,* 3 vols., trans. Pierales-sandro Casavini (Paris: Olympia Press, 1962), vol. 1, pp. 112f.

30 *Ibid.*, vol. 1, p. 71.

31 *Ibid.*, vol. 3, p. 222.

32 *Ibid.*, vol. 2, p. 113.

33 *Ibid.*, vol. 2, p. 57.

34 *Ibid.*, vol. 1, p. 55.

35 Georges Bataille, *Death and Sensuality* (New York: Walker and Co., 1962), p. 175.

36 Dinnage, *The Marquis de Sade,* p. 46.

37 Mario Praz, *The Romantic Agony* (New York: Meridian Books, 1956), pp. 95–186.

38 For a discussion of the role of Thanatos in Gothic fiction, see Brigid Brophy, *Black Ship to Hell* (New York, 1962), pp. 298–325.

39 *Death and Sensuality,* p. 188.

40 Dinnage, *The Marquis de Sade,* p. 43.

41 Seaver and Wainhouse, *The Marquis de Sade,* p. 246.

42 *The Other Victorians,* pp. 195f.

43 Susan Sontag, "The Pornographic Imagination," in *Styles of Radical Will* (New York: Farrar, Straus and Giroux, 1969).

44 *Black Ship to Hell,* p. 299.

45 Seaver and Wainhouse, *The Marquis de Sade,* p. 611.

46 *Ibid.*, p. 60.

## CHAPTER II

### *INTERLUDE: From 'Pataphysics to Surrealism*

1 Roger Shattuck, *The Banquet Years* (Garden City, New York: Doubleday-Anchor Books, 1961), p. 42.

2 André Breton, *Anthologie de l'humour noir* (Paris: Jean-Jacques Pauvert, 1966), pp. 358f.

3 *The Banquet Years,* p. 188.

4 Alfred Jarry, *Le Surmâle,* in *Oeuvres complètes,* (Monte Carlo and Lausanne: Éditions du Livre, 1948), vol. 3, p. 203.

5 *The Banquet Years,* p. 241.

6 Alfred Jarry, *Gestes et opinions du docteur Faustroll*, in *Oeuvres complètes*, vol. 2, p. 217.

7 Alfred Jarry, "On the Futility of the 'Theatrical' in the Theatre," in *Ubu Roi*, trans. Barbara Wright (Norfolk, Connecticut: New Directions, 1961), p. 181.

8 William Butler Yeats, *Autobiographies* (London: Macmillan, 1955), p. 349.

9 *Ubu Roi*, p. 164.

10 *Ibid.*, p. 169.

11 Breton, *Anthologie de l'humour noir*, p. 358.

12 Alfred Jarry, "Douze Arguments sur le théâtre," in *Tout Ubu* (Paris: Librairie Général Française, Le Livre de Poche, 1962), p. 148.

13 "Questions of the Theatre," in *Ubu Roi*, p. 174.

14 "Nous n'aurons point tout démoli si nous ne démolissons même les ruines!" *Tout Ubu*, p. 269.

15 *Ibid.*, p. 16.

16 "Song of Disembrainment," in *Ubu Roi*, p. 170.

17 Guillaume Apollinaire, "The New Spirit and the Poets," in *Selected Writings of Guillaume Apollinaire*, trans. Roger Shattuck (New York: New Directions, 1950), p. 232.

18 "Je juge cette longue querelle de la tradition et de l'invention De l'Ordre de l'Aventure." *Selected Writings*, p. 194.

19 Quoted by Shattuck, *The Banquet Years*, p. 268.

20 Apollinaire, "The New Spirit and the Poets," p. 237.

21 *Selected Writings*, p. 246.

22 "J'aime votre talent depuis longtemps et je l'aime d'autan plus que vous m'avez fait l'honneur de le diriger dans une voie où je vous précède mais ne vous dépasse point." *Guillaume Apollinaire*, ed. Michel Décaudin, *La Revue des lettres modernes*, Nos. 104–107 (1964), p. 7.

23 "IL MARQUE UNE ÉPOQUE. Les belles choses que nous allons pouvoir faire;—MAINTENANT!" *Ibid.*, p. 46.

24 Hans Richter, *Dada: Art and Anti-Art* (London: Thames & Hudson, 1965), p. 25.

25 *Ibid.*, p. 33.

26 *Ibid.*, p. 76.

27 *Ibid.*, p. 89.

28 *Ibid.*, p. 182.

29 *Ibid.*, p. 191.

30 Dada est notre intensité: qui érige les baïonnettes sans conséquence

la tête sumatrale du bébé allemand; Dada est la vie sans pantoufles ni parallèles . . .

Dada n'est pas folie, ni sagesse, ni ironie, regarde-moi, gentil bourgeois . . .

Nous déchirons, vent furieux, le linge des nuages et des prières, et préparons le grand spectacle du désastre . . .

Je nomme jem'enfoutisme l'état d'une vie ou chacun garde ses propres conditions, en sachant toute fois respecter les autres individualités. . . .

Liberté: DADA DADA DADA, hurlement des douleurs crispées, entrelacement des grotesques, des inconséquences: LA VIE. . . .

Ce que nous voulons maintenant c'est *la spontanéité*. Non parce qu'elle est plus belle ou meilleure qu'autre chose. Mais parce que tout ce qui sort librement de nous-même . . . nous représente. . . .

La simplicité s'appèlle dada. . . .

Dada, après avoir de nouveau attiré l'attention du monde entier sur la *mort*, sur sa présence constante parmi nous, marche en détruisant. . . .

Tristan Tzara, *Sept Manifestes dada* (Paris: Jean-Jacques Pauvert, 1963), pp. 15, 16, 26, 29, 35, 139, 142, 143.

31 Richter, *Dada: Art and Anti-Art*, p. 103.

32 *Ibid.*, p. 215.

33 ". . . notre dégoût de la civilisation, du *cacasosmos* organisé." "Dada c'est le germe du type humain nouveau." "Le mot Dada symbolise la relation la plus primitive avec la réalité environante. . . ." Raoul Hausmann, *Courier dada* (Paris: Le Terrain Vague, 1958), pp. 13, 21, 28.

34 "Dada était une révolte des non-croyants contre les incroyants." *Ibid.*, p. 145.

35 "Le système DD vous fait libre: brisez tout, visages camards. Vous êtes les maîtres de tout ce que vous casserez." Louis Aragon, *Les Aventures de Télémaque* (Paris: N.R.F., 1922), p. 36.

36 "Dada, lui, ne veut rien, rien, rien. . . . Les Dadaists ne sont rien, rien, rien, bien certainement ils n'arriveront à rien, rien, rien. . . ." Quoted by Anna Balakian, *The Literary Origins of Surrealism* (New York University Press, 1965), p. 132.

37 "Lâchez tout
Lâchez Dada
Lâchez votre femme, lâchez votre maîtresse
. . . . . . . . .
Partez sur les routes."

André Breton, *Les Pas perdus* (Paris: N.R.F., 1924), p. 132.

38 Quoted by Marcel Raymond, *From Baudelaire to Surrealism* (New York: Wittenborn, Schultz, 1950), p. 270.

39 Ernest Hemingway, A *Farewell to Arms* (New York: Scribner's, 1929),

p. 191. See the parallel statement of Tzara in René Lacote, *Tristan Tzara* (Paris: Pierre Seghers, 1952), pp. 17f.

40 "Pour la première fois le Dadaisme ne se pose plus d'une manière esthétique devant la vie." *Courier dada*, p. 28.

41 Quoted by Raymond, *From Baudelaire to Surrealism*, p. 273.

42 *Ibid.*, p. 282.

43 ". . . il appartient dans ses innombrables variations au spectateur. Pour son créateur, il est sans cause et sans théorie." Tzara, *Sept Manifestes dada*, p. 25.

44 "La poupée rejetée par l'enfant ou le chiffon coloré sont des expressions plus nécessaire que celles d'un âme quelconque. . . ." *Courier dada*, p. 38.

45 Pour faire un poème dadaiste
Prenez un journal
Prenez des ciseaux
Choisissez dans ce journal un article ayant la longueur que
vous comptez donner a votre poème
Découpez l'article.

*Sept Manifestes dada*, p. 64.

46 "Je ferme, j'ouvre, je crache. Attention! C'est le moment ici de vous dire que j'ai menti. S'il y a un système dans le manque de système—celui de mes proportions—je ne l'applique jamais. C'est-à-dire je mens." *Ibid.*, pp. 49f.

47 Quoted by Richter, *Dada: Art and Anti-Art*, p. 42.

48 *Ibid.*, p. 219.

49 *Courier dada*, p. 140.

50 ". . . l'art pour la diversité cosmique, pour la totalité, pour l'universel est innée dans celle-ci, la vie lente qui existe et dort même dans ce que d'habitude on nomme la mort." *Sept Manifestes dada*, p. 96.

51 Georges Hugnet, *L'Aventure dada: 1916–1922* (Paris: Galerie de l'Institut, 1957), p. 9.

52 Tristan Tzara, *La Première Aventure céleste de M. Antipyrine* (Zurich: Collection Dada, 1916), n.p. See also Tristan Tzara, *Le Coeur à gaz* (Paris: GLM, 1946), p. 31.

53 "Elle [la poésie] est elle-même une réalité. . . . Mais pour être valable, elle doit être inclusé dans une réalité plus large, celle du monde des vivants." Tristan Tzara, *Le Surréalisme et l'après-guerre* (Paris: Nagel, 1947), p. 34.

54 "La strélitzie aux doigts, l'esprit même de l'humour remonte en marchant sur des oeufs le cours des années de la 'dernière' guerre, le corps bien de face et le visage de profil." *Anthologie*, p. 493.

55 Quoted by Hausmann, *Courier dada*, pp. 72f.

56 *Dada*, p. 195.

57 André Breton, *Manifestoes of Surrealism*, trans. Richard Seaver and Helen R. Lane (Ann Arbor: University of Michigan Press, 1969), p. 241.

58 Quoted by Maurice Nadeau, *The History of Surrealism* (New York: Macmillan, 1965), p. 103.

59 *Ibid.*, p. 75.

60 *Ibid.*, p. 111.

61 *Manifestoes of Surrealism*, p. 26.

62 Quoted by Nadeau, *The History of Surrealism*, pp. 304f.

63 *Manifestoes of Surrealism*, pp. 125–126.

64 "Tout porte à croire qu'il existe un certain point de l'esprit d'où la vie et la mort, le réel et l'imaginaire, le passé et le futur, le communicable et l'incommunicable, le haut et le bas cessent d'être perçus contradictoirement." André Breton, *Situation du surréalisme entre les deux guerres.* (Paris: Éditions de la Revue Fontaine, 1945), n.p.

65 *Manifestoes of Surrealism*, p. 304.

66 *From Baudelaire to Surrealism*, p. 294.

67 *The History of Surrealism*, p. 223.

68 Quoted by Nadeau, *ibid.*, p. 315.

69 *Manifestoes of Surrealism*, p. 302.

70 Quoted by William S. Rubin, *Dada, Surrealism, and Their Heritage* (New York: The Museum of Modern Art, 1968), pp. 109–111.

71 Quoted by Nadeau, *The History of Surrealism*, p. 39.

72 *Manifestoes of Surrealism*, pp. 162, 297.

73 Quoted by Nadeau, *The History of Surrealism*, p. 250.

74 *Ibid.*, p. 274.

75 *Ibid.*, p. 313.

76 "Je repose la nuit sur un lit de verre aux draps de verre, où *qui je suis* m'apparaîtra tôt ou tard gravé au diamant." André Breton, *Nadja* (Paris: Gallimard, 1928), p. 20.

77 "A-t-on entendu chanter les oiseaux vers quatre heures de l'après-midi en avril? Ces oiseaux sont fous. C'est moi." André Breton and Paul Éluard, *L'Immaculée conception* (Paris: José Corti, 1930), p. 14.

78 "L'amour multiplie les problèmes. La liberté furieuse s'empare des amants plus dévoués l'un à l'autre que l'espace à la poitrine de l'air." *Ibid.*, p. 106.

79 "Les yeux baissés, nous portons le fardeau du silence depuis toujours et pour toujours." *Ibid.*, p. 78.

80 Jean-Paul Sartre, *What Is Literature?* trans. Bernard Frechtman (New York: Harper and Row, 1965), pp. 171f.

81 Anna Balakian, *The Literary Origins of Surrealism,* p. 18.

82 *The Banquet Years,* p. 331.

## CHAPTER III

## HEMINGWAY: *Valor Against the Void*

1 Ernest Hemingway, *A Moveable Feast* (New York: Charles Scribner's, 1964), p. 30.

2 Philip Young, *Ernest Hemingway* (New York: Rinehart & Co., 1952), p. 136.

3 Carlos Baker, *Ernest Hemingway: A Life Story* (New York: Charles Scribner's, 1969), p. 38.

4 *Ibid.*, pp. 44f.

5 Ernest Hemingway, *A Farewell to Arms* (New York: Charles Scribner's, 1929), p. 57.

6 Ernest Hemingway, *Green Hills of Africa* (New York: Perma Books, 1954), p. 101.

7 Baker, *Hemingway: A Life Story,* p. 85.

8 *Green Hills of Africa,* p. 51.

9 Baker, *Hemingway: A Life Story,* p. 214.

10 *Ibid.*, pp. 372, 374f.

11 A. E. Hotchner, *Papa Hemingway* (New York: Random House, 1966), p. 303.

12 Baker, *Hemingway: A Life Story,* p. 382,

13 *Ibid.*, p. 234.

14 *Ibid.*, pp. 267f.

15 Quoted by Carlos Baker, "Introduction," *Hemingway and His Critics,* ed. Carlos Baker (New York: Hill & Wang, 1961), p. 7.

16 Ernest Hemingway, *Death in the Afternoon* (New York: Charles Scribner's, 1960), p. 95.

17 "An Interview With Ernest Hemingway," *Hemingway and His Critics,* p. 19.

18 *Ibid.*, p. 37.

19 *A Moveable Feast,* p. 75.

20 Harry Levin, "Observations on the Style of Ernest Hemingway," *Hemingway and His Critics,* p. 110.

21 Elizabeth Sewell, *The Field of Nonsense* (London: Chatto & Windus, 1952), pp. 53f.

22 *A Moveable Feast,* p. 49.

23 Ernest Hemingway, *The Old Man and the Sea* (New York: Charles Scribner's, 1952), p. 114.

24 Ernest Hemingway, *The Short Stories of Ernest Hemingway* (New York: Random House, 1932), p. 481.
25 *Green Hills of Africa*, p. 102.
26 *Death in the Afternoon*, p. 122.
27 Carlos Baker, *Hemingway: The Writer as Artist* (Princeton: Princeton University Press, 1956), p. 71.
28 Ernest Hemingway, *In Our Time* (New York: Charles Scribner's, 1958), p. 9.
29 *Ibid.*, p. 21.
30 *Ibid.*, p. 117.
31 *Ibid.*, p. 67.
32 *Ibid.*, p. 68.
33 *Ibid.*, p. 90.
34 *Ibid.*, p. 179.
35 *Ibid.*, p. 186.
36 Malcolm Cowley, ed., *The Portable Hemingway* (New York: Viking Press, 1944), pp. xf.
37 *In Our Time*, p. 211.
38 *Ibid.*, p. 173.
39 Ernest Hemingway, *The Sun Also Rises* (New York: Bantam Books, 1954), p. 199.
40 *Ibid.*, p. 26.
41 *Ibid.*, p. 75.
42 *Ibid.*, p. 97.
43 *Ibid.*, p. 176.
44 *Ibid.*, p. 198.
45 *Ibid.*, p. 117.
46 A *Farewell to Arms*, p. 330.
47 *Ibid.*, p. 146.
48 *Ibid.*, p. 110.
49 *Ibid.*, p. 112.
50 *Ibid.*, p. 123.
51 *Ibid.*, p. 191.
52 *Ibid.*, pp. 338f.
53 *Hemingway: The Writer as Artist*, p. 63.
54 *The Short Stories of Ernest Hemingway*, p. 371.
55 *Ibid.*, p. 365.
56 Edmund Wilson, *The Wound and the Bow* (Boston: Houghton, Mifflin, and Co., 1941), p. 228.
57 *The Short Stories of Ernest Hemingway*, p. 505.

58 *Ibid.*, p. 506.

59 D. H. Lawrence, *Studies in Classic American Literature* (Garden City, New York: Anchor Books, 1955), p. 73.

60 Ernest Hemingway, *To Have and Have Not* (New York: Grosset and Dunlap, 1937), p. 105.

61 *Ibid.*, p. 168.

62 *Ibid.*, p. 224.

63 *The Short Stories of Ernest Hemingway*, p. 95.

64 *Ibid.*, p. vi.

65 Ernest Hemingway, *For Whom the Bell Tolls* (New York: Bantam Books, 1951), p. 370.

66 *Ibid.*, p. 324.

67 *Ibid.*, p. 176.

68 *Ibid.*, pp. 19, 306.

69 *Ibid.*, p. 281.

70 *Ibid.*, p. 179.

71 *Ibid.*, p. 403.

72 Ernest Hemingway, *Across the River and into the Trees* (New York: Charles Scribner's, 1950), p. 12.

73 *Ibid.*, p. 71.

74 *Ibid.*, p. 232.

75 *Ibid.*, p. 230.

76 *The Old Man and the Sea*, p. 9.

77 *Ibid.*, p. 27.

78 *Ibid.*, p. 55.

79 *Ibid.*, p. 102.

80 *Ibid.*, p. 140.

81 *Ibid.*, p. 83.

82 *Ibid.*, p. 110.

83 *Ibid.*, pp. 115f, 127.

84 *Green Hills of Africa*, pp. 22f.

85 *Ernest Hemingway*, pp. 139f.

## CHAPTER IV

### KAFKA: *The Authority of Ambiguity*

1 Albert Camus, "Hope and the Absurd in the Work of Franz Kafka," in *The Kafka Problem*, ed. Angel Flores (New York: Octagon Books, 1963), p. 251.

2 Franz Kafka, *Diaries: 1914–1923* (New York: Shocken, 1965), p. 210.
3 Franz Kafka, *Diaries: 1910–1913* (New York: Shocken, 1965), p. 197.
4 Franz Kafka, *Dearest Father* (New York: Shocken, 1966), p. 27.
5 Max Brod, *Franz Kafka* (New York: Shocken, 1960), p. 47.
6 *Diaries: 1910–1913*, p. 276.
7 Brod, *Franz Kafka*, p. 151.
8 *Ibid.*, p. 233.
9 *Ibid.*, p. 49.
10 *Ibid.*, p. 75.
11 *Ibid.*, p. 76.
12 Franz Kafka, *The Great Wall of China* (New York: Shocken, 1960), p. 284.
13 Erich Heller, *The Disinherited Mind* (New York: Farrar, Straus, and Cudahy, 1957), p. 219.
14 *Diaries: 1910–1913*, p. 11.
15 Franz Kafka, *Letters to Milena* (London: Secker and Warburg, 1953), p. 164.
16 *Ibid.*, p. 294.
17 Gustav Janouch, *Conversations with Kafka* (New York: Praeger, 1953), p. 101.
18 *Diaries: 1910–1913*, p. 296.
19 *Diaries: 1914–1923*, p. 167.
20 Quoted by Frederick J. Hoffman, *Freudianism and the Literary Mind* Baton Rouge: Louisiana University Press, 1957), p. 192.
21 *Diaries: 1910–1913*, p. 129; pp. 286f.; *Diaries: 1914–1923*, p. 206; Franz Kafka, *Parables and Paradoxes* (New York: Shocken, 1961), p. 149.
22 *Letters to Milena*, pp. 201, 186.
23 Heller, *The Disinherited Mind*, p. 226.
24 *The Great Wall of China*, p. 278.
25 Janouch, *Conversations with Kafka*, pp. 92f.
26 *Diaries: 1914–1923*, p. 77.
27 *Diaries: 1910–1913*, p. 33.
28 "Plus Kafka écrit, moins il est sûr d'écrir . . . plus il écrit, plus il rapproche de ce point extrême à quoi l'oeuvre tend comme à son origine." Maurice Blanchot, *L'Espace littéraire* (Paris: Gallimard, 1955), p. 62.
29 *Parables and Paradoxes*, p. 95.
30 *Ibid.*, p. 69.

31 *Ibid.*, p. 83.
32 *Ibid.*, pp. 133f.
33 *Ibid.*, p. 175.
34 Janouch, *Conversations with Kafka*, p. 92.
35 Martin Buber, "Kafka and Judaism," in *Kafka: A Collection of Critical Essays*, ed. Ronald Gray (Englewood Cliffe, N.J.: Prentice-Hall, 1962), pp. 161f.
36 *The Great Wall of China*, p. 264.
37 Heinz Politzer, *Franz Kafka: Parable and Paradox* (Ithaca, N.Y.: Cornell University Press, 1962), p. 81.
38 Franz Kafka, *The Penal Colony* (New York: Shocken, 1961), p. 62.
39 *Ibid.*, p. 67.
40 *Ibid.*, p. 132.
41 *Ibid.*, p. 87.
42 *Ibid.*, p. 225.
43 *Ibid.*, p. 96.
44 *Ibid.*, pp. 184f.
45 *The Great Wall of China*, p. 31.
46 *Ibid.*, p. 41.
47 *Ibid.*, p. 45.
48 *Ibid.*, p. 147.
49 Politzer, *Frank Kafka: Parable and Paradox*, p. 321.
50 *Diaries:* 1914–1923, p. 132.
51 Franz Kafka, *Amerika* (New York: New Directions, 1946), p. 1.
52 *Ibid.*, p. 120.
53 *Ibid.*, p. 162.
54 *Ibid.*, p. 233.
55 *Ibid.*, p. 266.
56 *Ibid.*, p. 265.
57 *Ibid.*, p. 182.
58 Franz Kafka, *The Trial* (New York: Knopf, 1959), p. 286.
59 *Ibid.*, p. 271.
60 *Ibid.*, p. 26.
61 *Ibid.*, p. 202.
62 *Ibid.*, p. 276.
63 *Ibid.*, p. 281.
64 *Ibid.*, p. 286.
65 *Ibid.*, pp. 183f.

66 Politzer, *Franz Kafka: Parable and Paradox,* p. 216.

67 *Diaries:* 1914–1923, p. 171.

68 Brod, *Conversations with Kafka,* p. xvii.

69 Franz Kafka, *The Castle* (New York: Knopf, 1965), p. 3.

70 *Ibid.*, p. 26.

71 *Ibid.*, p. 96.

72 *Ibid.*, p. 139.

73 *Ibid.*, pp. 209f.

74 *Ibid.*, p. 404.

75 *Ibid.*, pp. 122f.

76 Daniel-Rops, "The Castle of Despair," in *The Kafka Problem,* ed. Angel Flores (New York: Octagon: 1963), p. 184.

## CHAPTER V

### *INTERLUDE: From Existentialism to Aliterature*

1 Jean Paulhan, *Les Fleurs de Tarbes* (Paris: Gallimard, 1941), p. 72.

2 ". . . toute véritable transformation de la forme romanesque, toute féconde recherche dans ce domaine, ne peut que se situer à l'intérieur d'une transformation de la notion même de roman. . . ." Michel Butor, *Répertoire* (Paris: Éditions de Minuit, 1960), p. 11.

3 Jean-Paul Sartre, *The Words,* trans. Bernard Frechtman (New York: George Braziller, 1964), p. 153.

4 *Ibid.*, pp. 112, 235.

5 Francis Jeanson, *Sartre par lui-même* (Paris: Éditions du Seuil, 1956), pp. 61, 70, 117.

6 *The Words,* p. 180.

7 *Ibid.*, p. 253.

8 Jean-Paul Sartre, *Existentialism,* trans. Bernard Frechtman (New York: Philosophical Library, 1947), p. 32.

9 Everett W. Knight, *Literature Considered as Philosophy* (New York: Collier Books, 1962), p. 52.

10 Iris Murdoch, *Sartre: Romantic Rationalist* (New Haven, Conn: Yale University Press, 1959), p. 26.

11 Jean-Paul Sartre, *Literary and Philosophical Essays,* trans. Annette Michelson (London: Rider and Company, 1955), p. 127.

12 *Ibid.*, p. 142.

13 *Ibid.*, p. 153.

14 *Ibid.*, p. 162.

15 *Ibid.*, p. 142.

16 ". . . ils soutinrent que le but secret de toute littérature était la destruction du language et qu'il suffisait pour l'atteindre de parler pour ne rien dire." Jean-Paul Sartre, *Situations II* (Paris: Gallimard, 1948), p. 11.

17 Jean-Paul Sartre, *What Is Literature?* trans. Bernard Frechtman (New York: Harper and Row, 1965), p. 153.

18 *The Words*, pp. 253f.

19 *Ibid.*, pp. 251f.

20 Claude-Edmonde Magny, "The Duplicity of Being," in *Sartre*, ed. Edith Kern (Englewood Cliffs, N. J.: Prentice Hall, 1962), p. 30.

21 Henri Peyre, *The Contemporary French Novel* (New York: Oxford University Press, 1955), pp. 225f. Sartre's anticipation of techniques of the anti-novel is discussed by Edith Kern, *Existential Thought and Fictional Technique* (New Haven: Yale University Press, 1970), *passim*.

22 Jean-Paul Sartre, *Nausea*, trans. Lloyd Alexander (New York: New Directions, 1964), p. 29.

23 *Ibid.*, p. 56.

24 *Ibid.*, pp. 96f.

25 *Ibid.*, pp. 130f.

26 *Ibid.*, p. 137.

27 *Ibid.*, p. 174.

28 *Ibid.*, p. 134.

29 *Ibid.*, p. 6.

30 *Ibid.*, p. 232.

31 See Jeanson, *Sartre par lui-même*, p. 140; and Maurice Cranston, *Jean-Paul Sartre* (New York: Grove Press, 1962), p. 111.

32 Quoted by Murdoch, *Sartre: Romantic Rationalist*, p. 89. See also pp. 44, 97ff.

33 "Je n'ai jamais pu renoncer à la lumière, au bonheur d'être, à la vie libre où j'ai grandi." Albert Camus, "Discours de Suède," in *Essais*, ed. R. Quillot (Paris: Bibliothèque de la Pléiade, 1965), p. 1074.

34 "Préface," *L'Envers et l'endroit*, *ibid.*, p. 6.

35 Connor Cruise O'Brien takes a more critical view of Camus's relation to Communism, colonialism in general, and Algeria in particular. See his *Albert Camus: Of Europe and Africa* (New York: The Viking Press, 1970).

36 See the discussion of Camus's later politics, *ibid.*, *passim*.

37 Jean-Paul Sartre, "Tribute to Camus," in *Camus*, ed. Germaine Brée (Englewood Cliffs, N.J.: Prentice Hall, 1962), p. 174.

38 *Essais*, p. 13.

39 Albert Camus, *The Rebel* (New York: Vintage Books, 1956), p. 6.

40 Jean-Paul Sartre, "Reply to Albert Camus," *Situations*, trans. Benita Eisler (New York: George Braziller, 1965), p. 93. See also the statements of Germaine Brée, Henri Peyre, and Roger Quillot, in *Camus*, *passim*.

41 "Entre cet endroit et cet envers du monde, je ne veux pas choisir. . . . Le grand courage, c'est encore de tenir les yeux ouverts sur la lumière comme sur la mort." *Essais*, p. 49.

42 *Ibid.*, p. 13.

43 Serge Doubrovsky, "The Ethics of Albert Camus," in *Camus*, p. 74.

44 "Je comprends ici ce qu'on appelle gloire: le droit d'aimer sans mesure." "La mesure de l'homme? Le silence et les pierres mortes. Tout le reste appartient à l'histoire." *Essais*, pp. 57, 85.

45 Albert Camus, *Caligula and Three Other Plays*, trans. Stuart Gilbert (New York: Vintage Books, 1958), pp. vi. 8.

46 Albert Camus, *The Myth of Sisyphus and Other Essays*, trans. Justin O'Brien (New York: Vintage Books, 1959), p. 91.

47 *The Rebel*, p. 100.

48 *Ibid.*, p. 91.

49 Albert Camus, "The Renegade," *Exile and the Kingdom*, trans. Justin O'Brien, in *The Collected Fiction of Albert Camus* (London: Hamish Hamilton, 1960), p. 334.

50 *The Myth of Sisyphus*, p. 72.

51 *Ibid.*, p. 84.

52 *Caligula and Three Other Plays*, p. 14.

53 Albert Camus, "Create Dangerously," *Resistance, Rebellion, and Death*, trans. Justin O'Brien (New York: Knopf, 1961), p. 251.

54 *The Rebel*, p. 91.

55 *Ibid.*, pp. 92f.

56 *Ibid.*, p. 276.

57 Jean-Paul Sartre, "An Explication of *The Stranger*," reprinted in *Literary and Philosophical Essays*; and in *Camus*, pp. 108–121.

58 *Camus*, p. 119.

59 *Ibid.*, p. 120. C. Roland Wagner suggests a more dubious aspect of Camus's silence, "The Silence of *The Stranger*," *Modern Fiction Studies*, vol. 36, no. 1 (Spring 1970).

60 Nathan A. Scott, *Camus* (London: Bowes & Bowes, 1962), p. 85.

61 See also John Darzins, "Transparence in Camus and Kafka," *Yale French Studies*, no. 25, pp. 98–103, who argues that both writers

share an unhistorical sense of "expiation"; and Heinz Politzer, "Franz Kafka and Albert Camus: Parables for Our Time," *Chicago Review*, XIV, no. 1 (Spring 1960), pp. 47–76.

62 Albert Camus, *The Fall*, in *The Collected Fiction*, p. 269.

63 *Ibid.*, p. 261.

64 *Ibid.*, p. 292.

65 *Ibid.*, p. 294.

66 *Ibid.*, p. 295.

67 *Ibid.*, p. 304.

68 Philip Thody, *Albert Camus* (New York: Grove Press, 1957), p. 79.

69 Carl A. Viggiani, "Camus and the Fall from Innocence," *Yale French Studies*, pp. 66f.

70 *The Collected Fiction*, pp. 254, 264, 268, 281, 288.

71 *Ibid.*, pp. 276, 305.

72 *Ibid.*, p. 279.

73 *Ibid.*, p. 270.

74 *Ibid.*, p. 295. Other ambiguities of this novel, utilizing a frame within a frame, are discussed by Adele King, "Structure and Meaning in *La Chute*," *PMLA*, LXXVII, 3 (December 1962), pp. 660–667.

75 "Return to Tipasa," in *The Myth of Sisyphus*, p. 145.

76 Germaine Brée, "Novelists in Search of the Novel: The French Scene," *Modern Fiction Studies*, XVI, no. 1 (Spring 1970), pp. 7f.

77 Claude Mauriac, *The New Literature, trans. Samuel I. Stone* (New York: George Braziller, 1959), pp. 12ff.

78 See Geoffrey Hartmann, "Maurice Blanchot," in *The Novelist as Philosopher*, John Cruikshank (New York: Oxford University Press, 1962), pp. 147–154; and Nathan A. Scott, Jr., *Negative Capability* (New Haven: Yale University Press, 1969), pp. xiv, 8–88.

79 See Melvin J. Friedman, "Samuel Beckett and the *Nouveau Roman*," *Wisconsin Studies in Contemporary Literature*, vol. 5, no. 2 (Spring-Summer 1960), pp. 22–36; Nathalie Sarraute, *The Age of Suspicion*, trans. Maria Jolas (New York: George Braziller, 1963), pp. 17ff; and Kern, *Existential Thought*, pp. 241–243.

80 See John Sturrock, *The French New Novel* (London: Oxford University Press, 1969), pp. 24–32.

81 Lucien Goldmann, *Pour une sociologie du roman* (Paris: Gallimard, 1964), pp. 281–297.

82 Sturrock, *The French New Novel*, p. 33.

83 ". . . d'oeuvres vivaces et toutes négatives qu'on pourrait nommer des anti-romans." Nathalie Sarraute, *Portrait d'un inconnu* (Paris: Gallimard, 1956), p. 7.

84 Sarraute, *The Age of Suspicion*, pp. 13f.

85 *Ibid.*, p. 57.

86 *Ibid.*, p. 71.

87 *Ibid.*, p. 145.

88 *Ibid.*, p. 97.

89 Quoted by Ruth Z. Temple, *Nathalie Sarraute* (New York: Columbia University Press, 1968), p. 46.

90 *Ibid.*, p. 41.

91 Nathalie Sarraute, *Tropisms*, trans. Maria Jolas (New York: George Braziller, 1963), p. vi.

92 *Portrait d'un inconnu*, pp. 27, 47.

93 *Ibid.*, pp. 85–87.

94 "Je ne demande que cela, qu'ils me vident, qu'ils me délivrent." *Ibid.*, p. 74.

95 *Ibid.*, p. 124.

96 "Tout s'apaisera, peu à peu. Le monde prendra un aspect lisse et net, purifié. . . .
Après la mort? . . . Mais non, ce n'est rien, cela non plus . . . Même cet air un peu étrange, comme petrifié, cet air un peu inanimé disparaîtra à son tour . . . Tout s'arranger . . . Ce ne sera rien . . . Juste encore un pas de plus à franchir."
*Ibid.*, p. 238.

97 *Ibid.*, p. 137.

98 "Le réveil est paisible. La barre de savon, posée sur la planche au-dessus de l'évier, luit doucement au soleil matinal, comme le sable moiré de la plage après une nuit d'orage." *Ibid.*, p. 134.

99 The double aspect of Robbe-Grillet is later acknowledged by Barthes himself in his preface to the scrupulous study of Bruce Morrissette, *Les Romans de Robbe-Grillet* (Paris: Éditions de Minuit, 1963).

100 Bruce Morrissette, *Alain Robbe-Grillet* (New York: Columbia University Press, 1965, p. 6.

101 *Ibid.*, p. 5.

102 Dennis Porter, "Sartre, Robbe-Grillet, and the Psychotic Hero," *Modern Fiction Studies*, vol. 36, no. 1 (Spring 1970), p. 24.

103 Alain Robbe-Grillet, *For a New Novel*, trans. Richard Howard (New York: Grove Press, 1965), p. 14.

104 *Ibid.*, p. 19.

105 *Ibid.*, p. 24.

106 *Ibid.*, p. 59.

107 *Ibid.*, p. 108.

108 *Ibid.*, 37.

109 *Ibid.*, p. 107.

110 *Ibid.*, pp. 79–119, 127f.

111 *Ibid.*, p. 148.

112 *Ibid.*, pp. 166f.

113 See Roland Barthes, *Essais critiques* (Paris: Éditions du Seuil, 1964), pp. 102, 205.

114 See Bruce Morrissette, "The Evolution of Narrative Viewpoint in Robbe-Grillet," *Novel*, vol. 1, no. 1 (Fall 1967), pp. 24–33.

115 This apt term is Morrissette's, *Les Romans de Robbe-Grillet*, p. 112.

116 *Novel*, p. 29.

117 Alain Robbe-Grillet, *Two Novels: Jealousy and In the Labyrinth*, trans. Richard Howard (New York: Grove Press, 1965), p. 46.

118 *Ibid.*, p. 106.

119 *Ibid.*, p. 120.

120 *For a New Novel*, p. 154.

121 "Objective Literature: Alain Robbe-Grillet," in *Two Novels*, p. 22.

122 *Ibid.*, p. 126.

123 *Ibid.*, p. 137. Morrissette suggests certain parallels between that novel within a novel and Graham Green's *The Heart of the Matter*. See *Les Romans de Robbe-Grillet*, pp. 117f.

124 Bernard Dort, "Are These Novels 'Innocent'?" *Yale French Studies*, vol. 34, p. 23.

## CHAPTER VI

## *GENET: The Rites of Death*

1 Jean-Paul Sartre, *Saint Genet: Actor and Martyr*, trans. Bernard Frechtman (New York: George Braziller, 1963), p. 9.

2 *Ibid.*, p. 35.

3 Jean Genet, *Our Lady of the Flowers*, trans. Bernard Frechtman (New York: Grove Press, 1963), p. 83.

4 Jean Genet, *The Thief's Journal*, trans. Bernard Frechtman (New York: Grove Press, 1964), p. 70.

5 *Our Lady of the Flowers*, p. 94.

6 "Quand c'est le Mal, on ne sait pas encore de quoi l'on parle. Mais je sais qu'Il est le seul à pouvoir susciter sous ma plume l'enthousiasme verbal, signe ici, de l'adhésion de mon coeur." Jean Genet, "L'Enfant criminel," in *Les Bonnes* and *L'Atelier d'Alberto Giacometti* (Decines [Isère]: L'Arbalette, 1958), p. 162.

7 *The Thief's Journal*, p. 244.
8 *Ibid.*, pp. 172f., 175.
9 *Ibid.*, p. 13.
10 *Ibid.*, p. 84.
11 *Our Lady of the Flowers*, p. 235.
12 *The Thief's Journal*, p. 202.
13 *Our Lady of the Flowers*, p. 256.
14 *Ibid.*, p. 305.
15 Jean Genet, *Miracle of the Rose*, trans. Bernard Frechtman (New York: Grove Press, 1966), p. 37.
16 *Our Lady of the Flowers*, p. 69.
17 Richard N. Coe, *The Vision of Jean Genet* (New York: Grove Press, 1968), p. 19.
18 *Our Lady of the Flowers*, p. 235.
19 *Saint Genet*, p. 44.
20 "Introduction," *Our Lady of the Flowers*, p. 33.
21 *The Thief's Journal*,pp. 85f.
22 *Ibid.*, p. 94.
23 *Miracle of the Rose*, p. 46.
24 *The Thief's Journal*, p. 208.
25 *Our Lady of the Flowers*, p. 130.
26 *The Thief's Journal*, p. 110.
27 "Au peuple des morts, l'oeuvre de Giacometti communique la connaissance de la solititude de chaque être et de chaque chose, et que cette soltitude est notre gloire la plus sûre." Jean Genet, *Les Bonnes* and *L'Atelier*, p. 19.
28 *Ibid.* Also Jean Genet, "The Funambulist," trans. Bernard Frechtman, *Evergreen Review*, vol. 32 (April–May 1964), p. 46.
29 *Ibid.*, p. 47.
30 *Our Lady of the Flowers*, p. 63.
31 *Ibid.*, p. 71.
32 *Ibid.*, p. 72.
33 *Ibid.*, p. 82.
34 *Ibid.*, p. 181.
35 *Ibid.*, p. 186.
36 *Ibid.*, p. 184.
37 *Ibid.*, pp. 68f.
38 *Ibid.*, p. 266.
39 *Ibid.*, p. 307.

40 *Miracle of the Rose*, pp. 32f.

41 *Ibid.*, p. 71.

42 Jean Genet, *Funeral Rites*, trans. Bernard Frechtman (New York: Grove Press, 1969), p. 13.

43 *Ibid.*, p. 231.

44 *Ibid.*, p. 18.

45 "Enfin, pour être visible de vous, pour devenir un personage de roman, Querelle doit être montré hors de nous-même." Jean Genet, *Querelle de Brest*, in *Oeuvres complètes* (Paris: Gallimard, 1953), vol. 3, p. 182.

46 "Les glaces étaient vides, pures, étonnement proches de l'irréalité, n'ayant personne et presque aucune chose à refléter." *Ibid.*, p. 190.

47 *The Thief's Journal*, pp. 62, 109, 171–172, 205.

48 *Ibid.*, p. 45.

49 *Ibid.*, p. 86.

50 *Ibid.*, p. 21.

51 *Ibid.*, p. 268.

52 *Ibid.*, p. 170.

53 Jean Genet, "A Note on Theatre," *Tulane Drama Review*, vol. 7, no. 3 (Spring 1963), p. 37.

54 Quoted by Leonard Cabell Pronko, *Avant-Garde: The Experimental Theater in France* (Berkeley and Los Angeles: University of California Press, 1962), p. 146.

55 Jean Genet, *The Maids and Deathwatch*, trans. Bernard Frechtman (New York: Grove Press, 1961), p. 162.

56 *Ibid.*, p. 39.

57 *Ibid.*, p. 67.

58 *Ibid.*, p. 100.

59 *Ibid.*, p. 24.

60 Jean Genet, *The Balcony*, trans. Bernard Frechtman (New York: Grove Press, 1958), p. 31.

61 *Ibid.*, p. 1.

62 *Ibid.*, p. 4.

63 *Ibid.*, pp. 44f.

64 *Ibid.*, pp. 117f.

65 *Ibid.*, p. 68.

66 Jean Genet, *The Blacks*, trans. Bernard Frechtman (New York: Grove Press, 1960), p. 3

67 *Ibid.*, p. 39.

68 *Ibid.*, p. 42.

69 *Ibid.*, pp. 36f.
70 *Ibid.*, p. 102.
71 *Ibid.*, p. 126.
72 *Ibid.*, p. 90.
73 Jean Genet, *The Screens*, trans. Bernard Frechtman (New York: Grove Press, 1962), p. 52.
74 *Ibid.*, p. 192.
75 Marc Pierret, "Genet's New Play: *The Screens*," *Tulane Drama Review*, p. 97.
76 *The Screens*, p. 195.
77 *Ibid.*, p. 74.
78 Georges Batailles, *La Littérature et le mal* (Paris: Gallimard, 1957), p. 210.
79 *Our Lady of the Flowers*, p. 293.
80 *The Thief's Journal*, p. 11.
81 *Funeral Rites*, p. 170.
82 *Saint Genet*, p. 505.
83 *The Vision of Jean Genet*, pp. 119f.
84 *Ibid.*, p. 144.

## CHAPTER VII
## BECKETT: *Imagination Ending*

1 Samuel Beckett, "Letters on *Endgame*," *Village Voice*, March 19, 1958.
2 Hugh Kenner, *Flaubert, Joyce, and Beckett: The Stoic Comedians* (Boston: Beacon Press, 1962), pp. 72–78.
3 Peggy Guggenheim, *Confessions of an Art Addict* (New York: Macmillan, 1960), p. 50.
4 Quoted by Richard Ellman, *James Joyce* (New York: Oxford University Press, 1959), p. 662.
5 Quoted by F. N. Lees, "Samuel Beckett," *Memoirs and Proceedings of the Manchester Literary and Philosophical Society*, CIV (1961–1962), p. 5.
6 Quoted by Hugh Kenner, *Samuel Beckett* (New York: Grove Press, 1961), p. 21.
7 Quoted by Martin Esslin, *The Theatre of the Absurd* (Garden City, New York: Doubleday Anchor Books, 1961), p. 8.
8 *Our Exagmination round His Factification for Incamination of Work in Progress* (New York: Grove Press, 1962), p. 15.

9 Samuel Beckett, *Proust* (New York: Grove Press, 1931), pp. 1, 7.
10 *Ibid.*, pp. 4f.
11 *Ibid.*, p. 20.
12 Samuel Beckett, "Whoroscope," in *Poems in English* (New York: Grove Press, 1963), p. 4.
13 *Ibid.*, p. 4.
14 This term is coined and subtly defined by Kenner, *Samuel Beckett*, pp. 119f.
15 Samuel Beckett, *Molloy* (New York: Grove Press, 1955), p. 16.
16 Ludwig Wittgenstein, *The Blue and Brown Books* (Oxford: Basil Blackwell and Mott, 1958), p. 81.
17 Frederick J. Hoffman, *Samuel Beckett* (Carbondale, Illinois: Southern Illinois University Press, 1962), p. 63.
18 John Fletcher, "Samuel Beckett and the Philosophers," *Comparative Literature*, vol. 17 (Winter 1965), pp. 43f.
19 Samuel Beckett, *Malone Dies* (New York: Grove Press, 1956), p. 16.
20 A. J. Leventhal, "The Beckett Hero," *Critique*, vol. 7 (Winter 1964–65), p. 29.
21 *Molloy*, p. 41.
22 Samuel Beckett, *The Unnamable* (New York: Grove Press, 1958), p. 151.
23 Henri Bergson, "Laughter," in *Comedy*, ed. Wylie Sypher (Garden City, New York: Doubleday, 1956), p. 97.
24 *Ibid.*, p. 189.
25 Samuel Beckett, Georges Duthuit, and Jacques Putnam, *Bram Van Velde* (New York: Grove Press, 1958), p. 10.
26 *Ibid.*, p. 13.
27 *Proust*, p. 67.
28 Samuel Beckett, "Three Dialogues," *Transition* (1949), p. 102.
29 Samuel Beckett, *Murphy* (New York: Grove Press, 1957), p. 1.
30 *Ibid.*, pp. 6f., 9.
31 *Ibid.*, pp. 111f.
32 Samuel Beckett, *Watt* (New York: Grove Press, 1959), p. 79.
33 *Ibid.*, p. 215.
34 *Ibid.*, p. 168.
35 *Ibid.*, p. 203.
36 *Molloy*, p. 7.
37 *Ibid.*, p. 20.
38 *Ibid.*, p. 76.

39 *Ibid.*, p. 68.
40 *Ibid.*, p. 114.
41 *Ibid.*, p. 182.
42 *Ibid.*, p. 240.
43 *Ibid.*, p. 229.
44 Samuel Beckett, *Malone Dies* (New York: Grove Press, 1956), p. 1.
45 *Ibid.*, pp. 2f.
46 *The Unnamable*, p. 3.
47 *Ibid.*, p. 4.
48 *Ibid.*, p. 18.
49 *Ibid.*, p. 129.
50 *Ibid.*, p. 79.
51 *Ibid.*, p. 179.
52 Edmund Husserl, *Ideas I*, trans. W. R. Boyce Gibson (London: George Allen and Unwin, 1931), p. 233.
53 Ruby Cohn, *Samuel Beckett: The Comic Gamut* (New Brunswick, New Jersey: Rutgers University Press, 1962), p. 118.
54 Quoted by John Fletcher, *The Novels of Samuel Beckett* (New York: Barnes and Noble, 1964), p. 194.
55 Samuel Beckett, *How It Is* (New York: Grove Press, 1964), p. 57.
56 *Ibid.*, p. 69.
57 *Ibid.*, p. 69.
58 *Ibid.*, p. 88.
59 *Ibid.*, p. 140.
60 *Ibid.*, p. 144.
61 *Ibid.*, pp. 146f.
62 *Ibid.*, p. 143-
63 *The Theatre of the Absurd*, p. 296.
64 *Ibid.*, p. 12.
65 Quoted by Edith Kern, "Drama Stripped for Inaction: Beckett's Godot," *Yale French Studies*, vol. 14 (Winter 1954–1955), p. 41.
66 *The Theatre of the Absurd*, p. xvi.
67 Samuel Beckett, *Waiting for Godot* (New York: Grove Press, 1954), p. 22.
68 *Ibid.*, p. 28.
69 *Ibid.*, p. 44.
70 *Ibid.* p. 60.
71 See Samuel Beckett, "Letters on *Endgame*," *Village Voice*, March 19, 1958.

72 The references to all these critics are: Leonard Cabell Pronko, *Avant-Garde: Experimental Theatre in France* (Berkeley and Los Angeles: University of California Press, 1962), pp. 45f; Lionel Abel, *Metatheatre* (New York: Hill & Wang, 1963), pp. 136f; Kenner, *Samuel Beckett*, p. 156; and Cohn, *Samuel Beckett*, pp. 230–241.

73 Stanley Cavell, *Must We Mean What We Say?* (New York: Charles Scribner's Sons, 1969), p. 149.

74 Samuel Beckett, *Endgame* (New York: Grove Press, 1958), p. 1.

75 *Ibid.*, p. 3.

76 *Ibid.*, p. 18.

77 *Ibid.*, p. 29.

78 *Ibid.*, p. 55.

79 *Ibid.*, p. 56.

80 *Ibid.*, p. 80.

81 *Ibid.*, p. 82.

82 Samuel Beckett, *Eh Joe* and *Film* in *Cascando* (New York: Grove Press, 1968), pp. 37, 76.

## POSTLUDE: *The Vanishing Form*

1 This vision is most thoroughly advanced in the writings of R. Buckminster Fuller and summarized by his disciple, John McHale, *The Future of the Future* (New York: George Braziller, 1969).

2 Antonio Porchia, *Voices*, trans. W. S. Merwin (Chicago: Big Table Publishing Company, 1969), p. 38.

3 Heidegger makes the point rather differently by identifying the origins of tragedy with violated or overwhelmed being. See Robert W. Hall, "Being and Tragedy," *Chicago Review*, vol. 14, no. 3 (Autumn–Winter 1960).

4 Nathan A. Scott, Jr., *Negative Capability* (New Haven: Yale University Press, 1969), pp. 85f.

5 Stephen Spender, "The Vision of the Modern," *Partisan Review*, vol. 24 (Summer 1962), p. 359.

6 William Burroughs, *Nova Express* (London: Jonathan Cape, 1964), p. 12.

7 John Barth, *Lost in the Fun House* (New York: Doubleday & Co., 1968), p. 106.

8 John Barth, "The Literature of Exhaustion," in *The American Novel since World War Two*, ed. Marcus Klein (Greenwich, Conn.: Fawcett Publications, 1969), p. 274.

9 I have discussed these works at some length elsewhere. See Ihab Hassan,

"Almost the Voice of Silence: The Later Novelettes of J. D. Salinger," *Wisconsin Studies in Contemporary Literature*, vol. 4, no. 1 (Winter 1963), pp. 5–20.

10 J. D. Salinger, *Raise High the Roof Beam, Carpenters and Seymour: An Introduction* (Boston: Little, Brown, and Co., 1963), pp. 78, 86.

11 *Ibid.*, p. 158.

12 Jack Kerouac, "The Origins of the Beat Generation," in *A Casebook on the Beat*, ed. Thomas Parkinson (New York: Thomas Y. Crowell, 1961), pp. 69f.

13 *Ibid.*, p. 67.

14 Allen Ginsberg, "Footnote to Howl," *Ibid.*, p. 12.

15 Allen Ginsberg, "Death to Van Gogh's Ear" and "The End," *Kaddish and Other Poems* (San Francisco: City Lights Books, 1961), pp. 62, 99.

16 Robert Bly, "Poetry in an Age of Expansion," *The Nation*, April 22, 1961, p. 352.

17 Vincent Canby, "When Irish Eyes are Smiling, It's Norman Mailer," *New York Times*, October 27, 1968.

18 Norman Mailer, "The Argument Reinvigorated," in *The American Novel since World War Two*, p. 77.

19 Harold Rosenberg, *Artworks and Packages* (New York: Horizon Press, 1969), p. 13.

20 *Ibid.*, p. 23.

21 Quoted by Calvin Tomkins, *The Bride and the Bachelors* (New York: The Viking Press, 1965), p. 19.

22 John Cage, *A Year from Monday* (Middletown, Conn.: Wesleyan University Press, 1967), p. 70.

23 Robert Lebel, *Marcel Duchamp*, trans. George Heard Hamilton (New York: Paragraphic Books, 1967), p. iii.

24 See André Breton, "The Lighthouse of the Bride," *ibid.*, pp. 88–94.

25 Quoted by Tomkins, *The Bride and the Bachelors*, p. 57.

26 *Ibid.*, p. 31.

27 *Ibid.*, p. 62. See also Cage, *A Year from Monday*, pp. 70f.

28 *A Year from Monday*, p. 70.

# Index